Praise for Crossword Puzzles For Dummies

"Crosswords! Cryptograms! Acrostics! No need to be puzzled any longer. This addition to the IDG library deciphers and reveals the secrets behind the grid. You find out how puzzles are constructed, plus you get insiders' steps and hints, puzzle makers' techniques, along with sample puzzles from the top constructors. Beginners and pros alike will enjoy Michelle Arnot's insight into the world's greatest pastime and will have you quickly join the millions of puzzlers who delight in word game addiction."

— Marilynn Huret, Editor, *At The Crosswords,* www.atthecrossroads.com

"It is a pleasure to endorse Michelle Arnot's sprightly written book, which opens the door to the adventure and joy that is puzzle solving."

— Trude Michel Jaffe, Editor, *Los Angeles Times* Syndicate Daily Puzzle

"Michelle Arnot is one of the clearest, liveliest, most entertaining writers in the world of puzzles. Here is an excellent beginner's guide to mastering the secrets of crosswords."

— Will Shortz, Crossword Editor, *The New York Times*

"If you're a committed puzzlehead, this book is a MUST. You've got to buy it. If you're not a puzzlehead, give your brain a break — an enchanting workout. Develop your vocabulary, impress your friends, and live happily forevermore!!"

— Thomas H. Middleton, Double Acrostics Constructor, *The New York Times* and *Harper's* magazine

"Michelle Arnot's *Crossword Puzzles For Dummies* seduces newcomers into cruciverbalsm and entertains acrossionados with a clear but comprehensive approach to the subject. She writes with authority about the culture and history of crossword puzzles from their origins to where you can find them today on the Web, gives helpful advice for solving various styles of American and British puzzles, and tests your skills with quizzes and sample puzzles. This is a great book!"

— John J. Chew, III, Chairman, National SCRABBLE® Association Dictionary Committee, www.math.utoronto.ca/jjchew

"I give a hearty bravo to *Crossword Puzzles For Dummies*. I especially enjoyed Chapter 13, "Deciphering the Cryptic Crossword," and encourage everyone of all ages to check it out."

— Frank W. Lewis, "Setter" for the *Nation* Cryptic Crossword

References for the Rest of Us!™

BESTSELLING BOOK SERIES

Do you find that traditional reference books are overloaded with technical details and advice you'll never use? Do you postpone important life decisions because you just don't want to deal with them? Then our *...For Dummies®* business and general reference book series is for you.

...For Dummies business and general reference books are written for those frustrated and hard-working souls who know they aren't dumb, but find that the myriad of personal and business issues and the accompanying horror stories make them feel helpless. *...For Dummies* books use a lighthearted approach, a down-to-earth style, and even cartoons and humorous icons to dispel fears and build confidence. Lighthearted but not lightweight, these books are perfect survival guides to solve your everyday personal and business problems.

"More than a publishing phenomenon, 'Dummies' is a sign of the times."

— The New York Times

"...you won't go wrong buying them."

— Walter Mossberg, Wall Street Journal, on IDG Books' ...For Dummies books

"A world of detailed and authoritative information is packed into them..."

— U.S. News and World Report

Already, millions of satisfied readers agree. They have made *...For Dummies* the #1 introductory level computer book series and a best-selling business book series. They have written asking for more. So, if you're looking for the best and easiest way to learn about business and other general reference topics, look to *...For Dummies* to give you a helping hand.

1/99

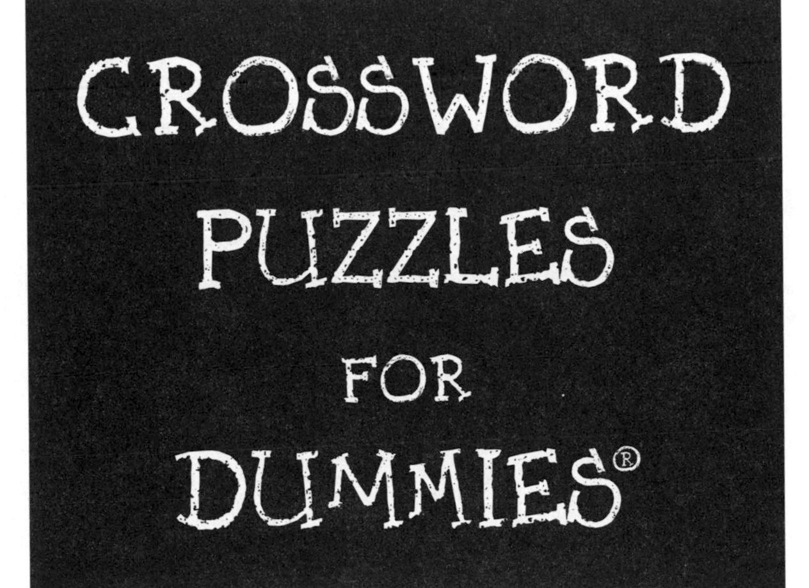
CROSSWORD
PUZZLES
FOR
DUMMIES®

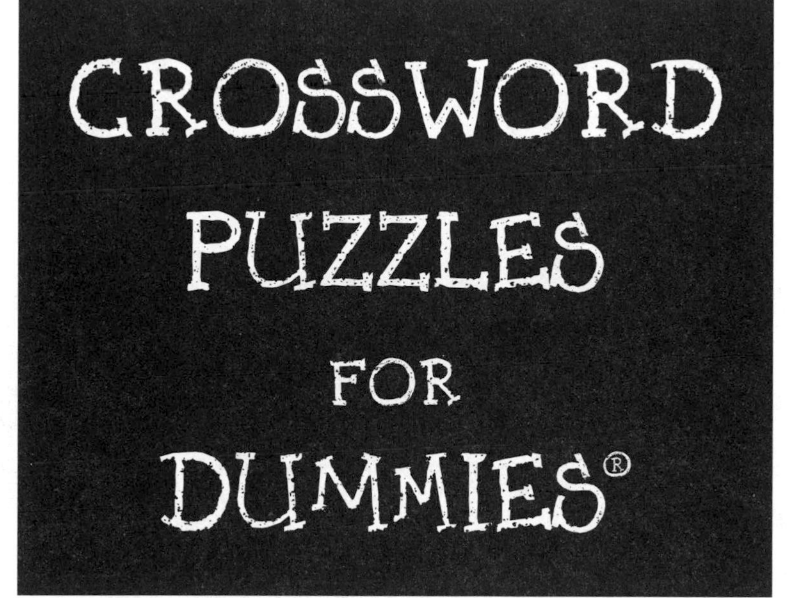

by Michelle Arnot

IDG Books Worldwide, Inc.
An International Data Group Company

Foster City, CA ♦ Chicago, IL ♦ Indianapolis, IN ♦ New York, NY

Crossword Puzzles For Dummies®

Published by
IDG Books Worldwide, Inc.
An International Data Group Company
919 E. Hillsdale Blvd.
Suite 400
Foster City, CA 94404
www.idgbooks.com (IDG Books Worldwide Web site)
www.dummies.com (Dummies Press Web site)

Library of Congress Catalog Card No.: 97-81240

ISBN: 0-7645-5067-5

Printed in the United States of America

10 9 8 7 6 5 4 3 2

1B/TQ/QT/ZZ/IN

Distributed in the United States by IDG Books Worldwide, Inc.

Distributed by CDG Books Canada Inc. for Canada; by Transworld Publishers Limited in the United Kingdom; by IDG Norge Books for Norway; by IDG Sweden Books for Sweden; by Woodslane Pty. Ltd. for Australia; by Woodslane (NZ) Ltd. for New Zealand; by TransQuest Publishers Pte Ltd. for Singapore, Malaysia, Thailand, Indonesia, and Hong Kong; by ICG Muse, Inc. for Japan; by Norma Comunicaciones S.A. for Colombia; by Intersoft for South Africa; by Le Monde en Tique for France; by International Thomson Publishing for Germany, Austria and Switzerland; by Distribuidora Cuspide for Argentina; by Livraria Cultura for Brazil; by Ediciones ZETA S.C.R. Ltda. for Peru; by WS Computer Publishing Corporation, Inc., for the Philippines; by Contemporanea de Ediciones for Venezuela; by Express Computer Distributors for the Caribbean and West Indies; by Micronesia Media Distributor, Inc. for Micronesia; by Grupo Editorial Norma S.A. for Guatemala; by Chips Computadoras S.A. de C.V. for Mexico; by Editorial Norma de Panama S.A. for Panama; by American Bookshops for Finland. Authorized Sales Agent: Anthony Rudkin Associates for the Middle East and North Africa.

For general information on IDG Books Worldwide's books in the U.S., please call our Consumer Customer Service department at 800-762-2974. For reseller information, including discounts and premium sales, please call our Reseller Customer Service department at 800-434-3422.

For information on where to purchase IDG Books Worldwide's books outside the U.S., please contact our International Sales department at 317-596-5530 or fax 317-596-5692.

For consumer information on foreign language translations, please contact our Customer Service department at 1-800-434-3422, fax 317-596-5692, or e-mail rights@idgbooks.com.

For information on licensing foreign or domestic rights, please phone +1-650-655-3109.

For sales inquiries and special prices for bulk quantities, please contact our Sales department at 650-655-3200 or write to the address above.

For information on using IDG Books Worldwide's books in the classroom or for ordering examination copies, please contact our Educational Sales department at 800-434-2086 or fax 317-596-5499.

For press review copies, author interviews, or other publicity information, please contact our Public Relations department at 650-655-3000 or fax 650-655-3299.

For authorization to photocopy items for corporate, personal, or educational use, please contact Copyright Clearance Center, 222 Rosewood Drive, Danvers, MA 01923, or fax 978-750-4470.

About the Author

A funny thing happened to Michelle Arnot on her way to a Master's degree in 18th Century French literature at Columbia University: She ended up making a career of her hobby in crosswords. Instead of writing a thesis, Michelle constructed a crossword. When the puzzle was accepted for publication, she switched gears and has been involved with puzzles ever since.

Michelle has been omnipresent in the world of puzzles since the publication of her book *What's Gnu: The History of the Crossword Puzzle* (Vintage Books, 1981). She served as Editor and Publisher of dozens of national puzzle magazines, most notably for *The Herald Tribune* and the Kappa Publishing Group. Additionally, she taught seminars on solving for the New School For Social Research and the Learning Annex. Her editorial career gradually extended into the marketing of puzzle magazines in the direct mail arena.

In her other life, Michelle is a health writer who specializes in subjects of interest to women. She's written books on topics as diverse as infertility and foot care.

When she's not at the word processor, Michelle is often found tramping the hills around Sandisfield, Massachusetts where she and her family keep busy with their 150-year-old house. An avid birdwatcher, Michelle likes to match faces to the avian references she reads about in puzzles. You can easily identify Michelle in warm weather by her T-shirt adorned with a crossword grid.

ABOUT IDG BOOKS WORLDWIDE

Welcome to the world of IDG Books Worldwide.

IDG Books Worldwide, Inc., is a subsidiary of International Data Group, the world's largest publisher of computer-related information and the leading global provider of information services on information technology. IDG was founded more than 30 years ago by Patrick J. McGovern and now employs more than 9,000 people worldwide. IDG publishes more than 290 computer publications in over 75 countries. More than 90 million people read one or more IDG publications each month.

Launched in 1990, IDG Books Worldwide is today the #1 publisher of best-selling computer books in the United States. We are proud to have received eight awards from the Computer Press Association in recognition of editorial excellence and three from Computer Currents' First Annual Readers' Choice Awards. Our best-selling *...For Dummies®* series has more than 50 million copies in print with translations in 31 languages. IDG Books Worldwide, through a joint venture with IDG's Hi-Tech Beijing, became the first U.S. publisher to publish a computer book in the People's Republic of China. In record time, IDG Books Worldwide has become the first choice for millions of readers around the world who want to learn how to better manage their businesses.

Our mission is simple: Every one of our books is designed to bring extra value and skill-building instructions to the reader. Our books are written by experts who understand and care about our readers. The knowledge base of our editorial staff comes from years of experience in publishing, education, and journalism — experience we use to produce books to carry us into the new millennium. In short, we care about books, so we attract the best people. We devote special attention to details such as audience, interior design, use of icons, and illustrations. And because we use an efficient process of authoring, editing, and desktop publishing our books electronically, we can spend more time ensuring superior content and less time on the technicalities of making books.

You can count on our commitment to deliver high-quality books at competitive prices on topics you want to read about. At IDG Books Worldwide, we continue in the IDG tradition of delivering quality for more than 30 years. You'll find no better book on a subject than one from IDG Books Worldwide.

John Kilcullen
Chairman and CEO
IDG Books Worldwide, Inc.

Steven Berkowitz
President and Publisher
IDG Books Worldwide, Inc.

Eighth Annual Computer Press Awards 1992

Ninth Annual Computer Press Awards 1993

Tenth Annual Computer Press Awards 1994

Eleventh Annual Computer Press Awards 1995

IDG is the world's leading IT media, research and exposition company. Founded in 1964, IDG had 1997 revenues of $2.05 billion and has more than 9,000 employees worldwide. IDG offers the widest range of media options that reach IT buyers in 75 countries representing 95% of worldwide IT spending. IDG's diverse product and services portfolio spans six key areas including print publishing, online publishing, expositions and conferences, market research, education and training, and global marketing services. More than 90 million people read one or more of IDG's 290 magazines and newspapers, including IDG's leading global brands — Computerworld, PC World, Network World, Macworld and the Channel World family of publications. IDG Books Worldwide is one of the fastest-growing computer book publishers in the world, with more than 700 titles in 36 languages. The "...For Dummies®" series alone has more than 50 million copies in print. IDG offers online users the largest network of technology-specific Web sites around the world through IDG.net (http://www.idg.net), which comprises more than 225 targeted Web sites in 55 countries worldwide. International Data Corporation (IDC) is the world's largest provider of information technology data, analysis and consulting, with research centers in over 41 countries and more than 400 research analysts worldwide. IDG World Expo is a leading producer of more than 168 globally branded conferences and expositions in 35 countries including E3 (Electronic Entertainment Expo), Macworld Expo, ComNet, Windows World Expo, ICE (Internet Commerce Expo), Agenda, DEMO, and Spotlight. IDG's training subsidiary, ExecuTrain, is the world's largest computer training company, with more than 230 locations worldwide and 785 training courses. IDG Marketing Services helps industry-leading IT companies build international brand recognition by developing global integrated marketing programs via IDG's print, online and exposition products worldwide. Further information about the company can be found at www.idg.com.

1/24/99

Dedication

To my daughter, Astrid Brown, and the next generation of solvers.

Author's Acknowledgments

The author extends her sincere thanks to all the good people at IDG Books Worldwide, Inc. and Dummies Press for creating this unique opportunity. A special thanks to Mark Butler for taking the project off the shelf, and to Heather Albright and Nickole Harris for their strenuous efforts on my behalf. Above all, thank yous to my editor, the serene and supremely talented Mary Goodwin. Her insight, patience, direction, good humor, and genuine interest created a productive working relationship that made the writing and editing process easier and (almost) enjoyable. And to think there's another great lady just exactly like her in the world — she's got a twin!

The game of crosswords is a journey with no specific destination. As I've traveled in the land of puzzles through the years, I've been fortunate to make the acquaintance of scores of puzzle people in all aspects of the field. These people have influenced me and generously shared their knowledge. Among the many talented editorial people, who are too numerous to list here, special thanks go to Will Shortz, Stan Newman, Marilyn Huret, Trude Jaffe, and Mary Lou Tobias. Also thank you to the Kappa Publishing Group, which I've had the pleasure of being affiliated with for more than decade. Most especially, hats off to my technical editor, Nancy Schuster. Her technical know-how pumped life into the more advanced chapters of this book, and her comments and humor infused some otherwise dry subjects with levity. Thank you, Nancy.

Many talented people contributed top-notch puzzles to help illustrate points in this book, including Janet Dobkins, Marilyn Huret, Fred Piscop, Jay Sullivan, and Alfio Micci.

Last but not least, thanks to my family for giving me the time and space to see the project through (including weekends, holidays, and many meals). Special thanks to my sister, Jacqueline Arnot, Web site designer extraordinaire and able guide through the Internet.

Publisher's Acknowledgments

We're proud of this book; please register your comments through our IDG Books Worldwide Online Registration Form located at http://my2cents.dummies.com.

Some of the people who helped bring this book to market include the following:

Acquisitions, Development, and Editorial

Project Editor: Mary Goodwin

Acquisitions Editor: Mark Butler

Copy Editors: Christine Meloy Beck, Rowena Rappaport

Technical Editor: Nancy Schuster

Editorial Manager: Elaine Brush

Editorial Assistant: Paul Kuzmic

Production

Project Coordinator: E. Shawn Aylsworth

Layout and Graphics: Steve Arany, Lou Boudreau, Maridee V. Ennis, Angela F. Hunckler, Anna Rohrer, Brent Savage, M. Anne Sipahimalani, Rashell Smith, Michael A. Sullivan

Special Graphics: Lou Boudreau, Drew R. Moore, Anna Rohrer

Proofreaders: Michelle Croninger, Joel K. Draper, Janet M. Withers

Indexer: Sharon Hilgenberg

General and Administrative

IDG Books Worldwide, Inc.: John Kilcullen, CEO; Steven Berkowitz, President and Publisher

IDG Books Technology Publishing: Brenda McLaughlin, Senior Vice President and Group Publisher

Dummies Technology Press and Dummies Editorial: Diane Graves Steele, Vice President and Associate Publisher; Mary Bednarek, Director of Acquisitions and Product Development; Kristin A. Cocks, Editorial Director

Dummies Trade Press: Kathleen A. Welton, Vice President and Publisher; Kevin Thornton, Acquisitions Manager

IDG Books Production for Dummies Press: Michael R. Britton, Vice President of Production and Creative Services; Cindy L. Phipps, Manager of Project Coordination, Production Proofreading, and Indexing; Kathie S. Schutte, Supervisor of Page Layout; Shelley Lea, Supervisor of Graphics and Design; Debbie J. Gates, Production Systems Specialist; Robert Springer, Supervisor of Proofreading; Debbie Stailey, Special Projects Coordinator; Tony Augsburger, Supervisor of Reprints and Bluelines

Dummies Packaging and Book Design: Patty Page, Manager, Promotions Marketing

♦

The publisher would like to give special thanks to Patrick J. McGovern, without whom this book would not have been possible.

♦

Contents at a Glance

Cartoons at a Glance
By Rich Tennant
The 5th Wave
By Rich Tennant
"No wonder the glacier was able to overtake him."
page 121
The 5th Wave
By Rich Tennant
IT WAS THE LAST TIME EMILY SERVED ALPHABET SOUP TO HER WORD PUZZLE PLAYING HUSBAND.
CEDE, CEIL, CEBUS, LICE CUBES...
OBSESSIVE, FIXATED, FANATIC, COMPULSIVE...
page 261
The 5th Wave
By Rich Tennant
You shouldn't be having that much trouble, Daddy. I helped by blackening in some of the squares this morning before you got up.
page 213
The 5th Wave
By Rich Tennant
Daily Bugle
"Looks like we used the wrong grid with the crossword again."
page 5
The 5th Wave
By Rich Tennant
ESKIMO CROSSWORD PUZZLE
page 67
The 5th Wave
By Rich Tennant
"Can't I just give you riches or something?"
page 177
Fax: 978-546-7747 • E-mail: the5wave@tiac.net

Table of Contents

Introduction

Almost 50 million Americans work crosswords each year. Of course, some people work the puzzles with greater success than others. At some point most people hit a wall that they can't seem to get over alone. If you're one of these people, you may start to take an either-you-have-it-or-you-don't attitude toward the puzzle. Before you toss puzzles aside, realize that this book provides you with everything you need to break through your crossword congestion.

Consider this book your new friend, the one that always polishes off the crossword in ink. Unlike other puzzle books, *Crossword Puzzles For Dummies* is not a compilation of puzzles. Rather, it is your puzzle guide to everything in the exciting world of puzzles — the book offers tips on deciphering clues, planning strategies, and getting a grip on those special words that seem to appear only in crossword grids.

Of course, you could just ram right into the grid, blindly scanning the clues for entries you already know, hoping that you can fill in enough of the grid to help you out on the harder clues. However, after a while, you may grow tired of the frustration that usually develops from approaching the grid so haphazardly. With time, you may realize that having a game plan, plus a working knowledge of the language of crosswords, minimalizes your frustration — and maximizes your pleasure with — the grid. That's when you should turn to this book.

How to Use This Book

You find the information in this book organized into parts, which focus on general crossword topics (such as the language of crosswords), and chapters, which focus on specific aspects of those general topics.

In each chapter, you use the headings to locate the subjects that really interest you. You don't need to start reading at Chapter 1 — just glance through the Table of Contents or simply flip through the book and start reading wherever you want to jump in.

I include a number of puzzles and practice exercises throughout the book. When it comes to working these puzzles, you can forget everything your teachers ever told you about marking in your book. Feel free to take pencil in hand and have at it right on these pages (this book uses a special kind of paper that is meant to be marked on).

Because puzzles are portable, feel free to carry this book with you to help control your blood pressure while you wait in the checkout line at the grocery store or pass the time at the dentist's office. It's also a great travel companion on any airline flight. Just don't be surprised if you find yourself asking the person next to you for a four-letter word that answers to "Georgia Peach."

Part I: Getting Started with Puzzles

The four chapters that comprise Part I get you up to speed with puzzles — even if you've never seen a crossword before in your life or if you've never gotten past square one. Here you can find your place in the Puzzle Universe. You discover the fundamentals of the grid and how to comb the clues for optimum solving success. I also tell where to find the puzzles you'll need to feed your habit, and I touch on those "other" types of puzzles — ones that don't look quite like your average crossword.

Part II: Mastering Crosswordese

Many of the words that appear in the crossword puzzle are not words you hear everyday in school, on the news, or among friends. The people who put puzzles together use certain kinds of words that fit well with other words in the grid — they have to use crosswordese in order to construct puzzles.

Crosswordese comes from any number of sources, and because new words and names are invented every day, crosswordese changes just as quickly as any other language. In this part of the book, I let you in on the words that comprise crosswordese today.

Part III: Building Your Sunday Puzzle Power

Hit this part of the book for insight on working that most daunting of puzzles — those you find on the Sunday puzzle page. I tell you everything you need to know to take the bite out of (and put the fun back into) Sunday-size crossword puzzles, diagramlesses, acrostics, and cryptic puzzles (all of which are regulars on the pages of the Sunday editions of many newspapers). I also talk about the Puns and Anagrams puzzle, which occasionally appears on some Sunday puzzle pages.

Part IV: Other Pieces of the Puzzle

At some point, you may not experience the same thrill you once got from filling in the last square of your daily puzzle. You may begin to yearn for puzzle stuff beyond the pen, paper, and puzzle associated with the average crossword experience. Just turn to this part of the book to read about some extra fun stuff that comes along with being a puzzle addict — stuff like constructing your own puzzles, entering crossword competitions, building your solving strength by playing other games, pulling puzzles off the Internet, and meeting other puzzled people (both on and offline).

Part V: The Part of Tens

The chapters in this part of the book present a hodgepodge of puzzle info — some of it's just for entertainment, and some of it's downright useful. You can turn here to find out all about important people in the puzzle world. You also find a small collection of puzzles, a list of answers to the questions I hear most about crossword puzzles, and a compact list of solving tips.

Part VI: Appendixes

Instant answers await you in this part of the book. Appendix A gives you the answers to the puzzles and exercises you find scattered throughout the book, and Appendix B gives you a running list of the most popular grid words, organized alphabetically and by the length of the word.

Conventions Used in This Book

To make it easier for you to pick out the important info in this book, I use the following conventions:

- All entries (the answers to the clues) appear in CAPITAL LETTERS. Of course, when you write entries into the grid, you can use all small letters, all capital letters, or a combination of both — whatever suits your personal style.
- All clues appear in quotations marks. For example, I may refer to the clue "Northern lights." (The quotation marks just make it easier for you to see where the clues start and where they end. In actual crossword puzzles, clues don't appear in quotation marks.)
- When I refer to particular clues, I use a shorthand that also appears in crossword puzzles — I refer to a clue as "1 Across" or "6 Down." The number refers to the number of the clue, and "Across" and "Down" refer to the direction of the entry (more about that in Chapter 1).

Icons Used in This Book

To help me highlight the key points I want you to take with you after you close this book, I use the following icons:

As in any game, in puzzles there are rules, both written and unwritten. Just to make sure that you're on your toes, this icon marks the stuff to keep in the back of your mind as you work a puzzle.

Okay — some stuff about puzzles is kind of technical (and therefore unessential!), and so I mark any info like that with one of these if you want to glide on by.

This icon marks advice and information that can make you a savvier solver so that you won't miss it.

Common pitfalls that may frustrate you are spelled out along the way to stop you from crushing your own pencil.

If you're looking for an extra challenge, you may want to time yourself against suggested limits. If you don't want to, ignore the whole exercise.

I include a few fun games to help you sharpen your solving skills.

Sometimes I give you a few answers to help you get started on a puzzle in the book. I put one of these icons right next to that information in case you don't want any help. Just steer clear of anything with this icon next to it, and you'll be doing the puzzle alone.

Look for this icon when you need advice on specific puzzle products. I recommend various sources and brand names throughout the book.

Puzzle fans come from many walks of life — this icon highlights favorite anecdotes by famous fans who share your predilection for puzzles and allow their lives to become an open book on the subject.

A Shameless Plug for Some Great Puzzle Books

I did such a wonderful job of writing this book that the folks at IDG Books let me put together a collection of some of my favorite puzzles. The result — *101 Crossword Puzzles For Dummies,* Volume 1, published by IDG Books Worldwide, Inc., which offers puzzles for every level of solver. I include 101 of the best daily- and Sunday-size crossword puzzles, cryptograms, diagramless, and acrostics I could find. I also offer solving hints and tips throughout the book to give you a boost when you need it.

After you work your way through *101 Crossword Puzzles For Dummies,* Volume 1, keep an eye out for the exciting sequels, Volumes 2 and 3.

Part I
Getting Started with Puzzles

"Looks like we used the wrong grid with the crossword again."

In this part . . .

If you're a true puzzle novice, then this part of the book can acquaint you with the ground-zero fundamentals of working crossword puzzles, including a look at the grid, the clues, and some basic strategy. Even if you've worked a few puzzles before in your time, I bet this part of the book can still show you a few tips and tricks to make you a smarter solver!

Also in this part, I tell you about some great places to find the puzzles you'll need to fulfill your puzzle cravings. I also tell you briefly about the "other" types of puzzles out there — including fill-ins, cryptograms, jumbles, and hidden words.

Chapter 1

Breaking Out of Crossword Gridlock

In This Chapter

- Finding your way around a crossword grid
- Examining the anatomy of a crossword puzzle
- Planning your approach to the puzzle
- Getting the green light on cheating
- Examining the various types of puzzles
- Exercising your brain for puzzles

Crosswords and other grid games amuse, distract, teach, and — above all — gratify. Puzzles let you expand your mental horizons in concentrated spurts without requiring a big time commitment. They give you an icebreaker at the office or anywhere you may find yourself. They test your powers of recall and challenge your wits.

You can start exploring this exciting universe of puzzles by taking an insider's look at the standard crossword — the well-known checkered grid with clues. In this chapter, I explain the elements of the common crossword grid and its underpinnings. Breaking down the game into its components may also answer some of your basic questions about the mechanics of solving the puzzle.

In addition, I give you a leg up on planning your crossword puzzle strategy, and I soothe any fears that you may have about consulting an outside source for help when (and if) you need it. (In fact, I condone any proactive behavior that improves your game.)

Getting Past Square One

Imagine sitting back with a crossword puzzle for ten minutes and completing it in pen, correctly, all in the comfort of your commute to work. Or, better yet, being able to answer your kids' and friends' questions about puzzles. Taking a close look at what goes into a puzzle can be a good start to making these dreams come true.

In the realm of the American crossword (as well as the British cryptic-style puzzle, which you can read about in Chapter 13), all solvers follow one important rule: Have fun. Actually memorizing the rules of the game belongs strictly to the domain of the two people behind the scenes which include the following:

- **The constructor:** The person who brainstorms the clues and answers and how they fit together in the grid for the ultimate enjoyment of the solver.
- **The editor:** The person who makes the final decision as to presentation of a puzzle, including making sure clues are phrased clearly and that the answers to the clues are correct.

As a solver, you don't have to worry too much about the work of the constructor or the editor; a solver just needs to be aware of a few basic guidelines that the constructor and editor use to build a puzzle.

Think of the American-style crossword as a friendly Q&A quiz — kind of a skewed vocabulary test spiced up with a dash of pop culture trivia. Specifically, the following three elements make up the common crossword puzzle:

- **Clues:** The question part of your friendly Q&A, the numbered clues appear beside or below the grid. A crossword consists of 37 to 55 clues in each direction (Across and Down), depending upon the grid size.
- **Entries:** Think of entries as the answer part of your Q&A. Entries read in two directions: Across answers read from left to right, and Down answers read from top to bottom. The way the entries interlock (key) to spell out answers in both directions gives the grid a kind of beauty and elegance.
- **Grid:** You fill in the entries (answers) in their assigned places indicated by a number in the grid. Black squares show you where the entries end. Why black in this age of Technicolor? Because most reading materials are still printed in black ink. (If you're lucky enough to have access to the Internet and the World Wide Web, you can visit some sites that treat you to multicolored puzzles. Turn to Chapter 16 for some hints on good puzzle-related Web sites.)

To start your exploration of a typical crossword puzzle, take a look at Puzzle 1-1 (if you get curious about the answers, you can find them in Appendix A). You may recognize the crossword by its black and white grid pattern with an accompanying list of numbered clues.

Picking your puzzle

Crossword puzzle has erroneously come to be used as the generic term for all puzzles, including those that require the solver to circle or fill in entries. Technically, *crossword* refers specifically to the grid-and-clues Q&A pencil game that I explore throughout most of this book.

Under the black-and-white umbrella of the term *crossword puzzle,* you find the straightforward, good old American crossword and its cousins:

- **The cryptic:** The cryptic is the British-version of the crossword, which you can read about in Chapter 13.
- **The diagramless:** This puzzle lists clues without any grid: The solver must determine the pattern. Turn to Chapter 11 for more about this puzzle.
- **The acrostic:** You try to fill in a rectangular grid containing a literary excerpt that reads across only. The initial letters of the clue answers spell out the author and source when read vertically. For more information on this type of puzzle, see Chapter 11.

Puzzle 1-1

Crosswords often use abbreviations at the end of clues. For example, "wds" stands for words, and "abbr." stands for abbreviation.

Across

1 Hardwood tree
4 Plays on words
8 Exceeded 55 mph
12 Singer Rawls
13 *Laugh-in* funnyman Johnson
14 Use the loudspeaker
15 Stay put: 2 wds
17 Press, as a blouse
18 Whole
19 — and feather (old-time punishment)
21 Mr. Skelton
22 Stop it!
26 Used a VCR
29 Weep
30 Monkey —, monkey do
31 Amongst
32 Fuel for a car
33 Actress Rowlands
34 "Velvet Fog" — Torme
35 Mont Blanc, for one
36 Use a menu
37 Magician's term
39 Vacation destination
40 — Vegas
41 Fiesta fixture in Mexico City
45 Ming, for one
48 Represent: 2 wds
50 — vera (sunburn cream)
51 Ireland, poetically
52 Cash machine: abbr.
53 Word with egg
54 Sunflower or poppy product
55 Cowboy Rodgers

Down

1 Or —! (fighting words)
2 Cut of meat
3 Mixed-breed dog
4 Matched, as socks
5 Strongly recommended
6 Extreme degree
7 Irish dog
8 Former VP Agnew
9 Golfer's term
10 Type of maniac
11 TV room
16 Weary
20 "Have you — wool?"
23 Formerly owned, as clothing
24 Kelly or Hackman
25 Learn of
26 Pack down, as clay
27 Continent: abbr.
28 Velvety surface
29 Baseball headgear
32 Lip balms
33 Type of piano
35 One — time (singly)
36 Gave an opinion
38 Wintry forecast
39 Word with tire
42 Distant
43 *Wizard of Oz* pooch
44 The Salvation —
45 "Moondance" Morrison
46 Pub order
47 Distress signal: abbr.
48 Formal neckwear

Exploring the grid

You can count on four givens about crossword grids:

- They are square.
- They always consist of an odd number of squares across and down, such as 13 or 15.
- They contain symmetrical (mirror-image) patterns. If you draw a diagonal line through a grid from the top-left corner to the bottom-right corner, the pattern on top mirrors the one below. The diagonal from top-right to bottom-left works the same way. Whether you hold the diagram upside down or right side up, the pattern remains the same.

  GRIDLOCK BUSTER

  Remembering the symmetrical pattern of the grid can actually make you a more efficient solver; check out "Navigating the Grid: Basic Crossword Strategy" in this chapter for the details.
- They typically contain five-sixths white squares and one-sixth black squares.

All grids may look the same to you at this point, but grids vary in size. Four common puzzle sizes exist. Typical daily newspaper crossword grids measure either 13 x 13 or 15 x 15 squares, which include no more than 28 or 38 black squares, respectively. Sunday-size grids weigh in at 21 x 21 (about 140 entries) or 23 x 23 (about 170 entries); these diagrams include 70 to 85 black squares. The more white squares you see, the more advanced the challenge — the puzzle contains longer entries and fewer *repeaters*.

A *repeater* is a crossword cliché — an entry that you'll find time and time again in your solving routine. Throughout this book, I list the most common repeaters along with the clues that they are usually clued with.

Go ahead and familiarize yourself with the basic layout of the crossword, starting with a 13 x 13 grid (as shown in Puzzle 1-1), the compact model in the crossword universe. Count the squares across the top line, starting at the box with 1 in the corner, to determine that the grid has 13 squares. Familiarizing yourself with the crossword layout gives you confidence and a feeling of comfort that you won't encounter anything too tricky in it.

Strolling through the clues

Clues are numbered in sequence and listed beside the grid in two lists, Across and Down. In a word or two, clues convey the essential meaning of the entries. Tight puzzle layouts keep space at a premium, so the numbers next to the clues often appear in boldface. Then, clues are set in nonbold to help you distinguish between the two.

Each corresponding number shows you where the answer entry begins in the grid plus whether the entry is Across or Down. After reading a clue, you refer to the grid to determine how many letters (white spaces) the corresponding answer contains. Check out the first clue on the Across list in Puzzle 1-1 — "Hardwood tree" — for example. You find three spaces allocated in the grid. Okay, nature-lover — your job is to determine which three-letter tree name belongs in the puzzle as the entry.

I'm taking you on a quick tour of the puzzle now, and that's why I have you look at Square 1. When actually solving puzzles, you don't have to start your solving at 1 Across. Crosswords aren't like books that you begin reading on page one. No rules govern where to begin your solving, and you don't need to solve methodically from top to bottom. You don't miss anything in the plot by starting in the middle with crosswords. Instead, work your way through the puzzle by looking for types of clues first. I give you my secret formula for conquering the clues in Chapter 2. For now, just concentrate on 1 Across and that three-letter tree.

The Across entry's connected to the Down entry

Entries (answers) get assigned places in the grid in either Across or Down positions. Every letter reads (keys) in both directions so that it belongs to an Across entry and a Down entry. You never find a single letter off on its own, not if you're working an American crossword. (But after you travel to Great Britain, that policy changes; see Chapter 13 for more on the British cryptic puzzle.)

But not every clue number functions in both directions. Some numbers appear only in the Across direction, because that number doesn't begin a Down word. Only numbers with a black square (or border line) to their left begin an Across word; only numbers with a black square (or border line) above them begin a Down word. Consequently, Across clues may outnumber Down clues, because every single letter reads across.

Through practice, you can come to recognize the basic types of clues. I discuss the following clue types at length in Chapter 2, but as a part of your tour of the puzzle, please take a look at some examples of the various clue types you can find in Puzzle 1-1:

- **Synonyms:** A straightforward dictionary definition for the entry — see 1 Across.
- **Missing-words:** These clues usually feature a dash. Just fill in the word represented by the dash, and you have your entry — see 44 Down. (Sometimes constructors make things a bit harder on you with *implied missing-word clues*. Instead of a giveaway dash, the missing word is referred to in combination with another word — check out 53 Across.
- **Proper names:** Names of celebrities, both given names and surnames, usually contemporary or at least perennially popular — see 33 Across.
- **Foreign words:** Throwing in a few everyday foreign words spices up the process and offers more short word options — see 41 Across.
- **Wordplay:** These clues are like mini riddles in the grid, and to solve them you need to look at the words in the clue from different perspectives. For example, a clue like "Hawk's penthouse" may make you scratch your head for a few minutes until you decipher the riddle and come up with the four-letter entry NEST. (Sorry, you won't find any of these in Puzzle 1-1.)
- **Themes:** Over the past three decades, crosswords have become more than a collection of random words — *themes* (a thread that ties together two or more clues in the same puzzle) and wordplay have gained popularity. In fact, themes are the standard nowadays. The theme may be a play on words or a related group of items. You can spot a theme in the grid by looking for longer entries in parallel parts of the puzzle. Most often, theme entries appear in both Across and Down positions. Sunday-size puzzles have titles that clue you in to what the theme is about (see Chapter 10 for more information on working the Sunday puzzle). In Puzzle 1-1, a pair of Across entries (15 and 47) forms the theme of the puzzle.

Where clues are plural, entries are as well. Where clues are phrased in the past tense, entries are, too.

You may have noticed that clues are very short and to the point. The crossword format doesn't allow spelling out a definition as a complete sentence. A kind of crossword code packs in all the information. Through practice, you can come to understand how the code operates like mini-riddles.

Coming up with the entries: Repeaters give you a hand

Due to the limited size of the grid, about two-thirds of the entries fall in the three-, four-, or five-letter range. (Beginner-level puzzles may include two-letter entries in some sources.) Due to the limited length of crossword words, the same entries appear over and over in crossword after crossword. These *repeaters* make up a special lexicon of entries and act as filler for the majority of white squares.

You find repeaters in every category of clue. Because most puzzles really try to minimize obscure terms, repeaters are now being drawn from today's world; however, some repeaters are obsolete in spoken English; you only find use for these words in crossword puzzles — unless you have a SERF (a typical crossword repeater) keeping house for you.

Really obscure repeater words are on the way out in puzzles. Clues won't refer to a strange genus or heraldic term as often as they used to. Instead, today's constructors draw repeaters from the well of cultural knowledge held by the typical solver, which includes familiar words like the names of brands and celebrities.

Often when solving, you find that the words in the grid alternate consonants with vowels for maximum interweaving potential. When you're in a bind inside the grid, test a vowel following a consonant that you've filled into the grid and vice versa. Then refer back to the clue list and try again.

Unless you've already taken pencil in hand and started working the previous puzzle, you don't see any entries in Puzzle 1-1. The puzzle is just waiting for you to solve it. When you answer a clue correctly, you get confirmation when the entry fits properly with the letters from the intersecting entries. In other words, when everything goes right, the Across and Down entries all read correctly and click with the clues. Every single letter interlocks in two directions — namely, Across and Down — so you have two opportunities to check that you have the correct answer.

In Puzzle 1-1, for example, 1 Across — ELM — crosses sensibly with 1 Down — ELSE.

Pen or pencil? Does it really matter?

Yes, pen or pencil matters, but only because you're up a creek if you decide to use pen and you make a mistake. I can think of only three good reasons to use ink over pencil:

- You've jotted all the entries in the margin of the clues and you know that they're right.
- You're solving a cryptic, in which case each clue has only one possible solution (see Chapter 13 for more info on the cryptic).
- You don't have a pencil.

Champion solvers have spoken on this subject ad nauseam. I guess that when you're a champion, you can afford to discuss such matters.

Peeking at the answers

Solutions (answer grids) show the letters filled into the appropriate boxes in the grid without the corresponding numbers. (Because answer grids are usually a reduced version of the solving grid, the boxes don't have room to include both letter and number.) When checking the answers for a specific word, you just have to use your crossword "compass" to figure out where that word falls in the grid.

Working a crossword in a newspaper offers an extra challenge that you don't find when solving a collection of crosswords: The newspaper publishes the answers the following day (except for Sunday puzzles, which require a week of waiting until the answers appear). So when you find yourself in a jam with a newspaper puzzle, you have to wait until the next morning to look at the answers. When the solutions are in the back of the book — for example, in Appendix A, as they are in this book — you can get yourself unstuck immediately.

If you can't wait until the next day to get the answer to a clue that's slowing you down, some newspapers offer the option of dialing a 900 number for same day answers. If you're really stuck on a clue, and you don't have a 900 number to help you, sometimes a reference book can help you with the entry you need — see "Is It Really Cheating If No One Sees You Do It?" in this chapter for assurance that it's okay to hit the books from time to time. Chapter 9 also gives you some ideas about which reference books are most helpful to solvers.

Navigating the Grid: Basic Crossword Strategy

When you pick up a book, you normally start reading on page 1. When solving a crossword, you can start working anywhere in the grid. You can quickly scan the clues, starting with either the Across or the Down clues, and fill in the entry for any clue you can figure out, whether it's 4 Across or 34 Down.

Until you gain confidence about your answers, scribble your guesses in the margin next to the clues before you enter them in the grid. Think of this technique as a way to warm up for the actual workout (and as a warm-up for attempting the diagramless; see Chapter 11 for more information on diagramless puzzles).

A puzzle novice's common *opener* (or first move) is looking for clues that require plural entries and filling in every possible S as the final letter of each entry. (In Puzzle 1-1, clues that require plural entries include 4 Across and 32 Down.) I don't recommend going this route for a couple of reasons. First, although chances are good that S is the final letter of a plural word, exceptions — such as MEN — do exist. Second, having a single letter off by itself when you get stumped proves distracting. (Plus, filling in S's can get discouraging when they're the only letter you get. Nothing makes you feel worse more quickly than a grid with stray S's floating in it like unwanted algae.) The one time that inserting the S is very helpful is at the end of a Down entry when it starts the crossing word.

Making all the right moves

Constructors may do their best to trip you up with tricky misleading clues that send you in the wrong direction. With experience you can train yourself to recognize these pitfalls. However, when you first start out with the puzzle, stick to the basics by getting a handle on the roster of repeaters. With this ammunition at your fingertips, you can make greater progress in the grid before you run out of answers.

The following steps give you a straightforward attack plan on any crossword puzzle you care to pick up — be it a daily or a Sunday-size puzzle. I tell you both the general steps you should take, and I apply those steps to Puzzle 1-1 so that you can see them in action (just read the bolded parts of the following list if you don't want any hints about Puzzle 1-1):

1. **Walk through the clues, picking out the clues you can easily answer.**

   In Chapter 2, I outline my foolproof plan for scanning the clues. For now, start by looking for missing-word clues, which most people find to be the easiest clues to solve.

   You can usually spot a missing-word clue by the "—" hanging out in the clue (read "Strolling through the clues" in this chapter for the lowdown on clues). How about 30 Across: "Monkey —, monkey do"? Three letters. Remembering the old rhyme, you hopefully come up with SEE, which you can fill in immediately.

   Feel free to tick off the completed clues. Hey, cross them out. Empower yourself!

   Keep looking for a missing-word clue until you find one — every editor includes some missing-word clues in easy-to-solve crosswords.

2. **After you enter an answer for one clue, work on the clues that connect to the clue you already answered.**

   In Puzzle 1-1, to confirm that SEE is correct, read the clues for the entries that intersect SEE. How about 24 Down: "Kelly or Hackman," four letters. Most moviegoing audiences have seen one or the other well-known GENE in various big-screen guises. (The alternate spelling JEAN can be ruled out because a J at the end of 25 Across is unlikely.) Yup, GENE fits in nicely on the grid.

   Answer as many clues that cross SEE as you can until you run out of ideas.

3. **Scout around for other three- or four-letter entries in the grid.**

   You may find shorter entries in corners where Down clues are generally shorter than Across ones. Witness the lower-left corner in Puzzle 1-1. Take a clue such as 46 Down, "Pub order," with three letters assigned to the grid. Question: What are you most likely to order in a pub? Beer comes to mind, but that's four letters. Besides, beer is something you drink at an American bar, and pubs are more often connected with England. Next question: What is a three-letter pub order in England? With a little thought (or a call to a friend in England), you come up with that ever-popular crossword repeater beverage, ALE.

   Your search for each answer begins with the query: What's another word for this? In the case of 51 Across, for example, Emerald Isle may spring to mind, but that answer doesn't fit. With a clue like "Ireland" and an entry of four letters, two possible answers are EIRE or ERIN. The "poetically" part of the clue tells you that the proper answer is EIRE. (Ireland is the destination of choice for many crossword solvers, but more about that in Chapter 8.)

   Each clue has only one correct solution. You know that you have a confirmed correct answer when the interlocking answers match the corresponding clues both Across and Down. On the other hand, you know that you've guessed wrong when the interlocking answers don't mesh properly. When you don't come up with common letters between interlocking words, think again. Don't waste your time trying to make wrong guesses work. Even when your first guess matches the number of squares in the grid, as soon as you find that the words don't interlock, erase it. Otherwise, you end up running in circles on the crossword treadmill.

How do you know if an entry is correct? If it's the obvious answer, as with a missing word, then it's a simple choice. Or you may be absolutely sure about one of the answers because it's a dictionary definition. Or it may just be a hunch. Of course, you may end up erasing a correct answer and coming back to it later. It's all in the way you play the game.

4. **Investigate one of the corners, such as the bottom-right corner.**

   The shorter entries in corners make the clues in corners generally easy to crack. After you write in ALE for 46 Down, you want to check the clues that interlock with it — 45 Across, 45 Down, 47 Down, 50 Across, and 53 Across. Another missing-word clue at 50 Across — great! Anyone who has ever had a burn may have firsthand knowledge of the soothing sensation of ALOE. The L interlocks, which confirms that all is well in each direction. Two interlocking words with common letters verify that you've found the correct answers.

5. **Check out the mirror image of a corner that you have already solved.**

   After you unravel a corner of a crossword, you may find that the counterpart corner in the other half of the diagram is equally accessible. The symmetry of the grid seems connected to this strategy, although I have no hard evidence.

6. **Continue until you've successfully filled each square.**

   Sometimes you may complete a puzzle without reading and answering every clue. That's the way interlocking letters work: By answering the clues in the opposite direction, words begin to emerge even before you get a chance to read the clue.

Is It Really Cheating If No One Sees You Do It?

The concept of cheating doesn't exist in puzzle solving. If you derive pleasure from browsing through reference books in search of an answer, then that search is all part of the way you play the game. Whether you answer the clues right off the bat or you turn to another source (meaning a dictionary or simply someone else within earshot) depends on your personal taste. Besides, even if you do cheat, who knows except you?

For example, looking at a map to find the answer to 35 Across in Puzzle 1-1 may take you on a journey that brands Mont Blanc upon your memory bank forever. Consulting the almanac for the given name of Nixon's VP (8 Down) may refresh your memory about the Watergate era of U.S. history. Turning to references supports the theory that puzzles are brain food. Certainly, they can be informative if you choose to pursue that route.

Professional acrossionado Stan Newman attributes his outstanding career as a puzzle tournament winner to hitting the books. The key to puzzle prowess? Looking it up! — whatever *it* is. A healthy curiosity about words and where they come from helps you build a strong vocabulary that serves you well puzzle after puzzle.

Of course, you may decide to sneak a peek at the answer section in the back of the book. I call checking out the answer grid *cheating*. But what I don't know won't hurt you.

A puzzle a day

Combine a checkered grid with a list of clues and — presto! — you have a window on the workings of the human brain. That's why the father of French psychology, Jacques Lacan, opened his training sessions with the mysterious dictum: "Do puzzles."

Certainly, an aptitude for puzzle solving signifies that your brain is functioning. Being good at puzzles means that you're brainy, *n'est-ce pas?* Puzzle people want to believe so. In any case, medical wisdom has confirmed that puzzle solving on a regular basis keeps the brain sharper and defies the aging process.

In 1980, linguist Robert Oliphant, a professor at California State University, Northridge, proclaimed crossword solving to be an excellent mental exercise designed to keep your memory in tip-top shape. Why? Because puzzle solving requires an active pencil-and-paper response that's preferable to the passive nature of reading. What's more, Professor Oliphant believes that puzzles build your recall of what's happening in the world around you. Searching those memory banks for the specific answer requires effort, and that process corrects the natural tendency to forgetfulness that comes with age. A diet of a puzzle (plus an apple) a day gets you results!

Jogging guru James Fixx (author of *The Complete Book of Running and Games for the Superintelligent)* believed that puzzles allow the mind to do its best work. Because the mind doesn't work in a linear way, he reasoned, working puzzles offers different perspectives on problem solving in a controlled setting. Research on Mensa, the high IQ society founded at the end of WW II by a pair of British barristers, confirmed his hunch. The common denominator among its diverse members? A passion for puzzles.

Spinning the Wheel: Looking at Popular Letters

TV's *Wheel of Fortune* taps into humans' age-old fascination with filling in the blanks. Vanna, one of the show's hosts, reveals the number of squares in the puzzle along with a vague clue about the solution. The quest to identify a familiar word or phrase that reads only from left to right forms your challenge — like tackling a single Across entry.

Acrossionado Merv Griffin, who created *Wheel of Fortune,* introduced a roulette wheel into the solving equation. Then he raised the stakes to suit 20th century tastes — he threw in the additional incentive of winning money by filling in the correct letters.

Watching *Wheel of Fortune* can help make you a better crossword solver? Amazing but true — by raising your consciousness about the frequency with which certain letters appear in the English language. You don't have to be a good speller to anticipate which popularly used letters such as S and R are more likely to appear and where they fall in the composition of a word. For example, you don't expect J to end a word.

The crossword solver uses a specialized alphabet. If you stay tuned to *Wheel of Fortune,* you see Vanna turn over the letters E, S, and R with amazing frequency. These letters may appear anywhere in a word, while letters such as J and M appear more often at the beginning of words. Other letters appear most often at the end of words, while a small group of letters rarely appears at all.

The Crossword Alphabet's Most (and Least) Popular Letters

Most used letters:	S, R, E, T, D, A, I, L
Least used letters:	J, Q, X, Z, F, V, W

PUZZLE PEOPLE

The origins of the crossword: It all started in NYC

'Twas the week before Christmas 1913 when newspaperman Arthur Wynne found himself desperate to fill the eight-page Fun supplement of *The New York Sunday World.* A native Liverpudlian, Wynne had been an avid solver of Victorian puzzles. The Fun section formed a testimonial to his upbringing — chock-a-block with picture puzzles *(rebuses),* riddles, and anagrams (words rearranged to make new words). For a change of pace, Wynne devised something new for the holidays: The *Word-Cross,* a diamond-shaped grid with numbered clues. Each entry listed two numbers to indicate where the entry began and ended in the grid. The simple instructions below the grid read: "Fill in the small squares with words which agree with the following definitions." *Sunday World* solvers went bonkers. Before long, with its syllables switched, the Cross-Word became a weekly feature.

Within two months, Wynne solicited contributions from among his solvers and established the newspaper tradition of having a puzzle editor and getting the puzzles via freelance contribution that continues to this day.

Chapter 2

Scoping Out the Clues

In This Chapter

- Looking for missing words
- Scanning for proper names
- Figuring out synonyms
- Searching for foreign-language clues
- Playing with words
- Picking up on themes
- Gaining control of the squares

Why does the 80/20 rule always apply? With crosswords, 80 percent of the grid contains the *repeaters* (the words that follow you from puzzle to puzzle), while variables make up the remaining 20 percent. Some words recur continuously in crosswords, so when you get a little basic lingo under your belt, your solving strength certainly improves.

Although approaching a crossword is an art with few rules, you can help yourself by selecting clues for optimal solving success. I'm going to share some tricks of the trade related to working with the clues in this chapter.

Crossword entries fall into six general categories:

- **Missing words**
- **Proper names**
- **Synonyms**
- **Foreign words**
- **Wordplay**
- **Themes**

Abbreviations appear in all categories, and some categories contain a few subsets. In this chapter, I familiarize you with how to identify each of the six different types of clues. If you look for and solve clues in the sequence I suggest, you can improve your solving skills.

Never Start with the First Clue, 1 Across

Never say never in the world of puzzles. Sure, if you know the answer to 1 Across it is the logical place to start. But the winning strategy is to look for types of clues rather than going through them in sequence. Although you won't always know the answer to 1 Across, chances are good that you'll know the answers to certain other types of clues if you attack them in order of difficulty.

The beauty of the crossword lies in the way the entries intersect. Every time you take a guess at an entry that you're unsure about, you can double-check that it works against the answers that cross it. When you first look at a crossword, you're drawn to the shorter entries first. This is a natural tendency because the shorter words may be easier to solve. With the way words interweave in the grid, often your best bet is to approach a corner that offers you at least a couple of clues that you know the answers to. With two intersecting answers, you have some letters to build upon. If one of those clues happens to be 1 Across, fine, but you don't necessarily have to start there.

Beginning methodically at 1 Across doesn't give you any advantage — successful solving isn't like reading a text from start to finish. After you solve either two overlapping entries (either parallel Across or Down clues or two intersecting clues) anywhere in the grid, you can begin to see the letter combinations emerge in the other direction. Sometimes, if you are left with one blank square, just testing out letters of the alphabet in that place leads you to the correct answer even before you read the clue.

If you know the answer to a clue, regardless of clue type, fill in the answer in the grid. The strategy of solving by type of clue works just as well after you've depleted the answers that you know off the bat as before. (There is no right or wrong in crosswords, just suggested approaches to successful solving.)

Step #1: Start with a Missing Word

You can recognize a missing-word clue by the telltale dash (—) that takes the place of a word that is missing from the clue. You just have to come up with the missing word, and you have your answer.

As a rule, missing-word clues offer the easiest way to get into a crossword. If a puzzle doesn't have even one missing-word clue, you can expect that the constructor has made the puzzle a toughie.

If the answer to the first missing-word clue eludes you, continue reading the clues until you find one you know. Constructors design these clues to be accessible, and finding the answer to one is your access route into the puzzle.

Sometimes you know the answer instantly, as in "Bric-a- —" (BRAC) or "— and that" (THIS). Like a syllable acted out in a charade, the missing link becomes clear almost immediately as part of a bigger concept such as a popular pair or saying.

Missing-word clues come from a wide variety of sources, including, but not limited to, the following:

- **Book titles:** For example, *"A — of Two Cities"* (TALE)
- **Film titles:** For example, *"— of a Mad Housewife"* (DIARY)
- **Foreign languages:** For example, "Como — usted?" (ESTA)
- **Geography:** For example, "Costa —" (RICA)
- **Names:** For example, "Joyce Carol —" (OATES)
- **Names of plays:** For example, *"— Misbehavin'"* (AINT)
- **Popular duos:** For example, "Ike and —" (TINA)
- **Popular sayings:** For example, "You can't — 'em all" (WIN)
- **Song titles:** For example, *"The Star Spangled —"* (BANNER)

Rock music is working its way into the clues in this category. Even Madonna can find her work memorialized forever in puzzles with her controversial song *"— Don't Preach"* (PAPA)

- **TV shows:** For example, *"— in the Family"* (ALL)

Flex your mental muscle with these common missing-word clues. You can find the answers in Appendix A:

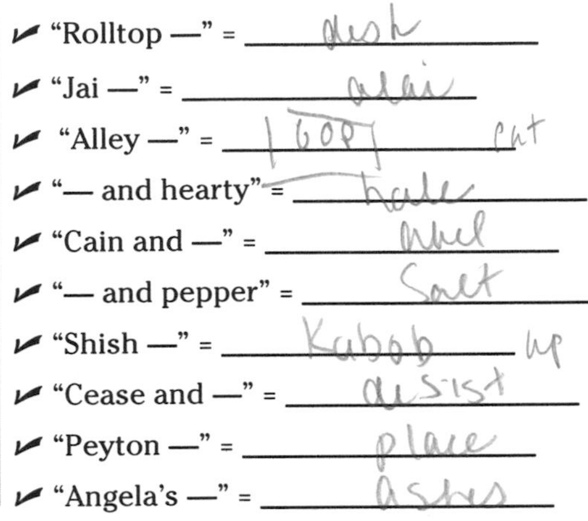

- "Rolltop —" = ____________
- "Jai —" = ____________
- "Alley —" = ____________
- "— and hearty" = ____________
- "Cain and —" = ____________
- "— and pepper" = ____________
- "Shish —" = ____________
- "Cease and —" = ____________
- "Peyton —" = ____________
- "Angela's —" = ____________

Sometimes a constructor implies a missing link rather than clearly depicting it with a dash, which requires you to read the clues more closely after you review the ones with dashes. Instead of "— and hearty," the implied clue may sometimes read as "Hearty's companion" or "Word with hearty"; rather than "— tide," the clue may read "Type of tide." Regardless of how the clue reads, it asks for the same solution: the missing word.

Step #2: Name the Proper Name

After you fill in all the missing-word clues that you can find, moving on to the proper names makes a good strategy. The Crossword Hall of Fame consists mainly of the same one- or two-syllable faces that continue to appear prominently throughout your solving history, consult Chapter 6 for a complete look at proper name repeaters.

What's in a name?

In real life, a proper name is the name you go by. In crosswords, a proper name may be a first or last name of a celebrity, past or present. It may be someone you know of or someone you have only heard about in the world of puzzles.

Beware of celebrities whose names may be mistaken for everyday words. One prime example is TIGER WOODS. If you encounter a clue such as "Woods, for example," the name TIGER may not instantly pop to mind. Constructors love to tease you with this sort of deliberate wordplay, which may stump you if you're not careful. Another tricky clue, "Woody, for one," may disguise the entry ALLEN, as in the film director.

The unwritten rule among constructors and editors is *good news rules.* Where a constructor faces the choice between IDA Lupino, the 1940s actress, and Ugandan ruler IDI Amin, IDA may have the edge. (Enough time has elapsed, however, so that IDI appears to be making a comeback in the world of acceptable puzzle entries.) The woman who set the rules for crosswords, Margaret Farrar (fondly known as "Mrs. Crossword"), established the ground rule that this pastime should lift your spirits, not remind you of life's unpleasantries.

Actress Celeste HOLM once confessed to me that she never ceases to get a tremendous thrill when entering her surname in the squares. Likewise, the wife of the Cosa Nostra chronicler, Peter MAAS (author of *Serpico* and *Underboss*), reports that many friends call in with congratulations when they see her husband's name in a puzzle.

To get some practice dropping names in the puzzle, try your hand at matching the following first and last names. You can find the answers in Appendix A:

First names	***Last names***
COCO	PHILBIN
IRA	LAUDER
ARLO	BAGNOLD
GREER	DEE
ENID	BOMBECK
INA	GUTHRIE
MIA	CHANEL
KEN	GERSHWIN
ERMA	BALIN
ESTEE	KESEY
REGIS	GARSON
RUBY	FARROW

Looking for monograms

You may find the following initials becoming embroidered on your subconscious through their repeated appearances in puzzles:

- **DDE** = "After HST" or "Before JFK"
- **FDR** = "Predecessor of HST"
- **GBS** = "Shavian monogram"
- **JFK** = "After DDE" or "NYC airport"
- **WJC** = "White House monogram"

Step #3: Go for the Synonyms of Repeatersville

Synonyms are essentially two terms that share the same definition. Your job is to match two like words or phrases. For example, as you read down the clue list, the clue "Hawaiian dance" evokes HULA. "Distress call" in three letters reminds you of SOS. "Personality" in three letters makes you think EGO. You read the clue "Hot brew," and in three letters you think TEA.

In the interest of dressing up a synonym clue for a simple entry, constructors often present examples of the entry. For example, in the case of TEA, you may find a clue such as "Earl Grey, for one." This clue references a blend of tea leaves. Of course, the clue is deliberately misleading because it sounds like a man's name if you're not familiar with that type of tea.

Sometimes the constructor offers an "either/or" example that gives you twice the opportunity to get a simple synonym. For TEA, the two blends may be "Oolong or Lapsang." Again, this way of presenting a synonym increases the challenge a bit.

Where the clues come from

Synonyms are drawn from everywhere, with every subject fair game for a clue. Some general topics that you encounter in the entries include the following:

- **Animals:** HEN, EWE, RAM, and SOW and their remarks (BAA, MAA, and OINK) make frequent trips from the barnyard to the crossword puzzle. Animal sounds may answer to the clue "Barnyard sound."
- **Birds:** Yes, I know — birds are also animals, but the crossword puzzle uses so many bird-related words, I just have to give birds their own category. Specifically, ANI, AUK, DAW, EMU, ERN, LOON, MOA, RAIL, and TERN appear in the puzzle with amazing frequency. Example synonym clues involving the bird's nest are "Black bird" (ANI or DAW); "Flightless bird" (EMU or MOA); and "Seabird" (AUK, ERN, LOON, RAIL, or TERN).
- **Bones:** Here's where you get a chance to recall your high school anatomy classes. ULNA (arm), RIB, and TIBIA (shin) all. The clue may read simply "Bone," or it may be more specific as in "Below a humerus" (ULNA).
- **Flowers:** You find ASTER, IRIS, and ROSE sprouting up in the puzzle frequently. For example, the clue may be vague as in "Bloom," tricky as in "Bloomer," or specific as in "Fall bloomer" (ASTER).
- **Moods:** The human element makes an appearance in IRATE or ELATE/D, as in "Riled" or "Gladdened."
- **Musical terms:** Constructors add a musical tone to the puzzle with words such as CLEF, FLAT, REST. Any may answer to the clue "Musical term."
- **Schools:** CEE and DEE and CRAM as in " Poor grades" and "Prep for a final."
- **Skirt styles:** Skirt fashions are very popular in the grid, including MINI, MIDI, MAXI, and A-LINE. The clue for any of these may be terse as in "Skirt."
- **Trees:** ASH, ELM, OAK. You may encounter a vague clue as in "Tree" or more specific as in "Tree of the olive family" (ASH).

Because synonym clues are essentially straightforward definitions, you can often find the answer in the dictionary. For example, if you look up a clue like "Spasm" in the dictionary, you find the three-letter synonym TIC.

Wherever you solve crosswords, you encounter a plethora of three-letter entries beginning with E in the synonym category. These entries key well in both directions and are a comfort to find after you come to expect them. Here are some key entries and clues to keep on hand:

- **E'ER** = "Poetic contraction" or "Poetic adverb"
- **E'EN** = "Poetic contraction" or "Poetic time of day"
- **EKE** = "Squeeze by, with out"
- **ELL** = "Building addition"

- **EMU** = "Flightless bird"
- **ERE** = "Before, poetically"
- **ERG** = "Unit of work"
- **ERN** = "Seabird"
- **ESE** = "Vane direction" or "Compass point"
- **ESS** = "Curve" or "Double curve"
- **ETC** = "Common catchall abbr."

Test your handle on synonyms by matching the entries in Column A with the clues in Column B. You can find the answers in Appendix A.

Column A	*Column B*
AGAR	"Copycat"
ASEA	"Asian governess"
AWAY	"Taj Mahal city"
ASTA	"Word with code"
AERO	"Not in"
AGRA	"At a distance"
ALOE	"Mine entrance"
AMAH	"Without a clue"
AFAR	"Prefix with dynamics"
ARIA	"Seaweed substance"
AREA	"Operatic solo"
ADIT	"Nora Charles' pet"
APER	"Skin cream additive"

Abbreviations

Synonyms also include shortened words. If an entry is an abbreviation, the clue may openly say so by indicating "abbr." — for example, "Cash machine: abbr." As anyone who uses banks today knows, bank cards give 24-hour access to your money through the use of an ATM (automated teller machine).

Open identification that the entry is an abbreviation instantly tips you off to the fact that the skill level of the crossword is introductory. As soon as you notice the absence of colons throughout the clues, you know that you're treading in deeper puzzle waters. Replacing the obvious "abbr." with a phrase that hints at the abbreviation takes the solver to a more challenging level.

You may also find "Cash machine, for short." The word *short* tips you off to the fact that you need a shortened form of the answer. Escalating the challenge, at the third level, the clue itself may start to look like a telegram by abbreviating a part of the clue, as in " 24 hr. banker." Just as when speaking a foreign language, after you tune in to the accent, you understand what's being said.

Step #4: Interpreting Foreign-Word Clues

After you check the three easiest clue categories (missing words, proper names, and synonym repeaters), you venture into other languages. Because entries with three to five letters make up so much of the crossword grid, the standard puzzle vocabulary extends beyond the shorter words found in the dictionary. I call this aspect of solving the "Berlitz" section — after the publishing house that puts out those handy phrase books and tapes for people traveling abroad. Technically, interpreting foreign-word clues is matching simple translations into English from another language. You find basics to help you get by with foreign languages in Chapter 7.

Constructors use foreign languages to diversify the basic lexicon of puzzles, especially where the language provides a letter pattern not available in English. Mostly constructors call on French and Spanish, with a smattering of Italian and German. Sometimes you see the clue presented in its straightforward form with attribution to the language, as in "Water: Fr." (EAU) or "Street: Fr." (RUE).

You may encounter a missing word combined with a foreign language, as in " — de grace (final blow)" for the entry COUP. Most puzzles italicize the clue when it's in a foreign language unless the entry has become accepted in English as in the phrase "— d'etat" (also COUP).

Sometimes the constructor implies that the entry is in a foreign language by referring to a city of the country in question within the clue — for example, "Boyfriend, in Paris" for AMI. Or a language may be implied by a reference to a name in that language within the clue, such as "Girlfriend, to Pierre" for AMIE. In Spain, the typical reference name may be Jose.

Try matching up the following clues in Column A with their entries in Column B. (Don't forget that I tell you all about foreign languages in Chapter 7.) You can also peek at the answers in Appendix A if you want some quick help:

Column A	*Column B*
"Me, in Metz"	CRI
"Love, in Roma"	TIO
"Place: Fr."	VIE
"Dernier —"	AMORE
"Nino's uncle"	CASA
"Life: Fr."	SAN
"Home, to Jose"	PRO
"German article"	MOI
"Saint: Sp."	DER
"Quid — quo"	LIEU

Roman numerals

Generally, Roman-numeral clues refer to dates in ancient history, as in "Year in Nero's reign." Although you may not know these answers off the top of your head, you probably know the seven key letters — M = 1,000, D= 500, C = 100, L = 50, X = 10, V = 5, and I = 1. Some combination of any three or more of these numerals yields the entry.

Step #5: Check for Wordplay

Clues involving wordplay function as riddles rather than straightforward definitions. Take a clue such as "Mont Blanc, for one," with three letters in the grid. To the novice solver, the first guess may be ALP. After all, what acrossionado doesn't covet a trip to that stunning slope? On closer examination, however, the correct answer emerges as a pricey writing utensil: PEN.

The phrasing of a clue measures the difficulty of the puzzle. At the most elementary level, the crossword is a synonym-matching game — ACE answers the clue "Top card," for example. The same entry in a more advanced crossword may be clued as "Winner for Sampras." This is a two-stage solving process: first, you need to know who Sampras is, and then you need to understand the tennis term for winner. Tennis fans instantly get the reference to contemporary court king Pete. The process becomes less clear-cut when the entry moves away from dictionary words.

A question mark at the end of a clue is a giveaway that you're reading a riddle or bit of wordplay.

Test your wits by answering some strange questions as posed by some of my favorite puzzle constructors — Emily Cox, Henry Rathvon, and Henry Hook from *The Boston Globe Sunday* puzzle page. I indicate the number of letters in the entries in parentheses following the clue. You can find the answers in Appendix A:

Column A	***Column B***
A frame up? (3 letters)	LEASE
Turn red? (5 letters)	CRIB
Complains in a fishy way? (5 letters)	EIRE
Flat piece of paper? (5 letters)	RIPEN
Respectable people? (6 letters)	NAP
Green land? (4 letters)	CARPS
Ram's dams? (4 letters)	EWES
Pest's rest? (3 letters)	ELDERS
Tot's cot? (4 letters)	ART

Step #6: Picking Up on Themes

Advanced crosswords offer solvers more than a collection of unrelated words. The added element appears in the form of a theme. A theme may connect as few as two lengthy entries that appear in symmetrical positions within the grid, with the balance of clues not theme-related. Most Sunday-size puzzles weave a theme into the puzzle and its title and have 8 to 12 theme entries.

Theme entries may run across the width and/or length of the grid. Even in a non-Sunday-size crossword (see Chapter 10 for more information on the Sunday puzzle), a theme may include more than one word, as in related phrases such as SIT TIGHT or STAND FOR.

Most solvers save the theme clues for last because they assume that those clues are the most difficult ones. Certainly, attacking the theme clues first isn't a winning strategy. However, you don't necessarily have to hold off to the end. Some experts recommend reading the theme clues first (and the title, if there is one) and letting the information seep into your subconscious while you go about filling in the missing words and synonym matching. If you're lucky, the theme clue makes sense to you and gives you the entry to one of the longer clues. That way, you can fill in more squares and make greater headway into completing the puzzle. If you're really lucky, you understand the theme and are able to figure out the other theme clue(s) quickly, too.

If an entry includes a two-word phrase, the clue may openly say so at the end of the definition, as in "Stay put: 2 wds." Easy puzzles always give you a tag at the end of the clue to let you know how many words are required. The answer — SIT TIGHT — doesn't have a space between the two words. You have been alerted to the fact that more than one word appears in this entry, so you won't be surprised. On the other hand, depending on your puzzle editor, you may get no indication that two words appear in the entry. Take a clue such as "One — time (singly)." The answer, AT A, fills three squares in a row as a single entry without any tip-off. These days, you can expect to find a multiple-word entry without any warning.

Crossword punctuation allows for this type of multiple-word run-on due to the constrictions of the grid. You understand the entry as two words, but when you fill it into the grid, it appears as one. Popular short phrases that repeat in crosswords in addition to AT A include I SEE ("Understanding words"), AS IS ("Sale sign"), and ON A ("— Clear Day").

Remembering Double Missing Words

Very often, words run together in the grid. Using combinations of two short words opens up the grid even further for the constructor.

Many double missing words include the single-letter word "A" within the pair.

These pairs of words are often clichés, as in "Wedding vow" (I DO). Newly minted terms adapt well to crosswords, as in "60s fad" for OP ART and "Current communique" for E-MAIL.

A handy phrase to keep in your back pocket is I SEE, which answers to the clue "Understanding words." (It also works as a response to someone who is trying to help you crack the code.)

In the following list, you find the missing pairs of words that you most need to know to increase your PQ (puzzle quotient). You can find the answer in Appendix A:

Column A	*Column B*
"I cannot tell —"	A LOT
"— bad example	IN IT
"Stuck in —"	IN ONE
"Put — on it!"	IF AT
"What's — for me?"	A LIE
"— first you don't succeed . . ."	A LID
"— was saying . . . "	A RUT
"Thanks —!"	A BUG
"Hole —"	A BAT
"Snug as —"	SET A
"Blind as —"	AS I

Chapter 3

Finding a Puzzle to Work

In This Chapter

- Feeding your daily habit
- Scanning the newspapers for puzzles
- Leafing through magazines
- Browsing the shelves for puzzle books

After you catch the solving bug, you need a handy and steady supply of crosswords. Luckily, today's solver is never far from a crossword puzzle. Marketing experts have discovered that adding a crossword to the pages of any publication gives it an instant audience of reliable solvers. You'd be hard-pressed to find a newspaper without a crossword. Most magazines are following suit. In fact, have you ever picked up a magazine in the doctor's office and found the puzzle page has been torn out? Solvers can be ruthless when it comes to their favorite indoor sport.

I'd bet dollars to donuts that if you look at the reading material on your coffee table right now, you'd find a treasure trove of crosswords. After you exhaust the supply of puzzles in your house, you may want to purchase a puzzle book or magazine (or several).

With so many puzzles to choose from, getting overwhelmed is easy. In this chapter, I list various puzzle sources by level of challenge from easy to medium to expert. Knowing where to find the type of puzzles that are right for you is half the battle. Solving, of course, is the second (more fun) half.

A puzzle must fit into the context of the publication it appears in. While each editor lends some personal touch to the crossword, the trend is to maintain the tradition of the crossword itself, whatever the tradition of that publication may be. For example, *The New York Times* crossword, which has the reputation of being a more challenging puzzle, won't ever become an easy crossword no matter who the editor is.

Leafing through the Newspaper: The Syndicates

What's the single most popular feature in any newspaper? According to all sources, the puzzle page — which includes the crossword and its cousins, the jumble and the hidden-word puzzle (see Chapter 4 for more information on the jumble and hidden-word puzzle). Sources at various publications report that on the rare occasion when the crossword doesn't get to press, a hue and cry arises from the readership. (In fact, the presses were once stopped at *The New York Times* in mid-run in order to add the missing crossword puzzle — or so the story goes.)

At least one of four newspaper readers is hooked on the puzzle page, which explains why nearly every American daily includes something for this audience. Typical of the daily solver is eminent newspaperman, best-selling author, and confirmed acrossionado Ben Bradlee, who got hooked in the 1930s and has yet to meet a newspaper puzzle he can resist.

In the past five years, big-city newspapers have introduced 900-number phone services to help those solvers who "hit the wall" and need help to complete the puzzle. These services typically offer up to three clue answers per call. (Think of the money you save by staying the course with this book.)

Only two newspapers have their own daily puzzles — *The New York Times* and *Newsday*. Other newspapers rely on syndicates to supply daily features such as cartoons, crosswords, and other word puzzles. A *syndicate* is a company that operates as the source of certain types of features. As the supplier, the syndicate enlists the talent (meaning the crossword constructors, cartoonists, and astrologers, among others) and sells the work throughout the nation. Well-known syndicates include Creators Syndicate, *The New York Times,* the *Los Angeles Times,* Tribune Media Services, United Features Syndicate, and King Features.

Some syndicates supply puzzles under the byline of a single constructor, while others supply puzzles under the byline of a single editor. After you develop a taste for a particular puzzle constructor or editor, you can scan the newspapers for his or her name. Identification allows you, the solver, to become familiar with constructors and editors and perhaps develop your own personal favorites. For the constructor, having a byline is part of the Andy Warhol formula of 15 minutes of fame.

Sometimes you need sharp eyes to catch the bylines. They may appear in small type under the lower-left corner of the grid. Or they may appear at the top of the puzzles as in *Newsday* or *USA Today.*

Beginning-level newspaper puzzles (King Features Syndicate)

I use the following criteria to judge whether a puzzle is beginner-friendly or better suited for a more advanced level. Generally, if the puzzle has the following two characterisrics, then it's okay for beginners:

- **The grid is small.** I mean below the standard 15 x 15 squares associated with the typical daily crossword. (While a daily measures 13 x 13 (or smaller) the Sunday grows to 19 x 19 or 21 x 21.)
- **The clues contain hints.** For example, if a clue calls for an entry to be in another language, the clue contains a hint (either following a colon or in parentheses) that says something like "House (Span.)" or "House: Span."

The puzzles produced by King Features Syndicate fit these criteria to a tee. One of the original syndicates, King Features Syndicate has provided a daily 13 x 13 crossword since the Roaring 20s. One of the original puzzle constructors, Eugene Sheffer, still impacts some of the puzzles published by King Features Syndicate.

Sheffer became the official King Features constructor decades ago when he still held a day job as a full professor in the French department of Columbia University; he worked on creating puzzles by night. The Sheffer daily crossword continues to be published to this day, guided by top constructor Henry Hook, following general guidelines that he established.

Sheffer's original rules for constructing puzzles with a simple challenge include:

- Short clues (three words, maximum)
- One foreign word per puzzle (maximum)
- One whimsical clue (for example, "Pest's rest" for NAP)
- Hints (technically called "tags") where needed (for example, "abbr." or "2 wds" to tell you that the entry is an abbreviation, or is two words, respectively.)

The tradition in King Features puzzles is to draw on the solver's memory (rather than wordplay or riddles), which makes them suitable for beginners.

The tried-and-true formula of the King Features "Sheffer" crossword features set grid designs, with each design repeating 13 times a year. While the clues and their entries change, the diagrams remain the same. In fact, the same grid design repeats every four weeks.

At a constant 13 x 13 squares, the compact Sheffer puzzle is handy and quick to do. Some puzzles have themes (topics that tie together the lengthier clues), although it's not a requirement.

King Features also syndicates the Thomas Joseph crossword, an even more compact oblong grid at 11 x 13 squares. Due to the smaller size, two-letter words may appear in some patterns put together by Joseph, but as a rule, three letters are the minimum acceptable size.

Each King Features daily puzzle has a suggested solution time so that, if you want to, you have a measure of the time investment ahead. For example, for Puzzle 3-1, the solution time is estimated at 24 minutes. (You can find the answers to Puzzle 3-1 in Appendix A.)

After you work the King Features daily-size puzzle often enough, you may yearn to move on to a slightly harder challenge. On Sundays, readers can look forward to The Premier Crossword (Sunday-size) by Donna Stone (also syndicated by King Features). In her puzzle, Stone blends the old with the new, creating an eclectic mixture in the clues and entires. In keeping with the "old," her puzzles sport titles that imply the theme, and her clues tend to be straightforward. In keeping with the "new," the themes incorporate wordplay in a clever manner.

In Puzzle 3-2, I share a Stone puzzle with a theme about chocolate, which is a generous offer for a cocoa fanatic like me. Please note that the theme clues (longer entries) repeat the exact same phrase, "Chocoholic's treat." Some themes use the same clue for an extra solving hurdle. Enjoy the flavors, calorie free! (Check out Chapter 10 to discover how to get started with a Sunday puzzle and themes.) After you finish working the puzzle, check out the answers in Appendix A to get the unparalled satisfaction that comes with being right!

Puzzle 3-1

Across

1 Pop singer Loeb
5 Aries
8 One of the help
12 Pedestal statue
13 Kyoto sash
14 Sea eagle
15 Brunch, for one
16 Model
18 Fort wall
20 Author Verne
21 Undeniably
22 Petrol
23 Give a leg up
26 Pattern of excellence
30 "— Got a Secret!"
31 Serenade the moon
32 "A Chorus Line" song
33 Sunshade
36 Emulate Kristi Yamaguchi
38 "Oedipus —"
39 Story of a lifetime
40 The "final frontier"
43 Contradiction
47 Lover
49 Actor Neeson
50 Very eager
51 Wapiti
52 Rue the run
53 Erstwhile Persian
54 Affront, in slang
55 Bedazzle

Down

1 Walk unsteadily
2 Thought
3 Make like an eagle
4 Mitigates
5 Ring borders
6 Blind as —
7 Russian space station
8 One of the Gorgons
9 Seed coating
10 *Bus Stop* playwright
11 Reps.' Rivals
17 Open a bit
19 Favorite
22 Festive
23 Marceau portrayal
24 Eventual aves
25 "— the ramparts . . ."
26 Crony
27 — long way
28 Can. prov.
29 Born
31 Compete with Foreman
34 Videogame parlor
35 Appear
36 Round Table address
37 Eucalyptus eaters
39 Woof, bow-wow, arf, et al.
40 Hormel product
41 Macadamize
42 Saharan
43 Hungarian sheepdog
44 Steno's skill: abbr.
45 Honolulu's island
46 Comicbook super group
48 U.K. ref. bk.

Medium-level newspaper puzzles

I look for the following features when deciding if a puzzle is suitable for medium-level solvers:

- **Daily grid:** You're looking at a grid that has grown by two squares in each direction (as compared to a beginning-level puzzle). In the scheme of crosswords, the standard daily grid measures 15 x 15. The bigger the puzzle, the bigger the challenge just because you have more clues to read and answer.
- **Sunday grid:** The average size is 21 x 21, although it sometimes expands to 23 x 23.
- **Clues:** The tone determines the level of your challenge in the clues. A medium-level puzzle tends to be straightforward in its clues — but that doesn't mean the clues are dull. It just means that things are pretty much as they appear; for example, where a solution is an adjective, it is referred to in the clue. You see "Word with herring" for RED, rather than a vague clue like "Herring, e.g." You may find hints on the clues to indicate foreign language or multiword entries. Or you may not.
- **Entries:** Themes are preferred. Sunday puzzles combine titles with themes for lively results.

The Los Angeles Times Syndicate

Back in 1978 when I sold my first puzzle, the pioneers of crosswords were still running the industry. Through Margaret Farrar, the woman who launched the entire industry, I met Trude Michel Jaffe, Mrs. Farrar's "amanuensis" (HELPER) and a longtime newspaperwoman. Over the decades, Jaffe has been the daily crossword editor for the *Los Angeles Times,* while Joyce Lewis recently began to handle the Sunday submissions.

The *Los Angeles Times* puzzle is an offshoot of *The New York Times.* The *L.A. Times* launched its puzzle shortly after Margaret Farrar reached the mandatory retirement age with *The New York Times* in 1969. Because the *L.A. Times* didn't have an age cap, Mrs. Farrar moved her prodigious energies to the other coast.

The *Los Angeles Times* puzzles have a reputation for offering a minimum of obscure, archaic, and foreign words. Editor Dan Michel calls the level of this puzzle "middle mind."

Clues in the *Los Angeles Times* puzzles tend to be straightforward, while cleverness emerges in the entries. These puzzles feature themes and topicality heavily. Many of the same folks who submit puzzles to *The New York Times* supply material to the *L.A. Times,* as you note if you pay attention to bylines.

If you solve a crossword from this syndicate, you may notice a few quirks:

- A clue may not contain the same number of letters as the entry word. This is a quirky requirement. For example, you won't see "Halt" as a clue for STOP but rather "Traffic sign."
- No parenthetical note or tag identifies multiple-word entries. For example, for ATA you find a clue like "One — time" without a tag like "2 wds."
- Entries that modify a clue word are stated clearly. For example, the clue for BLUE may be "Word with sky or moon."
- Entries that combine a prefix or suffix with a clue word are stated clearly. For example, the entry TRI may have the clue "Prefix with angle."

Puzzle 3-3 helps you understand why solvers look forward to the Sunday *L.A. Times* challenge. Puzzle 3-4 shows a sample of the ongoing contribution that Jaffe continues to make in the puzzle world. If you get stumped on a clue, or if you just want to check that you have the correct entry for a clue (or if you just want to cheat), flip to Appendix A in the back of the book for some help with the answers. (Chapter 10 offers tips and hints for working Sunday-size puzzles.)

Puzzle 3-2: For Chocoholics

Across

1 Java joint
5 Donahue of *Get a Life*
11 Poster abbr.
14 Moving man?
19 In a flash, in memos
20 Tebaldi or Scotto
21 Ford of football
22 Texas landmark
23 Chocoholic's treat
25 Incite Rover
26 Get cracking
27 McCarthy's trunkmate
28 Novelist Seton
29 South African politician
31 Tavern
32 The — Ridge Boys
34 Minuscule
36 Chocoholic's treat
39 Polenta ingredient
44 Pretentious
46 Nixon or Bush
47 Breakfast of centurions?
48 Snatch
50 Where to dance a saltarello
52 Cease
55 Chocoholic's treat
59 Eastern capital
61 Where Devils fight Flames
62 Knight's title
63 Pressure
65 Ichthyologist's concern
68 Shipbuilding wood
71 Mongrel
72 Sturm — Drang
73 Chocoholic's treat
78 Citrus cooler
80 Mrs. Eddie Cantor
81 Secure the ship
82 Sentry's shout
83 Meerschaum part
86 — vous plait
88 Actor Gunn
92 Contests
93 Chocoholic's treat
99 Soprano Frances
100 "— Street" ('63 song)
101 Tender
102 Southern constellation
103 Sty cry
105 Everett of "Medical Center"
107 Troubadour
110 Chocoholic's treat
114 TV's *Murder —*
115 Morning moisture
116 Hogwash
117 Summer fruits
119 Dana's *Two Years Before the —*
123 Sign of summer
127 Go in
130 Fairway accessory
131 Chocoholic's treat
133 Simpson of fashion
134 Dryden work
135 Journalist Fallaci
136 Mirth
137 Day or Duke
138 Ensnare
139 Fixed tightly
140 Nevada city

Down

1 Actress Peggy
2 Strong — ox
3 Mirror image?
4 *Sleepless in Seattle* director
5 Muff
6 "— Smile Be Your Umbrella"
7 Privy to
8 Not any, with "a"
9 Paul Anka's birthplace
10 *Norma —*
11 To boot
12 Moon or Richards
13 Pizza topping
14 Arrest
15 Seville shout
16 Like Mozart's flute
17 With 120 Down, protein component
18 Pescow or Dixon
24 Dutch export
29 St. John of "Horror Hotel"
30 Enjoyed these theme entries?
33 Beer barrels
35 Stoltz or Idle
37 Composer Franck
38 Eye-related
39 Musical finale
40 In excess
41 Praise a performance
42 Griffon greeting
43 Vientiane's nation
45 Run up the phone bill
49 "Otello" librettist
51 Italian commune
53 Soporific substance
54 Menial laborer
56 News, briefly
57 Secular
58 "I Can —, Can't I?" ('37 song)
59 — firma
60 Nonpartisan: abbr.

64 "That hurts!"
66 Short shows
67 Stevenson scoundrel
69 Commotion
70 Newsstand
73 Ward off
74 Stallone role
75 Corn holders
76 *Sesame Street* cutie
77 Mighty mite
78 Make like
79 Prima donna
84 Bestow
85 Laundry problem
87 Emerge
89 Practice punching
90 Joyce's land
91 Circus barker
94 Director Besson
95 Porthos's pal
96 Oland role
97 Sect starter
98 Man the bar
100 Kadiddlehopper's portrayer
104 Shot
106 Reserved
108 Golfer Ballesteros
109 Cramp
110 Roll or bagel, essentially
111 Sonata movement
112 Furry fisherman
113 Kid stuff
118 Come across
120 See 17 Down
121 '70s hairdo
122 Shoe size
124 Bagel or bialy
125 Nerd
126 Toast topper
128 Ivy Leaguer
129 Part of USAR
131 Archery item
132 Lear, to Cordelia

Puzzle 3-3: Dog Day

Across

1 Like Peck's boy
4 Give a darn
7 Job for the bunko squad
11 Dressed for the bench
16 Single-handedly
17 Historic time
18 Hawk home
19 Childish
20 They made "Fire"
23 Develop
24 Utterly senseless
25 Hwy. by Malibu
26 Bulls and Bears
28 Back talk
29 Flue-ish
30 3-3, e.g.
31 Gave birth to
32 Cairo cobra
34 Bambi's Faline
35 Calendar col.
36 The Spanish?
37 Hog haven
38 Golfer's doohickey
39 Thine and mine
40 Meat-and-potatoes dish
45 After dust and dish
47 Complies with
49 Salty sauce
50 Torture oneself
52 " — a Parade"
53 Bldg. unit
55 Have the slip to
56 Gave the slip to
59 She's a fox
60 Zeus's predecessor
63 ". . . and — my cap . . ."
65 Grab a cab
66 Hail, to Caesar

67 Bowling alley device
71 Manipulate heartstrings
72 Chump
74 Ariz. neighbor
75 Cajoles
76 Heather
78 Stop
80 The write stuff
82 Ore. neighbor
83 Soulmates?
84 Marry
86 Put two on the nose
88 Unskilled workers
89 Broadway Rose lover
90 50s teen wear
94 Compiegne co.
95 Eiger, e.g.
97 Sib, for one
98 Aye opposite
99 *Goodfellas* fellas
102 "Well — be!"
103 Future fish
104 37 Across occupant
105 Rostov's river
106 Befuddled
108 *Fantasia* frame
109 Cluster
111 Haul
112 Fast flyer's engine
113 Tuneful passage
116 Epithet for Hamlet
119 See 72 Across
120 Expert
121 Zero follower
122 Burly Burl
123 Vietnam area
124 Nerve network
125 Audible awe
126 Koppel

Down

1 Silly slip
2 Singer Moyet
3 Toroid
4 Future flower
5 Misadd
6 Petulant
7 Coterie
8 Canea citizens
9 Put on the radio
10 Flatland highland
11 Rpm pt.
12 An eye, foreign eye
13 Early Times?
14 Jealous
15 More profound
16 Flareup of feeling
18 Ex-ember
19 Rev. Jackson
21 Give it a shot
22 Puck's place
27 San —, Cal.
30 Go one better
31 Lamarr
33 Problem for Pauline
36 The French?
37 Debate side
40 Golfer Ballesteros
41 It's spotted in Africa
42 Bar, at the bar
43 Fido's foot
44 Lit
46 Cote d' —
47 Hardy or Stone
48 1900 uprising
51 Hawaii's state bird
52 One no-Trump?
53 Part of a *drame*
54 Condition
55 Greek peak
57 Draws forth
58 Impressionist painter
61 Cutlet?
62 *Cero* follower
64 "— deal!"
68 "— us a child . . ."
69 They'll take you out
70 Timer's button
73 He loved Lucy
77 Letters from Greece
79 Asparagus unit
81 Paleo's opposite
85 Place of berth?
86 Squandered
87 Sushi option
88 Get nosy
89 Plane wing part
91 Little drip
92 Expertise
93 Hans's cousin
94 Shrill insect
96 Corp. symbols
99 California desert
100 Lifted the lid
101 Bunches of bits
104 Napped leather
105 Fudd, to Bugs
106 Minstrel's song
107 Vague rumor
110 Poetic tentmaker
111 Cable choice
112 Took a plane
114 Two-kind link
115 Abacus result
117 Gibraltar simian
118 Lennon's lady

Puzzle 3-4

Across

1 First bids
8 Hung on string
15 Moon's nearest orbit path
16 Worship
17 Gleefulness
18 Puritan's helper
19 *The Sun Also* —
20 Face in the mirror
22 Squeeze out a living
23 Winner for Sampras
24 Self confidence
25 Blackbirds
26 Road cover
27 Last word in awful
28 Assemblage of eight
29 Make certain
31 London nail polish
33 Cooks' needs
35 Memorization
36 Whaler's way to blubber
38 Cease and —; stop
42 Follows came or went
43 Church altar areas
46 Japanese drama
47 Blaring
48 Hits a homer
49 Alt. choice
50 Humongous wine container
51 Journalist Alexander
52 Crinkly fabric
54 Sharp-cornered
56 Tropical ailment
58 Cold country
59 Commended
60 Starts up again
61 "Chicken" colonel

Down

1 Make it go
2 Big-beaked bird
3 Chalkboard accessories
4 Evening, in some ads
5 Sponsorship
6 Antique car
7 Graduate to-be
8 Catastrophe
9 Saw
10 Seward Peninsula cape
11 Certain "Day" color
12 Lesotho's coins
13 Book of the Bible
14 Loathe
21 Take and trust lead-in
24 Eliot and Angelou
25 Peaks
27 False
28 Joyce Carol —
30 Stand on its head
32 Swellings
34 Towards the coast
36 Wide ruffle
37 Lolls about
39 Turned upside down
40 Has more suds
41 Duds
42 Aquila's bright star
44 Peter or pipes
45 Familiar commemoratives
48 Role for Alan Ladd
51 Treat a door rudely
52 Jean Auel's *Cave Bear People*
53 Invader's job
55 Eskimo knife
57 The "altar" star

If you have access to the World Wide Web, you can access an archive of the *Los Angeles Times* Syndicate puzzles that catalogs puzzles from the last six months. Turn to Chapter 16 for more information about finding puzzles online.

Creators Syndicate

This puzzle, which is commissioned by *Newsday,* is syndicated nation-wide by Creators Syndicate.

This 15 x 15 puzzle actually offers a mission statement, which is "to provide American newspapers with a crossword having broad appeal to all age groups, lively language, and free of unusual and obscure words." Editor Stan Newman, who is also the Managing Director of Puzzles and Games for the Times Books division of Random House, Inc., considers himself a sort of "puzzle evangelist."

After *Newsday* discontinued Stan's puzzle in December 1996, the newspaper received over 10,000 complaints from disgruntled solvers. As a result, *Newsday* reconsidered and reinstated Stan in May 1997.

Newman diverges from providing popular fare on the weekends, when he escalates the tone of the clues to the expert audience. The Saturday *Newsday* puzzle is a 15 x 15 unthemed puzzle known as the "Saturday Stumper." Attempt it at your own risk. You'll find out how much a theme helps your solving technique under daily circumstances. Newman emphasizes wide open spaces on Saturday, which means longer entries and a minimum of crosswordese (crossword repeaters). What's more, clues are tougher. *Newsday* also gears its 21 x 21 Sunday themed puzzle toward the more experienced acrossionado.

Other characteristics of the Creators Syndicate crossword you should know about include the following:

- The puzzle allows no more than two obscure entries per daily puzzle, and no more than three on Sunday. By obscure entry, I mean something like ASTARTE, which answers to "Phoenician goddess."
- The puzzle offers parenthetical hints for missing-word clues that are titles. For example, you see "I — Rhythm (Clooney tune)." (The corresponding entry is GOT.)
- You find a balance of clues between contemporary and traditional references, such as clues related to rock and classical music mixed together.
- The puzzle uses colloquial terms to define everyday entries, such as "Out of sight" for HIDDEN.

Take a whack at Puzzle 3-5 to experience the thrill that Creators Syndicate crossword workers look forward to every day. Appenidix A contains the answers to Puzzle 3-5.

Newsday has a fantastic site on the World Wide Web where you can access archived puzzles and puzzle help galore. Just turn to Chapter 16 for more information about finding puzzle fun on the Web.

Puzzle 3-5: Hi Again

Across

1 Theme of this puzzle
5 Nick at Nite offering
10 Leaves town
14 Type like *this:* abbr.
15 Last Greek letter
16 Springy tune
17 A good way to take bad news
20 Sunday speech: abbr.
21 What the particular may pick
22 British cattle breed
23 "Zip- — -Doo-Dah"
24 Iowa city
25 Sun worshiper
28 French friends
29 Actor Holbrook
32 Vision-related
33 Struck down, old-style
34 A few
35 Treats casually
38 Moves quickly
39 Suspicious
40 Tilted
41 Commercials, for instance
42 Cindy Crawford ex
43 Colloquial
44 Hostile criticism
45 Tim of *WKRP*
46 *It All Started with Columbus* author
49 *Misery* star
50 Recipe phrase
53 Tropical island shrub
56 Take care of
57 Occupied
58 Shatner's best-known role
59 Nintendo rival
60 "A Boy — Sue"
61 Midmonth day

Down

1 Haunches
2 — *Jury* (Spillane novel)
3 It may be over your head
4 Under the weather
5 More optimistic
6 Overact
7 Sales personnel
8 "That's gross!"
9 Basketball inventor
10 Windshield material
11 Portrait medium
12 High-fashion mag
13 Underworld river
18 Next to bat
19 Stage signals
23 Sheriff Lobo portrayer
24 *Jaws* town
25 Former South African prime minister
26 Plant pest
27 Pigs' digs
28 Love, Italian style
29 *Crocodile Dundee* star
30 In the midst of
31 Southpaw
33 Lewis Carroll beast
34 Golf Hall of Famer
36 Does an inaugural job
37 Champaign athletes
42 Substance on stamps
43 Ocean floor
44 Mrs. Ted Turner
45 Uplift
46 New Testament book
47 '50s president of South Korea
48 Flash Gordon foe
49 Buddy
50 Corrosive chemical
51 Entice
52 Pops the question
54 Aunt in *Bambi*
55 Travel downhill, in a way

1	2	3	4	■	5	6	7	8	9	■	10	11	12	13
14				■	15					■	16			
17				18						19				
20			■	21				■	22					
■	■	■	23				■	24			■	■	■	■
25	26	27				■	28				■	29	30	31
32					■	33				■	34			
35					36					37				
38				■	39				■	40				
41			■	42				■	43					
■	■	■	44				■	45			■	■	■	■
46	47	48				■	49				■	50	51	52
53						54					55			
56				■	57					■	58			
59				■	60					■	61			

USA Today

Since its inception a decade ago, a single editor, Charles Preston, has managed the crossword in *USA Today.* Like many other newspaper crosswords, freelance constructors provide the basic material to Mr. Preston for selection.

The daily-size *USA Today* puzzle conforms to the 15 x 15 standard. To help you get familiar with the personality of the constructors, *USA Today* uses bylines to alert you to the day's constructor.

USA Today favors straightforward clues and themes, which is common at this level of solving. However, a couple of elements distinguishes *USA Today*'s puzzles from the other syndicates:

- The daily puzzles usually have themes (which are reflected in the titles), as you can see in Puzzle 3-6, called "Shivery."
- Clues offer more information rather than less. For example, for the entry ELKE, rather than a vague clue like "Sommer" you find "Ms. Sommer."

Puzzle 3-6 contains all the classic elements of a *USA Today* puzzle. As always, you find the answers to the puzzle in Appendix A.

Expert-level newspaper puzzles

Welcome to the big leagues! The expert-level newspaper puzzle may look suspiciously similar to medium-level and beginning-level puzzles, but upon closer examination, you begin to note the following differences:

- **The daily grid:** These grids tend to run 15 x 15, but they have patterns that keep black squares to a minimum. (The longer entries afforded by the lack of black squares keep the entries down to about 78 per grid.)
- **The Sunday grid:** You can look forward to a standard 21 x 21 or 23 x 23 grid, but again, constructors keep black squares to a minimum (typically to one-sixth of the grid). The entries in these puzzles number from 140 to 150 on the 21's, and from 70 to 180 on the 23's.
- **Clues:** The clues are what distinguish this puzzle from its brethern. Expert-level clues become more clever in composition. A clue for a simple entry like THE may be disguised as "A relative," which can throw you off if you follow "relative" and not "A." Wordplay becomes the norm, whereas wordplay is the exception at other levels of solving.
- **Themes:** Themes, which cover a wide range of topics, including music, movies, and circuses, emphasize wordplay. Pop culture (such as brand names) enters the puzzle through themes, with an emphasis on modern and cultural references. Wordplay may emerge in the entries through homonyms (INTRA-VENUS instead of INTRAVENOUS) or clever clues ("Prisoners of a kind" for CAPTIVE AUDIENCE).
- **Variety in the entries:** Constructors make an effort to insert rarely used letters (J, K, Q, W, X, and Z) in the grid. You may come across entries like STYX, JAZZ, or INXS in expert territory.
- **Everyday words:** Constructors resort to obscure entries at this level only when necessary to support a clever interlocking clue. Certainly, you won't see two intersecting obscure entries — for example, you'll be glad to know that you'll neven see a clue such as "Tree genus" intersect with the clue "Bulgarian town."

A brief history of Will Shortz

Readers of *Games* recognize Will Shortz as a member of the original editorial team. To listeners of Weekend Edition on National Public Radio, Shortz is the Sunday puzzle master. In his capacity as puzzle editor at *The New York Times,* Shortz has changed the course of the crossword in many positive ways since he took the reins in 1993. Perhaps more than any other puzzle editor, he has introduced many helpful and interesting innovations to puzzle. For example, Shortz was the first puzzle editor to allow bylines on daily puzzles, which were traditionally anonymous. And he condones the use of popular brand names as entries. Radical.

The New York Times (Times syndicate)

The reputation of *The New York Times* crossword puzzle is legendary. It has earned a certain mystique as the most difficult newpaper puzzle in the country. Certainly, the standard for this puzzle is intelligent entertainment for a literate readership. Freelance constructors from around the nation submit material, and the editor, Will Shortz, gives it all a thorough review.

When you travel abroad, you can always find a *New York Times* crossword in the pages of *The International Herald Tribune.*

The *New York Times* 15 x 15 daily crossword escalates in difficulty as the week progresses. Monday's puzzle is the easiest of all, gearing up day by day until the weekend. (The editorial reasoning behind this policy is that acrossionados deserve a break on Monday.) Expert solvers feel that the Saturday puzzle is truly the most difficult of all. The Sunday puzzle is, by definition, the most time-consuming because it has the largest grid size, expanding to 21 x 21 squares or 23 x 23 squares from the daily standard of 15 x 15 squares.

When you first pick up the *Times,* go for the Monday crossword — beginners can tackle a Monday puzzle with a measure of success. You may notice that it has more missing-word clues than Friday's puzzle, which means that you can solve quite a bit of the puzzle before you hit the wall. Until you gain some solving confidence, approach Saturday's puzzle with caution!

The *New York Times* puzzle distinguishes itself from other puzzles with the following characteristics:

- **More brand names:** You now see plenty of nationally recognized brand names in the entries (Nike, Chee-tos, and so on) that were taboo under prior editors (and in most other crosswords).
- **More humor:** The tone of the entries tends toward the lighthearted rather than dry, dictionary definitions.
- **More colloquial phrases:** Whether or not they appear in the dictionary, everyday phrases are breaking into the entries. Now you may see a clue like "Words before about" and "at 'em'."
- **Less emphasis on themes:** Wide-open patterns are welcome so that parallel entries may span 12 squares. The thrust is on weaving longer unrelated entries together rather than relying on a theme within the grid.
- **Less crosswordese:** The old lexicon of crossword stand-bys is on the wane as the *Times* grid embraces brand names and puns. "Flightless birds" may become extinct in more than one way. So long to EMU and MOA!
- **Fewer obscure entries:** Etruscan goddesses are definitely out in today's *Times* puzzles, as are the types of rope fibers.

Puzzle 3-6: Shivery

Across

1 Not with it
5 David's song
10 Out!
14 Stat, sort of
15 Tired out
16 Stockings
17 Operation —: naval Antarctica project
19 Utah resort
20 Compensations
21 Colette's Tuesdays
23 Tell a secret
24 Object with a tail
25 Cultivated land
27 Brat's outbursts
30 Bad habits
31 Paris patron
32 Bolger
33 Tucked in
34 Baby's woe
35 Pelt
36 Playing marble
37 Nostrums
38 Embarrassing display
39 Celestial phenomenon
41 Grandma's corset
42 Good grief!: var.
43 Leo's bragging
44 I do declare!
46 Chitterlings, e.g.
50 Ms. Sommer
51 California herbs
53 To shelter
54 — Semple McPherson
55 Roman statesman
56 Animal fat
57 Swiss veggie?
58 Adam's grandson

Down

1 Is on the go
2 Cruising
3 Highlander
4 Horrified
5 Outcast
6 Smooth
7 Pub drinks
8 Taylor, of the violet eyes
9 Memory trigger
10 *The Secret* —: Conrad
11 One way to quit
12 Italian wine region
13 Earl Grey and oolong
18 Is in a dither
22 Qtys.
24 Major or Minor
25 Leg bone
26 It gets the party going
27 Communicate, in a way
28 Water pipes
29 Auld lang —
30 Theda Bara, e.g.
31 Copperfield's wife, and others
34 Blind alley
35 Capone's sobriquet
37 Silent one
38 Stonewall
40 Assented
41 Added power, with up
43 Oar
44 It's a —!
45 Fitzgerald, of song
46 Body: prefix
47 — even keel
48 Von Bismarck
49 Brit awards
52 Washington medical agcy.

Essentially, a *Times* puzzle is a Q&A test that balances the measure of your vocabulary and your general knowledge from classical subjects to the contemporary.

Times Books produces *The Crossword Answer Book,* a word finder based on the typical clues and entries that you find in *The New York Times* puzzle. If you plan to work the *New York Times* puzzle on a regular basis, consider purchasing this book. Additionally, you can buy collections of the crosswords from past editors. For help with past puzzles, you may want to get *The New York Times Crossword Dictionary,* also from Times Books. (See Chapter 9 for more complete information.)

Puzzle 3-7 shows a good example of what makes Shortz one of the most popular puzzle editors in the "American-speaking" world.

The New York Times knows their puzzle is good. The *Times* makes it possible to access one of their puzzles day or night, from any location in the world, over the World Wide Web. See Chapter 16 for more information on this incredible feat of technology.

Tribune Media Services

One extremely seasoned editor, whose work as a constructor is well-known in the field, manages the Tribune Media Services syndicate out of Chicago. He recently assumed full-time duties after a stint as the daily editor. Specifically, you can look forward to a puzzle edited by Wayne Robert Williams all week; Herb Ettenson retired from his post as the Sunday editor in November 1997 after more than 30 years on the job.

(Since assuming the post of puzzle editor with Tribune Media Services, Wayne Robert Williams has been impressed by the volume of feedback he receives through e-mail at `tmspuzzle@aol.com`. Unlike editors who rely on mail, Williams finds he can respond quickly and promptly to reader's comments. What's more, there's nothing lonely about the job anymore!)

Regardless of the day you pick up the puzzle, the *Chicago Tribune* crossword focuses on cleverness and ingenuity. Entertainment and challenge serve as parallel goals in this puzzle. In addition, the *Tribune* crossword is known for the following two features:

- **Unusual-looking entries:** The editor likes to see an everyday word like FISHHOOK in the grid (with the double H configuration) versus an obscure term like ARNEBIA. Their philosophy is that solvers don't care about the "Genus of Asiatic herbs."
- **Pun-type clues:** For example, that crossword standby ALE is clued by something like "Stout relative."

Puzzle 3-7

Across

1 "Quite contrary" nursery rhyme girl
5 Sudden outpouring
10 June 6, 1944
14 Pinza of "South Pacific"
15 "Here — trouble!"
16 Straight line
17 Chest organ
18 Make amends (for)
19 Goat's milk cheese
20 '60s TV medical drama
22 Detective Lord — Wimsey
23 Guinness suffix
24 Shooting stars
26 World Wildlife Fund's symbol
30 *The Hairy Ape* playwright
32 Gets educated
34 Finale
35 Deep cut
39 Saharan
40 Writer Bret
42 Butter alternative
43 — contendere (court plea)
44 Kind of "vu" in a classified
45 Colossus of —
47 Hardy's partner
50 Get used (to)
51 Medicine injector
54 Neighbor of Syr.
56 Enough to sink one's teeth into
57 Pasternak hero
63 "— just me or . . .?"
64 Indian corn
65 Not theirs
66 Rat (on)
67 TV's *Kate &* —
68 Romance lang.
69 In — (actually)
70 She had "the face that launched a thousand ships"
71 Fuddy-duddy

Down

1 Blend
2 Côte d' —
3 N.H.L. venue
4 Cartoon bear
5 Oodles
6 Latke ingredient
7 Cupid
8 Rent-controlled building, maybe
9 WNW's opposite
10 British rock group since the mid-'70s
11 Because of
12 Take up, as a hem
13 Sophomore and junior, e.g.
21 Low-fat
22 — Club (onetime TV group)
25 Downy duck
26 Scheme
27 Prefix with dynamic
28 It gets hit on the head
29 1967 Rex Harrison film role
31 Moxie
33 Shoulder motion
36 Actor Alan
37 Trickle
38 Party thrower
41 Wiry dog
46 Spy Mata —
48 Unspecified one
49 Tin —
51 Wallop
52 O.K.'s
53 Train tracks
55 Luster
58 Streamlet
59 Empty
60 Garage occupant
61 Alum
62 Sonja Henie's birthplace
64 — jongg

1	2	3	4	■	5	6	7	8	9	■	10	11	12	13
14				■	15					■	16			
17				■	18					■	19			
20				21					■	22				
■	■	■	■	23			■	24	25					
26	27	28	29		■	30	31					■	■	■
32					33	■	34			■	35	36	37	38
39				■	40	41				■	42			
43				■	44			■	45	46				
■	■	■	47	48				49	■	50				
51	52	53					■	54	55		■	■	■	■
56					■	57	58				59	60	61	62
63				■	64					■	65			
66				■	67					■	68			
69				■	70					■	71			

Mastering the Magazines

Whoa! Have you noticed how many puzzle magazines are on the shelf at your local supermarket nowadays? Over 200 and counting. And at least half of these are monthly, while the rest come out less often — sometimes four to six times a year.

When I entered the puzzle field professionally 20 years ago, the selection of puzzle magazines was considerably smaller, about 100. But as publishers branched out into number-style puzzles and variety puzzle magazines, each new magazine develops a devoted readership that results in new niches and a proliferation of product (as they say in the biz).

What you get

Due to the shape of the puzzle layout, most puzzle magazines are smaller than your standard 8-x-10-inch magazine size. Pocket- (or pocketbook-) size portability is the idea. (This special size has given puzzle magazines prominence at the supermarket — or wherever you shop — in the special slots or "pockets" placed by the checkout counter. If that craving strikes while you're waiting in line, you may just go for a cute little crossword morsel at the last minute.) A typical puzzle magazine contains anywhere from 60 to 150 puzzles.

With puzzle magazine titles, you can count on much truth in labeling. If the title of the magazine uses words like *simple, easy,* or *fun,* you're in the beginner range. If the adjective modifying *crosswords* is any other word, you're on the next level of challenge. And when the magazine includes all 21 x 21 puzzles, chances are you've graduated to acrossionado.

Generally, magazines with a variety of puzzles are less popular because most solvers are pretty specific about which type of puzzle they prefer. If you can't enjoy every page, the book isn't as valuable to you. But if someone else in your house likes the cryptograms, for example, you've got it made. Or, you may discover that cryptograms are actually your cup of tea.

Selecting a puzzle magazine

Although a puzzle is a puzzle is a puzzle, to paraphrase Gertrude Stein, some brands of puzzle magazines have carved distinctive niches for themselves. Some brands specialize in different categories of puzzles; some brands make their name by offering puzzles of a specific level of difficulty.

Puzzle magazine sales are # 1 at the newsstand

Curiously, magazine sellers rely greatly on two profit centers: puzzle books and "adult" (X-rated) materials. Apparently when people are ready to plunk down their money for some entertaining reading, they think of one or the other of these two categories.

Did you ever notice that puzzles don't go stale? Whenever you get around to working on them, they seem "fresh" and interesting. Even last year's leftover crossword magazine can do the trick if you're in the mood for puzzles right now. That's why newsstands can stack up on them without fear. Unlike perishables, puzzles have no expiration date, although every two weeks they are replaced by the next month's crop. When the craving strikes, the puzzle magazine buyer has no trouble finding satisfaction at the store.

Most puzzle magazines fall into the easy- to mid-level range. Their editors design them to please rather than challenge (or frustrate).

When you're really thirsty, you drink whatever you find in the vending machine — within certain parameters (the choice suits your diet and pocketbook). Puzzle magazines are like Coca-Cola and Pepsi — would you refuse one when you're thirsty because you really prefer the other? Similarly, subtle differences in type styles or layouts may not be meaningful when you're in the mood for a puzzle.

Tables 3-1, 3-2, and 3-3 present a list of recommended beginning-level, medium-level, and expert-level puzzle magazines, respectively. Not all the magazines come out every month, because some readers only have time for six magazines per year.

I list magazines that have been around a while to help insure that when you go on your search, you can find them easily. I wish that I could advise you as to which specific magazine to choose, but your choice depends on your skill level and personal whims. Think of the decision like the choice between *Newsweek* and *Time:* The information is the same but the different formats suit different tastes.

Table 3-1 Beginning-Level Puzzle Books

Title	*Publisher*	*Price*
Big Crosswords	Harle	$1.95
Blue Ribbon Crosswords	JBH	$1.95
Dell Easy Crosswords	Dell	$1.99
Easy Crosswords	Harle	.99
Easy-To-Do	Harris	$1.35
Family Crossword Puzzles Plus	Penny Press	$2.95
Fast & Easy Crosswords	Penny Press	$1.49
Featured Crosswords	Official	$1.99
Fun 'N Easy Crosswords	Harris	$1.35
Good & Easy Crosswords	Harle	$1.25
Happy Crosswords	Harle	$1.25
Harle Crosswords	Harle	$1.25
Jiffy Crosswords	Harris	$1.35
Nice & Easy Crosswords	Penny Press	$1.25
Preferred Easy Crosswords	Official	.99
Quick & Easy Crosswords	Penny Press	$1.39
Quickie Crosswords	Harle	$1.39
Simple Crosswords	Harle	.99
Super Easy Crosswords	Harle	$1.50
TV Crosswords	Popular	$2.50

One really quirky detail about puzzle magazines

Each brand of puzzle magazine has a distinctive logo design somewhere on the cover that tips you off as to what you're holding even before you read the brand name. Usually the brand name squeezes into the shape of the logo somewhere in the upper-left corner.

- Dell: Square
- Harle: Cross shape
- Harris: Circle
- Official: Oval
- Popular: Sharpened pencil

Table 3-2 Medium-Level Puzzle Books

Title	Publisher	Price
Approved Crosswords	Penny Press	$1.25
Classic Variety Plus Crosswords	Penny Press	$2.50
Collectors Crosswords	Official	$3.50
Dell Crossword Puzzles	Dell	$1.79
Deluxe Crosswords	Official	$1.99
Herald Tribune Crosswords Puzzles Only	HT	$1.99
The National Observer	Ebb	$3.95
NY Herald Tribune Crosswords	HT	$1.95
Official Crossword Puzzles	Dell	$2.50
Pocket Crossword Puzzles	Dell	$1.49
Popular Crosswords	Popular	$1.59
Premium Crosswords	Popular	$1.95

Table 3-3 Expert-Level Puzzle Books

Title	Publisher	Price
Dell Crosswords Crosswords	Dell	$2.99
Dell Champion Crossword Puzzles	Dell	$1.99
Games	Games	$3.50
World Of Puzzles	Games	$2.95

One magazine that stands out in this field is *Games*. Everything about the way this puzzle magazine looks is different from the norm: *Games* is a full-size magazine (8 x 11 inches), and it includes a variety of puzzle types on different levels of challenge. Celebrating its twentieth anniversary in 1997, *Games* continues to publish high quality crosswords by well known top constructors such as Henry Hook and Trip Payne. Typically, the crosswords appear in its 16-page Pencilwise section. This section includes a range of puzzles in difficulty levels ranked from one to four stars; you also get the World's Most Ornery Crossword, which comes with two sets of clues (Hard and Easy) and a couple of British-style cryptic crosswords. Outside of this section, you find clever visual puzzles, reviews of new games (board and CD-ROM), contests and brain teasers of all sorts.

Under the leadership of editor Wayne Schmittberger, this magazine is back on course after a short hiatus in the mid-1990s. Books of *The Best of Games* are available from Times Books for $11.

Where to buy your magazines

You may have noticed that finding places that *don't* sell puzzle magazines is getting harder. Travelers expect to pick them up in airports and train terminals. Cold sufferers figure they can find a book or two at the drugstore along with tissues and decongestant. You see them hanging from the eaves of newsstands, and next to the cigarettes at cigar stores. No matter where life takes you, a puzzle magazine lies in your path. However, depending on what you're looking for, some venues may be better for you than others.

Supermarket chains

The supermarket is the most reliable place to go for your basic puzzle magazine shopping. Within the store are two magazine stops: the shelves in the magazine aisle and the check-out. All categories of magazines are displayed together as you cruise the aisles. Often you find a dozen or more different puzzle magazines on the shelf.

Because many puzzle magazines conform to the pocket size, you also find a few of the portable-sized ones in the special fixtures at the check-out counter — you know, the racks mostly devoted to *TV Guide.* The publisher pays a premium for this special placement, so you get only a limited selection in this spot. If you're like me, you're so pleased when you save a little on a pound of ham on sale that you're likely to treat yourself to an inexpensive magazine.

Discount superstores

Occasionally you can find puzzle books sold in bulk packs of three among the stacks of paper towels and other household items at discount stores. These books are most often generic collections at the beginner level. Technically, nothing is wrong with these puzzles to my knowledge. If you're a beginner who's just looking for practice and a little synonym matching, they may fill the bill. But you're not going to find any bargains on a more advanced level at this venue.

Bookstores

For the confirmed acrossionado, the bookstore is the ultimate source because it offers both magazines *and* the books. The puzzle book section usually spans across and down many shelves, with a variety of popular series in spiral-bound format. By the time you reach this level of expertise, you're willing to invest $10 for a collection of 50 crosswords put together by your favorite editor.

Two publishers dominate the puzzle magazine industry

Mergers and acquisitions have been the trend in the 1990s. Believe it or not, puzzle publishers are no exception to the gobbling up of one company by another.

Right now, two publishing titans (also known as "Olympians," in crosswordese) control the universe of puzzle magazines. Official Publications, established in the 1960s, mushroomed into the Kappa Puzzle Group in 1989 after acquiring such venerable imprints as Ebb, Games, Harle, Herald Tribune Crosswords, Popular Puzzles, and Quinn Puzzles.

Meanwhile, in 1996 the well established Penny Press line acquired the household name in puzzles — Dell. Depending on which publisher you ask, each dominates the market. Fact is, each sells mountains of magazines annually and each is privately held, which makes actual sales numbers a secret.

The bottom line: For $1.99, how can you go wrong?

In these days of the $9 movie ticket, I can't imagine a better bargain than a puzzle magazine. For about $2 you get as many as 100 puzzles, hours of diversion, a few chuckles, and an ego boost to boot. If you weigh the pluses and minuses, the benefits seem to win.

Among the pluses are the following:

- For two-puzzler households, magazines reduce the competition over who does the daily newspaper puzzle. You eliminate the need for two newspapers — a savings!
- You always have a handy distraction in your briefcase.
- Practice makes perfect, and here's the opportunity, complete with answers in the back of the book.

Minuses: Beware crossword obsession. After you have a book of crosswords, where do you draw the line? How many hours per day do you devote to the grid? During the peak of the "fever" in 1924, "Crossword Widow" Mary Zaba of Chicago sued her husband for neglect, for which the courts sentenced him to no more than three puzzles a day.

And may I add that for the price of admission, you can even qualify to win money? I'm referring to magazine subscription sweepstakes programs, like Publishers Clearing House and American Family Publishers, that fill your mailbox with their $10 million offers. I guarantee that you can find puzzle magazines among the selections on the stamp sheet. Just take a look at the next envelope that lands in your mailbox.

Topical puzzles in other types of magazines

Some magazines have puzzles hiding out in them, usually way in the back, close to the back cover where crossword fanatics like me can find them more easily. Here's a guide to the best and the brightest of the puzzles in these magazines, organized from easiest to hardest, solving-wise.

People (beginning level)

Anyone who doesn't have a stray issue of *People* magazine lurking on the coffee table must not be able to read English! The clues in the *People* puzzle feature celebrities that appear in the magazine's pages. Pop culture is the name of this game. One of the clues is a photo of a smiling film or television star.

Fran and Lou Sabin are co-constructors of this crossword, which is 13 x 13 squares. These puzzle pros are well-known as longtime collaborators of quality crosswords.

Puzzle 3-8 is a celebrity-oriented puzzle, similiar to one you may find in a *People* magazine.

TV Guide (beginning level)

If your expertise is television shows, then this puzzle is for you. Sources at *TV Guide* call the crossword its singlemost popular feature. On those rare occasions that *TV Guide* has appeared without a puzzle, readers kept the phones ringing with their complaints. (When you look forward to turning to the back page for that quick puzzle fix, you don't want to find some useless ad taking up the space.) So the editors are good about reserving the last interior page for puzzle fans seeking their weekly fun.

At 13 x 13, the *TV Guide* puzzle fits into the easy mold. Nearly every clue is a reference to TV or pop culture. And, if one a week isn't enough, you can find the *TV Guide Book of Crosswords* in the stores.

If you aren't yet acquainted with the *TV Guide* crossword puzzle, take a gander at Puzzle 3-9 to see what all the fuss is about.

TV Guide also makes its puzzles available on the World Wide Web. Consult Chapter 16 for more information on finding *TV Guide* puzzles, and puzzles from other publications, online.

Puzzle 3-8: Flic Faves

Across

1 *Star* — (1979 sci-fi classic)
5 *Cheers* setting
8 *In and* — (1997 Kevin Kline flic)
11 Amo, amas, —
12 Pitcher — Hershiser
14 Greek letter
15 — *With the Wind* (1939 film classic)
16 Missing some marbles?
17 Bond creator, — Fleming
18 Costar of *L.A. Confidential* (2 wds)
21 *To*— , *With Love* (1967 film classic)
22 Actor — Mineo
23 *Mr.* — (Michael Keaton comedy)
26 *The* — *Couple* (Lemmon-Matthau comedy classic)
28 Robin's costar in *Mrs. Doubtfire*
32 Dutch cheese
34 — *of the Needle* (1981 spy flic)
36 Letterman, to friends
37 Dancer Kelly and actor Hackman
39 Santa's helper
41 *Gunga* — (Cary Grant classic)
42 Norma — (role for 28 Across)
44 Pacino and namesakes
46 Costar of *L.A. Confidential* (2 wds)
51 *Ransom* star Gibson
52 Barbra Streisand 1987 drama
53 TV actress Barbara —
55 *Raiders of the Lost* —
56 — *Grit* (John Wayne classic)
57 Longest river
58 Country of origin for *The Crying Game*: abbr.
59 Final screen word
60 Prefix with vision

Down

1 — *the Dog* (1997 Dustin Hoffman flic)
2 Run — (lose control)
3 Rajah's consort
4 Rose features
5 Actor Dirk —
6 Coach Parseghian and namesakes
7 Kathie Lee's TV cohost
8 TV role fo Ron Howard
9 Barren land
10 The — Man (Oz character)
13 Cantrell and Turner
19 Popular AMC series
20 "Am I — to see you!"
24 Actress — Ryan of *Sleepless in Seattle*
25 A — For All Seasons (1988 film classic)
27 Take away the gray
29 Youth
30 56, to Caesar
31 Craving
33 TV impresario — Griffin
35 Passed, as time
38 Role for Roger Moore, with "The"
40 *Miami Vice* setting: abbr.
43 Get used to
45 — *of a Woman* (Pacino flic)
46 Deborah — of *The King and I*
47 Actress Sommer
48 Take by surprise
49 George Plimpton bestseller
50 Raise one's voice
51 Actress — Britt
54 Roseann Arnold, — Barr

Puzzle 3-9

Across

1 Frequent PBS supplier
4 *The Lion King* villain
8 Fairy-tale monster
12 Call them for a tow: abbr.
13 *Fernwood 2-Night* state
14 *Monopoly* document
15 *— and Tina* (2 wds)
16 1985 copy show *— Blue*
17 Beatles movie *Let —* (2 wds)
18 "— of the Universe"
20 Brooke plays her
21 *Dr. Katz* patient Philips
22 With 1 Down, Pebbles' playmate
23 Cagney played him in *Yankee Doodle Dandy*
26 Lassie, e.g.
27 Coach Parseghian
30 *Dukes of Hazzard* spinoff
31 Nolte film *Cannery —*
32 *Mystery Science Theater* "bot"
33 Actor Herbert
34 Julia Sweeney's *It's —*
35 James Brolin series, 1983-88
36 Rapper/*Players* star (hyph.)
38 He played Beaver's brother
39 *Speed —*
41 *Tattingers'* successor series *Nick and —*
45 Middle Eastern bigwig
46 Flicka's offspring, perhaps
47 *The Facts of Life's* Charlotte
48 Lymph —
49 *— McBeal*
50 *One — Million*
51 Uno, dos, —
52 *The Untouchables* hero
53 Disney comedy *— Bud*

Down

1 See 22 Across
2 Silent-film star Theda
3 *T.H.E.* and *Top*
4 Grave
5 "Goochie goochie" gal
6 Subject of HBO's *And the Band Played On*
7 *The — Rogers Show*
8 Loathing
9 '60s spy sitcom (2 wds)
10 *Tremors* actress McEntire
11 Genie portrayer Barbara
19 Leoni and pekoe
20 Actors' union: abbr.
22 Silent-film star Clara
23 Cartoon component
24 Yoko —
25 Andre Braugher series
26 — matrix printer
28 *— vs. Wade*
29 Pointed tool
31 George Segal film *King —*
32 West wore one on *Batman*
34 Revolutions — minute
35 Lauren and Hobby
37 Roman goddess of agriculture
38 TV-remote predecessors
39 *La Bohème* update
40 "— vincit omnia"
41 Courtney Love's band
42 Soprano's solo
43 Hindi queen
44 *A — in the Life*
46 Sports enthusiast

New York magazine (medium level)

For 20 years, the prolific puzzle constructor Maura Jacobson has consistently entertained solvers who know to look at the back of this magazine for a great 21 x 21 puzzle. Although her work appears in *New York* magazine, Jacobson doesn't necessarily draw from the subjects discussed in the magazine when constructing her puzzle. Her themes are wide-ranging, with the emphasis on fun and puns. Jacobson promises to not repeat clues within four months of a published appearance. Her work is available in books, for solvers outside the metro area, from Story Press ($9.99).

Scanning the Bookstore Shelves

Some solvers look for puzzles in books rather than newspapers or magazines. At this level, solvers have developed specific tastes: They're looking for certain names or brands. This readership can find a selection of puzzle collections sold in bookstores. Most of these collections are spiral-bound compilations with cardboard covers.

Clearly, the superior paper, spiral binding, and full-size pages of these collections means a larger investment. When you enter the bookstore, you're making a commitment to spend more on your new hobby. Of course, in the scheme of things, $8 to $10 is still a bargain when you're talking about hours of entertainment.

As a rule, crossword books are mid-level to expert, a notch or two above magazines. The typical book is spiral-bound, with an average of 50 puzzles per book. The word "omnibus" on the front cover of a puzzle collection implies that the book contains over 100 puzzles.

Crossword collections give you the opportunity to try puzzles that appear on the coast opposite the one you live on. For example, an East Coaster may want to try the rip-roaring puzzles by Merl Reagle that San Franciscans enjoy regularly in *The Examiner.* West Coasters may get a giggle out of Maura Jacobson's *New York* magazine masterpieces or the wonders of the Sunday Puzzle collection from Henry Hook and Emily Cox and Henry Rathvon of the *Boston Globe.*

When leafing through crossword books, you may note that bylines are the rule for each puzzle. Focusing on constructors provides the biggest difference between the average magazine and books. By the time you reach this level of interest, you probably have a passing acquaintance with some of the big names in construction. You may develop a preference for certain puzzle constructors, which ultimately guides your selection.

Tables 3-4 and 3-5 list my favorite puzzle books.

Moonlighting with puzzle collections

Constructors and puzzle editors who work for the newspaper syndicates also lend their hand to puzzle collections. For example, the following editors are famous for "moonlighting" on puzzle collections:

- **Stan Newman:** Creators Syndicate and Times Books
- **Charles Preston:** *USA Today* syndicate, magazines, and books
- **Will Shortz:** *The New York Times* and various book collections *(Brain Games, The Puzzle Master)*

PUZZLE PEOPLE

Columbia grads contribute puzzle collections to humanity

In 1924, two enterprising young Columbia graduates, Richard Simon and Max Schuster, noticed a need in the market for a book of crosswords. The crossword was a 10-year-old local feature known only to the readership of *The New York World.* The partners approached the editor from *The World,* a young woman named Margaret Petherbridge, with a request to compile this collection. An overnight bestseller, the slim volume launched the corporation known as Simon & Schuster and established Margaret Farrar as the promoter and arbiter of America's favorite indoor sport, as well as editor of the ongoing crossword series for the rest of her long and productive life.

Table 3-4 Mid-Level Puzzle Books

Publisher	Title	Price	Editors/Constructors
Fireside	*S & S Crossword Puzzle Book*	$8	John Samson
	Large Type Crosswords	$15	Eugene Maleska
	Super Crossword Series	$9	John Samson
	Crossword Treasuries	$8	Maleska and Samson
Story Press	*NY Magazine Crossword Puzzles*	$9.99	Maura Jacobson
Times Books	*Boston Globe Sunday Crosswords*	$9	Cox/Rathvon and Hook
	Best Pencil Puzzles	$11	*Games* magazine
	LA Times Sunday Crosswords	$9	Sylvia Bursztyn/Barry Tunick
	Crossword Omnibus	$10	Will Weng
	NY Times Daily Crosswords	$9	Eugene Maleska
	NY Times Puns and Anagrams	$9	Mel Taub
	Random House Sunday Crosswords	$9	Stan Newman

Table 3-5 Expert-Level Puzzle Books

Publisher	Title	Price	Editors/Constructors
Puzzle Works	*The San Francisco Examiner*	$7.95	Merl Reagle
Simon & Schuster	*S & S Crostics*	$9	Thomas H. Middleton
	Hooked on Cryptics	$9	Henry Hook
	Hooked on Puzzles	$9	Henry Hook
Times Books	*The Puzzlemaster Presents*	$12	Will Shortz
	Random House Masterpiece	$16	Stan Newman
	Random House Ultrahard Crosswords	$8	Stan Newman

Chapter 4

A Primer of Non-Crossword Puzzles

In This Chapter

- Looking away from crosswords
- Setting solving goals
- Circling hidden words
- Working fill-in-the-grid puzzles
- Decoding scrambled word puzzles

In this chapter I present four non-crossword puzzles: hidden words, fill-in-the-grids, jumbles, and cryptograms. After you get a handle on how each type of puzzle works, you can make an educated decision as to which type of solving suits you best. This chapter gives you a quick tour of the gamut of pencil puzzles outside of crosswords that may whet your appetite for some tempting new choices.

The beauty of the puzzles in this chapter is that all the information you need appears right on the page: You just have to use your eyes. No Q&A, no riddles — just putting together the elements that the constructor supplies for you.

Beware the condescending looks that crossword folks often shoot at the non-crossword contingent. Don't let them stop you. They just don't know what they're missing — yet.

Hidden Words: Practicing Your Loops

Remember those picture puzzles you did as a kid where the caption read "Find the hidden items"? Circling words in a grid of letters is the adult version of this early development game. Hidden-word puzzles test your ability to find words hidden in a grid on the page.

Each hidden-word puzzle functions as a mini-lesson based on a topic of general interest — a self-contained story based on a central theme. The subject can be general (for example, a holiday) or specific (say, a celebrity, a book, or a sport). Because all entries in the puzzle pertain to a single subject, this type of puzzle has an educational tone to it — your solving bonus. Some hidden-word puzzles also offer a hidden message that emerges in the grid.

Each hidden-word puzzle is comprised of two elements:

- **The grid:** The grid typically measures 15 x 15 letters, but you may find larger and smaller grids from time to time. Embedded within that grid, you can find the words from the word list.
- **The word list:** A list of about 30 words related to the theme appear in alphabetical order next to a grid of letters. The words concealed in the grid may appear in any of three directions: horizontal, vertical, or diagonal. Because the words may read in any direction, locating and circling each one becomes an eyeball-bending challenge.

Depending upon the publisher, this puzzle style has different brand names, including Word Find, Word Search, Loop a Word, Circle a Word, and Hidden Word. The only difference between these puzzles is their names.

Hidden-word puzzles have a very high profile

Hidden words are the mainstay of the puzzle industry, attracting the widest audience. This category of non-crossword puzzles captivates millions of Americans, if sales indicate anything. Newsstands everywhere carry puzzle magazines to fulfill the appetite of this popular pastime.

Even if you're not part of this enormous audience, you're probably related to someone who belongs to it. At the very least, in the recent past you've sat next to someone who was busily looping letters on a page.

Many people attribute the popularity of these puzzles to the fact that you can carry them wherever you go and enjoy the satisfaction of locating a few of the words in the list within the grid in a short span of time.

A longtime constructor of concealed puzzles confided to me that she personally knows many corporate big-wigs who loop words behind closed doors in some pretty impressive offices. The temporary distraction is welcome and relaxing.

When solving a hidden-word puzzle, watch out for the following items:

- Vertical entries may begin in the middle of the grid and read upwards.
- Diagonal entries may read upward.
- Words may read backward in a mirror image.
- Words often overlap, and letters may be used in more than one word.
- The only given with hidden words is that all the words read in a straight line. (Zigzag entries occur only in some rare variations.)

Every word that starts with a capital letter in the word list appears in the grid. Sometimes the puzzle constructor includes lowercase words in the word list to help put the entry in context. Lowercase words don't appear in the grid, so don't waste time looking for them.

The rule here (as with all puzzles) is no repetition: When you locate an entry, you know that it doesn't reappear within the grid. Feel free to draw a slash through each word on the list as you circle it in the grid.

Best opening move: Read the grid line by line from left to right to identify all the horizontal entries. These are the easiest ones to spot right off the bat.

Puzzle 4-1 shows you a great example of a hidden-word puzzle. You can find the answers to the puzzle in Appendix A.

If you're looking for magazines of hidden words, try *Superb Word Find* or *Variety Word Find* from *Official Publications; Dell Word Search Puzzles* or *Official Word Search Puzzles* from Dell Magazines are also quite good.

Puzzle 4-1: Great Sports

I'm about ready to jump start your solving by giving you some hints on where to look for some of the words. If you prefer to work the puzzle without any help, you should stop reading now.

If you start with S in the top left-hand corner of Puzzle 4-1, you see fine examples of entries that read horizontally (SOFTBALL), vertically (SAILING), and diagonally (SKATING).

Reading Puzzle 4-1 from left to right, you find two words in the top line right off the bat (SOFTBALL and DISCUS). As you read each line from left to right, the next time you see an entry from the word list is seven lines down — all the way towards the right side of the grid (POLO). Continue reading from left to right to the bottom, and you find four more entries: SOCCER, BOXING, KARATE, and ARCHERY.

ARCHERY
BADMINTON
BASEBALL
BOWLING
BOXING
CRICKET
DISCUS
DIVING
FISHING
FOOTBALL
GOLF
HOCKEY
JUDO
KARATE
LACROSSE
POLO
RACING
ROWING
RUGBY
SAILING
SKATING
SKIING
SOCCER
SOFTBALL
SQUASH
SWIMMING
TENNIS
TRACK
VOLLEYBALL
WRESTLING

S	O	F	T	B	A	L	L	D	I	S	C	U	S	Z
A	K	Z	Q	B	N	T	L	H	B	L	B	G	I	G
I	Z	A	S	H	G	O	R	A	L	G	Z	N	N	Y
L	N	O	T	N	I	M	D	A	B	Z	Q	I	N	E
I	H	Z	I	I	J	W	B	U	C	T	I	L	E	K
N	G	V	Q	H	N	Y	L	A	J	K	O	W	T	C
G	I	H	B	Z	E	G	A	Q	S	J	P	O	L	O
D	Z	G	V	L	H	C	C	V	Z	E	G	B	F	H
G	N	I	L	T	S	E	R	W	H	N	B	C	Z	V
R	S	O	C	C	E	R	O	I	I	S	G	A	G	C
U	V	Z	S	W	V	N	S	H	C	N	A	N	L	V
G	N	I	M	M	I	W	S	Z	I	K	I	U	G	L
B	O	X	I	N	G	I	E	W	Z	C	E	H	Q	V
Y	H	L	B	Z	F	V	O	K	A	R	A	T	E	S
V	Z	B	F	J	N	R	A	R	C	H	E	R	Y	J

Solvers come in all shapes and sizes

You don't need a Ph.D to be a successful solver. In fact, you don't even need a high school diploma. In 1981, Vivian Gomes, a seamstress, took first prize at a New England crossword contest. Because Gomes went to work at age 16, she had never finished high school. After winning that contest, she decided to go back to school and get her GED. Need I add that after three months in the classroom, she aced the exam? She credits crosswords with changing her life for the better.

Filling In the Grids: Backward Solving

If you crave jigsaw satisfaction, fill-in-the-grid puzzles challenge you to fit the pieces together in the correct position.

Depending upon the publication, this type of puzzle may be called a Fill-In or a Fill-It-In. It's a matter of copyright. Technically, this style is called Fill-In, but it's all the same to the solver.

Fill-in solving works in the reverse order from crossword solving: Like doing a crossword backwards, you begin with a set list of words, and your job is to figure out where the words fit in the grid.

A fill-in-the-grid puzzle is made up of the following elements:

- **The grid:** Instead of a standard crossword-solving grid, you begin with a blank answer diagram, as shown in Puzzle 4-2 (you can find the answers to Puzzle 4-2 in Appendix A). You see just a pattern of black and white squares. (Some puzzles fill in one word from the list to jump-start your solving.)
- **The word list:** You get a list of words rather than clues, and no numbers in either the grid or the list. Your job is to figure out how these entries interlock in the grid. Much like a jigsaw, you're looking for fit: Where the grid has a cluster of four-letter words, you have to determine which ones go where.

  The number of letters in the words divides the word list into categories, from three up to as many as 15 (the words appear alphabetized within each category, and shorter words predominate, as a rule). The word list doesn't tell you which words are Across entries and which ones are Down — you have to find out that information through trial and error, which may mean the vigorous use of your eraser.

The fewer categories per puzzle, the tougher the challenge. For example, a fill-in-the-grid with mostly four- and six-letter words requires more guesswork in identifying the correct position for each entry.

Start solving by focusing on the longest entries first (remember that a fill-in reverses standard crossword-solving practices). Because you have fewer 10- to 15-letter entries in the diagram, you can make judgment calls more quickly by testing out the long ones at the outset. Tougher fill-ins tend to contain entries that all fall into a smaller range of letters, which makes locating the correct position of each entry harder for you. As entries fall in place, cross them off the word list; each word appears only once in the diagram.

A *kriss-kross* is a tougher variant of the fill-in-the-grid format. While the fill-in uses the standard black and white crossword diagram, where each letter keys in both directions, the kriss-kross grid has unkeyed letters and no black squares. Sometimes called a skeleton, the entries intersect in just a few places like bones of the human body. Unkeyed letters heighten the solving challenge in a kriss-kross.

Puzzle 4-3 gives you another chance to enjoy a fill-in puzzle. (You can find the answer to Puzzle 4-3 in Appendix A.)

Puzzle 4-2

3 Letters

BOB
C.I.C.
DYE
HAE
HBO
IND.
IOU
JAG
JUS
L.B.J.
LIA
LYE
MAA
MOE
NAE
NAY
OBI
POP
REE
RUB
SIE
SOS
SSS
TES
TOP
UMW
UND
USM
WSW
YIP

4 Letters

AHOY
ALOU
CHER
COLE
DITE
GHEE
GOAS
IN RE
JIMS
MEGA
MOTO
N.C.O.'S
RAPS
RENE
RUHR
RUIN
SAKI
SCOT
SMEW
URSA

5 Letters

ADIEU
GENET
PAIRS
RESET
STEMS
URGES

6 Letters

POLKAS
TROOPS

7 Letters

ANEMONE
ANOINTS
BEECHER
DEPENDS

9 Letters

ABSCONDER
ANTIPATHY

Puzzle 4-3

3 Letters

AIX
AME
AWL
DES
ELI
ELL
ELM
ENC.
ENE
ENT.
ESE
ETE
EWE
HE'S
IER
III
LEI
NAT
NEA
NER
OLE
OTT
OVO
RAH
SCH.
SDI
SMU
VEE
XYZ

4 Letters

ANET
AQUA
A TO Z
CELT
CLEO
DAVY
EDDS
EINE
GAVE
GENA
GUNN
MENU
ONDE
ONES
PITA
SONY

5 Letters

DEALT
DOSES
EDDAS
SNEER
SNIDE

6 Letters

AT HAND
DONNAS
ENCAMP
ONEIDA
STUNTS
YODELS

7 Letters

ANGELES
CONDEMN

9 Letters

AD INTERIM
REEXAMINE

13 Letters

HEAD OVER HEELS
VERNAL EQUINOX

C
E
L
T

Numbers get in on the game

Basically, the fill-in tests your ability to fit entries together to make a coherent diagram, instead of drawing from your vocabulary or sense of humor. Fill-ins emphasize careful placement of letters in order to correctly fit each entry into the grid.

Because fill-in puzzles minimize the element of wordplay, these puzzles may also feature entries composed entirely of numbers. When you work an all-number fill-in, you heighten the jigsaw aspect of the solving experience as you determine how the numbers intersect to create a coherent diagram.

You have to rethink the way you read numbers when you solve a number fill-in. Categories are sorted by length in number sequence, not by value of the number. As a result, you see headings that range from "3 numbers" to "15 numbers" with the list beginning at 1 plus 2 to 14 digits. Don't think of the actual numerical value. Nothing adds up: It's just a pattern of numbers.

In the standard crossword grid, each letter participates in two words — one that reads across, and another that reads down. Technically speaking, constructors say that the letters *key* or *check* in two directions. This principle also applies to fill-ins that use the standard black and white diagram. Diagrams with words that key are easier to crack.

Jumbles: Instant Gratification

Sometimes you just want a word snack to satisfy that craving for getting the right answer, and a jumble can be just the ticket. As most newspaper readers know (jumbles often appear on the puzzle page of daily newspapers), the jumble is a really fun puzzle that only takes a few minutes.

A jumble consists of the following elements:

- **Jumbles:** Unlike an *anagram,* which makes a sensible word from another one (for example, TEAM = MATE), jumbles are not words. Your mission is to create a word from the jumbled-up, random-looking series of letters provided by the constructor. You have to determine the correct order of letters to make the jumble into a real word. Each jumble has only one correct answer. A jumble may be a single word or a series of scrambled words.
- **Answer blocks:** When you unscramble the "jumble," you pencil it in to an answer block, usually located directly underneath the "jumble." Some of the blocks have circles in them, meaning that the letters you sketch into those blocks are part of the final solution.
- **A cartoon:** The cartoon depicts some cryptic situation and often contains a question that you answer by unscrambling the letters you sketched into the circled blocks in the answer block.

Puzzle 4-4 shows a prime example of a jumble (you can find the answer to Puzzle 4-4 in Appendix A).

Solving the jumble measures your spelling knowledge. If you see a J or V in the lineup, your spelling sense saves you from putting either one in last place, because you know that these letters don't take this position in English words.

Puzzle 4-4

Use this space to jot down possible answers to the jumbles as you work on them.

Cracking a Secret Code in Cryptograms

Cryptograms are all about letter replacement. Letters in cryptograms have been switched around, creating a funky-looking message that you need to decipher.

In a cryptogram, every letter stands for a different one (and only one) throughout the message. For example, "B" may represent "T" through the cryptogram, where "T" may mean "C." Although the pattern of the sentence looks familiar, the "words" read as if they've been written in some kind of secret code.

The "code" changes from puzzle to puzzle, as though the alphabet flies up in the air, with the letters landing in different places, for each puzzle. Unfortunately, cracking the code on one puzzle doesn't give you a Rosetta Stone that you can apply to all other crytograms.

Cryptogram words are exact replicas of the actual words they disguise. For example, if you see a three-letter word as part of a cryptogram, you know that a three-letter word appears in the quote or phrase hidden within the puzzle.

Typically, a cryptogram message is a quotation complete with punctuation. The author's name may appear at the end of the cryptogram. Puzzle 4-5 shows a typical cryptogram in full swing (you can find the answers to the puzzle in Appendix A). Note that some cryptograms offer a hint by revealing the identity of one of the disguised letters. You may want to ignore the help, or you may welcome a helping hand until you get the hang of it.

To work a cryptogram, follow these steps:

1. **Jot down the alphabet on scrap paper.**

   You need to do a little prep work first. You use this list to keep tabs on the letters you have already matched up, and consequently, which letters are still "unused."

2. **Scan the cryptogram for one letter words, which are typically A or I.**

   Of course, you won't know which of the letters is the right one until you work a little more into the puzzle, but if you have a good feeling about one letter over the other, go ahead and pencil it into the appropriate place.

3. **After you crack the code on a letter, pencil in all occurrences of that letter in the puzzle. For example, where you find L to replace A, identify all the L's as A's through the cryptogram.**

   And I do mean pencil! You need to experiment many times before you actually match up a letter. Don't attempt to work a cryptogram with a pen unless you really enjoy the smell of white out.

You have another chance to practice your cryptogram solving skills with Puzzle 4-6.

A spooky alternative name haunts cryptograms

For short, puzzleheads refer to cryptograms — a bit ghoulishly — as *crypts.* Constructors are known as *cryptographers.*

Puzzle 4-5

In this puzzle, S = W.

```
"GE BNPAP GM X IGMUHBP KPBSPPQ X LHMGRGXQ XQI
"__ _____ __ _ _______ _______ _ ________ ___
LOMPDE,GB GM MPBBDPI XLGRXKDO. G SGQ!"
______,__ __ _______ ________. _ ___!"

— IXQQO YXOP
— _____ ____
```

Puzzle 4-6

To give you a head start, here's a hint: C = M.

```
"MLOX MO JOCOCVOJ MO PJO PBB CPF,HLO
"____ __ ________ __ ___ ___ ___,___
CNGHOJUOG FUGPSSOPJ PXF BUAO GHPXFG ODSBPUXOF."
_________ _________ ___ ____ ______ _________."

— CPJQ HMPUX
— ____ _____
```

4. **Scan the cryptograms for two letter words, and then three letter words, and so on, matching letters up as you go.**

   As each grouping of letters turns into a word, the message should come more and more into focus.

Table 4-1 lists the most common words that appear in cryptograms; the words in each length category are listed in frequency of appearance.

Table 4-1 Cryptogram Repeaters

Number of letters	*Repeaters*
1	A and I
2	IT, IN, IS, IF, AT, ON, TO, OF, AS, and AN
3	THE, AND, FOR, ARE, and BUT
4	THAT, THIS, THAN, and THEN

You also need to be on the lookout for the following patterns as you work your way through the cryptogram:

- **Apostrophes:** Where an apostrophe appears at the end of a word followed by a single letter, your choice is limited to S or T. When it follows a single letter, that letter must be I to give you I'd, I'll, or I've. Where it is followed by two letters, your choice opens to 'LL, 'RE and 'VE.
- **Double letters:** Check for EE, OO, FF, LL, SS, TT and MM, in that order.
- **Final letters:** Check for E, T, S, D, N, and R at the end of words.
- **Initial letters:** Check for T, A, O, M, H, and W at the beginning of words.
- **Suffixes:** Check for ING and LY in longer words.

When solving a crypt, the alphabet of frequently used letters consists of a dozen members. Listed in the order of frequency with which letters appear in the English language, you're looking at an abbreviated ABCs that go something like this: E, T, A, O, I, N, S, H, R, D, L and U.

Magazines of cryptograms aren't in great demand, but Official Publications produces one quarterly for gluttons.

Some cryptograms aren't just fun and games

During World War II, the Germans sent messages to their various armed forces overseas using a hard-to-crack secret code called *Enigma.* The Allies recruited legions of cryptographers to break the code in order to get the inside information on what the Germans were planning. Indeed, after the Allies deciphered the code, the tides turned for the Axis nations and the world at large.

One tricky thing you must remember about cracking a cryptogram — its alphabet may not contain all 26 letters of the alphabet, depending on which letters show up in the message. A cryptographer may try to confuse you by deliberately eliminating some letters from the message altogether.

The key to cryptogram decoding, according to Laura Z. Hobson, author of the classic novel *Gentleman's Agreement* as well as scores of cryptograms, is to bear in mind that the most commonly used letter in English is E. Experienced crypt solvers, such as the narrator of Poe's "The Gold Bug," often begin the decoding process by looking for E first. The most popular consonant is T. After you determine which letters represent E and T, you can move on to the next group of commonly used letters. Expert consensus ranks O and S in that category. M follows, according to Hobson. Meanwhile, according to Norman Hill, noted crossword expert, runners-up are A, I, and N.

Part II
Mastering Crosswordese

In this part . . .

A look at one just one crossword puzzle shows you that puzzles definitely have their own special language. For example, you don't very often use a three-letter word for toothpick in everyday conversation (unless you're a real toothpick enthusiast). After working a few puzzles, you begin to see that some of these special words repeat from puzzle to puzzle. Getting a grasp on these repeaters (as I like to call these frequent guests in the puzzle) goes a long way in increasing your puzzle power.

That's where this part of the book comes in. I cover the most frequently-used grid words, plus I tell you about parts of words that pop up in the grid.

And to further boost your solving power, I recommend some great reference books to help you when you get stuck on a clue.

Chapter 5

Parts of Words That Give You a Leg Up

In This Chapter

- Discovering how prefixes and suffixes combine in the grid
- Discovering the unions that puzzle pros need to know
- Attending crossword class
- Getting poetic
- Testing the puzzle winds

Puzzles are full of three- and four-letter entries. Some of these entries aren't necessarily words but are, instead, letter combinations that you may be familiar with as *parts* of words. Any commonplace combination is fair game in the grid, as long as the clue can telegraph the meaning to you in about four words or less.

One of the best ways to harness the power of puzzle repeaters is to try to anticipate the obvious ones. You quickly discover that with the help of even a single prefix, you can gain a foothold into the grid. You don't need to fret about memorizing strings of word parts — you're bound to see the same ones over and over (that's what makes them repeaters).

In this chapter, I show you the parts of words that give you a quick "in" to the grid.

Exploring Prefixes and Suffixes: Repeated Hangers-On

A prefix, as you know, is a syllable that you attach to the beginning of a word to refine or change its meaning. Suffixes are those appendages at the end of words. For crossword purposes, prefixes and suffixes provide a rich category of three- and four-letter possibilities.

With repeaters, you encounter the usual suspects time after time. In the prefix and suffix divisions, you're scouting for three- to four-letter entries. Of course, that measure applies to many repeaters. The big differences with a prefix or a suffix are that they're part of a word and that the constructor presents them as such.

Seeing what the clues look like

A clue for a prefix or a suffix can appear in one of two ways:

- **A straightforward definition:** These clues list the definition of the prefix or suffix and then tell you whether it's a prefix or suffix. For example, for a prefix like TELE, the clue may be "Distant: pref."
- **Associated with another word:** These clues tell you whether you're looking for a prefix or suffix, and then they list a word that is commonly combined with the prefix or suffix. For example, for a prefix like TELE, you see "Prefix with gram."

When you spy a single word followed by a colon and *prefix* or *suffix,* you may be able to find the answer to this clue by looking in a crossword dictionary. For a clue such as "Within: pref.," a crossword dictionary leads you straight to ENDO. However, because this clue is a straightforward dictionary definition with minimal room for wordplay, you won't bump into examples like this one every other clue. Constructors try to keep dictionary definitions to a bare minimum — a couple of clues per diagram.

Until I became an acrossionado, I'd never heard of the variation of a prefix or suffix called the *comb. form* (combining form, abbreviated) that you see at least once in the average crossword instead of *prefix.* A clue identified as a *comb. form* simply means a word part that combines with another word to form a compound word. For example, a clue such as "All: comb. form" yields OMNI from Latin. When combined with PRESENT from the English, you get OMNIPRESENT. You don't need to know the language of origin — you just need to keep in mind that the entry is a type of prefix or suffix. In fact, some puzzles have dropped the distinction and just use the terms "prefix" and "suffix."

Perusing prefixes that proliferate

When you solve enough puzzles, you see the following prefixes so often that you start chanting them in your sleep. Until that fateful day, you can use this list to give you a head start on popular puzzle prefixes:

- **ENDO:** Appropriately, medical science is rife with word parts. You don't have to look far for ENDO, which a constructor often clues as "Within: comb. form" or with its descriptive clue — "Prefix with cardium." The opposite of ENDO is ECTO, which most often appears as in "Prefix with morph."
- **EPI:** You often see EPI presented without any disguise, as in "Outer: pref." Or it may be offered as a description with the word that it attaches itself to — for example, "Prefix with dermis."
- **NEO:** Some prefixes look very nearly like their definitions. NEO, for one, means "new." Rather than the transparent "New: comb. form," the constructor may dress up the clue with a request for "Prefix with natal."
- **TELE:** Here's a combining form from the Greek. As a dictionary definition, you see the clue "Far: comb. form." As the implied missing prefix, you see "Prefix for graph."

Spotting suffixes you can't live without

Unlike other tailgaters you may come across, you'll be happy to spot any of the following suffixes in your puzzle:

- **ANA:** Although relatively rare in comparison to other suffixes that start with "A," you still come across "Collection: suffix" as a frequent clue for ANA, as in Americana.
- **ANE and ENE:** For puzzle purposes, medical science comes to the rescue in the suffix department. I'm talking about the famed ANE and ENE, which describe different carbon compounds. What they are doesn't matter, just which suffix the grid calls for. The dictionary-definition clue refers to "Carbon compound suffix." Or you may see these suffixes clued as "Hydrocarbon: suffix."

  You may not be able to discern which hydrocarbon you need in the diagram until you complete the entry that interlocks with the first letter of the suffix.

  The carbon suffix ANE also answers to the French word for *donkey.*
- **ITE:** You bump into ITE with great frequency. ITE most often goes by the dictionary definition of "Native: suffix." Sometimes you see it described as "Suffix with Brooklyn."
- **ITIS:** You see this one clued as "Inflammation: suffix." (Sometimes ITIS may be broken down into two words and appear in a missing-word clue such as, " How sweet —!")
- **STER:** Rather than by dictionary definition, the clue for STER may call for "Ending with gang" or "Ending with young."
- **"S" suffixes:** Suffixes made up of a trio of letters with S between two vowels, as in ASE, ESE, and OSE, are also very common. Both ASE and OSE fall into the scientific category: ASE answers to "Enzyme suffix," and OSE to "Sugar: suffix," as in *glucose.* ESE is a suffix related to a nationality, as in "Suffix with Japan."

Sometimes clues indicate suffixes and prefixes in devious ways. A word like "start" may indicate a prefix as in the clue "Start to form?" (UNI), while "ending" or "follower" may indicate a suffix as in "Trick ending?" (STER). The question mark tips you off that there is more to such a clue than meets the eye. (The question mark may or may not appear, depending on the challenge level of the puzzle.)

The suffix ESE also reads as a geographical direction. In this alternate sense, it may answer to a clue such as "Vane direction" or "Dir. from Baltimore to Myrtle Beach," describing the relationship of one town to another. (The abbreviation of "direction" tells you that the answer is an abbreviation as well.)

Getting Professional

For puzzle purposes, the following professional organizations provide fodder for three-letter entries, most of which end in A for Association:

- **ABA (American Bar Association)** = "Lawyers' org."
- **AMA (American Medical Association)** = "MDs' group"
- **ILA (International Longshoreman's Association)** = "Stevedores' org."
- **NEA (National Educational Association)** = "Teachers' org."

Some sports associations also pop up in the puzzle, including the following two, which are the most popular:

- **NBA (National Basketball Association)** = "Basketball org."
- **PGA (Professional Golfers Association)** = "Org. for Tiger Woods"

When you see the word "org." in a clue, you can make an educated guess that the entry is an abbreviation with an A in last place for *Association.*

Two other worthwhile abbreviated groups that enjoy good publicity in the grid are the BSA (Boy Scouts of America) and GSA (Girl Scouts of America), which you frequently find clued as "Boys' org." and "Girls' org.," respectively.

Enrolling at Crossword U.

Abbreviations in crosswords often refer to various courses you may find listed in a grad school course catalogue:

- **ACAD:** Short for academy, as in "Part of USNA"
- **ANAT:** Short for anatomy, as in "Med. school course"
- **BIOL:** Short for biology, as in "Med. student's course"
- **ECON:** Short for economy, as in "MBA's course"
- **ENGR:** Short for engineer, as in "MIT grad"
- **MBA:** Short for Masters of Business Administration, as in "Grad. degree"
- **USNA:** Short for U.S. Naval Academy, as in "Training ground for an Ens."

The Crossword Calendar

Another source of abbreviations in crosswords is the calendar, which includes the seven days of the week (MON, TUES, and so on) as well as the months (mainly SEPT) Abbreviated units of time also count the following:

- **HRS**: Short for hours, as in "24 in a day"
- **MIN:** Short for minute, as in "Part of an hr"
- **MOS:** Short for months, as in "Cal. units"
- **SEC:** Short for second, as in "Part of a min."
- **YRS:** Short for years, as in "'97 and '98, e.g."

Taking Advantage of Crossword Poetry

As noted by author and cryptographer Laura Z. Hobson, E is, without a doubt, the most used letter in the English language. Poetic touches come through in the world of E entries. Often the clue is straightforward yet oblique, as in "Poetic term." Any of the following poetic entries may answer to this vague (and therefore irritating) clue:

- **E'RE/E'ER:** E'ER is sometimes read as ERE, as in "Before: poetic." Or EER may be clued as a suffix, indicated by "Suffix with auction."
- **E'EN:** A clue may read as "Poetic time of day" (evening), as in "Time of day to Keats" or "Poetic contraction."
- **ENOW:** The clue may read as "Enough: archaic."
- **O'ER:** This one may answer to the missing-word clue "— the ramparts we watched. . . ."

Sometimes a clue uses the name of a well-known poet to let you know that the entry is a poetic term. In that case, you may see a clue for ERE like "Before, to Emily Dickinson."

Feeling Which Way the Wind Blows

Another common nonword three-letter entry refers to which way the wind is blowing. Weather Channel viewers are familiar with the vagaries of the wind, and weather watchers will be happy to spot common wind directions in the grid.

The vague clue "Wind direction" asks for any of the following directions. Very often, you need to fill in some connecting letters to determine which way the wind is blowing:

- **ENE:** The crossword weather vane most often points east northeast.
- **SSW:** A close second to ENE, you often feel a gust in the grid coming from south southwest.
- **ESE:** Less popular in the grid, the direction east southeast pops up only occasionally. (More often you see ESE as the entry for the clue "Suffix with journal.")
- **NNE:** North northeast only offers one E, making it a somewhat limited choice for constructors.
- **NNW:** The W at the end of the direction north northwest limits its use in the grid.
- **WSW** and **WNW:** Constructors use the directions west southwest and west northwest only rarely due to the hard-to-interlock presence of the two W's in these entries.

Any of the preceding wind directions can also be clued as directions on a compass. Sometimes the constructor tries to jazz up the clue by describing the direction of one location en route to another. For example, you may see "Dir. from Boston to Toronto" for WNW. The abbreviated clue indicates that the entry is also abbreviated.

Chapter 6

Crossword Celebrities

In This Chapter

- Hearing names that make news (puzzle news, that is)
- Getting to know celebrities famous only among acrossionados
- Discovering puzzle VIPs in fact and fiction

One of the richest mother lodes of recognizable three-, four-, and five-letter entries for puzzles come from names, which may seem unfair, because you won't find many names in the dictionary (you don't get as many opportunities to cheat with names). You will, however, find these names in a crossword dictionary or in the People section of *Information Please Almanac* (see Chapter 9 for more information on crossword-friendly reference books).

You won't often find name-related entries vaguely clued as "Girl's name" or "Boy's name." The clue references specific people with one outstanding quality: a puzzle-friendly name. From ALAN ("Alda or King") to ZENO ("Paradox man"), folks from every field and era frequent the squares until they become repeaters. With enough exposure, they graduate to the Puzzle Hall of Fame.

Although the daily news exposes you to the spelling of today's names, the acrossionado also needs a passing familiarity with celebrities of bygone days. When it comes to the grid, time is suspended — all that matters about a person is the letters that appear in his or her name.

As Claude Rains said so succinctly in *Casablanca,* "Round up the usual suspects." I hope you enjoy meeting the Hall of Fame gang as much as I enjoyed rounding up this motley crew.

What's In a Name?

Generally, a Hall of Fame clue consists of two words: a descriptive modifier ("actor," "author," "painter") plus the name, either first or last, such as "Actress Cannon" (DYAN) or "Crooner Perry" (COMO). In easier puzzles, a dash indicates the missing name as in "Crooner — Crosby."

More important than reputation, achievement, or wealth, where names are concerned, the constructor is looking for the easy-to-key (commonly used) letters: E and S rule, followed by R, T, D, N, A, and O. Those ever-popular letters in the English language have a wonderful new opportunity to combine in different configurations in names for a whole new set of repeaters.

Names that alternate E with any variety of popular consonants are ideal. For example, take IRENE, as in "Actress Dunne," who seems to be one of the few well-known women by that name. In addition, the French philosopher Descartes remains alive by his first name RENE.

People you know

Constructors get excited to put new faces to the same old names. According to puzzle editor Norman Hill, it was a relief to retire ALI Baba in favor of boxer Muhammad ALI. And what a treat when actress ALI MacGraw came on the scene and offered a third possible clue. Another name enjoying a revival is MEL, expanding from the standard "Crooner Torme" and "Baseball great Ott" to include "Actor Gibson" and "TV Actress Harris."

People you don't know from ADAM

Constructors also use names that never got passed along and are limited to one person from the past. For some solvers, these obscure folks present a stumbling block. I'm referring to repeaters such as Actress UNA Merkel, whose films may not merit the longevity of her specially-spelled name, and passe puzzle perennial Singer EDIE Adams (also known as "Mrs. Kovacs"). What a versatile E word EDIE provides, no matter when she last performed in public. And then there's the 1950s star "Actor Mineo," the most recent SAL of note.

Puzzle editor Norman Hill calls these folks the "ersatz" celebrities, because they are almost entirely forgettable if not for the spelling of their names. But they're not artificial at all — they are important links in the crossword grid.

Men among Men

Crossword puzzles do have a kind of popularity contest, but in this contest, the most popular men aren't judged by what clothes they wear or how well they mix a martini. In this realm, you measure popularity by looking for a couple of top vowels mixed together with a couple of top consonants, alternating if possible for a sexy and well-keyed mix. Even money can't buy this ideal kind of name.

First names: Omar, Eero, Erle, Ira, and Art

An informal survey of puzzle experts said that the number one man's name in the grids of the late 1990s is OMAR. With the perfect composition to fit into a corner and key well with other entries, OMAR is a dream come true. What's more, OMAR answers to a number of clues. Antiquated clues like "Khayyam" or "Tent maker" are all but banished from the realm. Instead, OMAR may surface in clues about new faces; for example, baseball's "Pitcher Daal" has stepped up to the plate. "General Bradley" is running a close second at the moment, but I'm concerned that the all-time top clue "Actor Sharif" is getting second billing at this juncture. Perhaps it's time for Sharif to take a break from Bridge and make a new film so that he can graduate from "Dr. Zhivago star."

The runner up in the grid's popularity contest is IRA. The clues associated with IRA have some variety, from "Gershwin" to "Playwright Levin" to "*Mad About You* role" to "Retirement acct." (meaning individual retirement account).

Then there are the two popular E names: EERO ("Architect Saarinen" or just plain "Saarinen") and ERLE Stanley Gardner ("Perry Mason author").

When it comes to male nicknames, the winner is ART, as in "Carney," "Jazzman Tatum," or "Columnist Buchwald."

Last names: Pei

As for a repeater surname, I wish I had a nickel for each time I've filled in the letters PEI (pronounced *pay*) for "Architect I.M." This esteemed man has given solvers a legacy of structures around the world as well as an easy-to-spell handy three-letter entry. (Between Mr. PEI and EERO Saarinen of Finland, the architecture field receives regular exposure in puzzledom.)

An alternate clue for EERO is "Eliel's son."

The Most Popular Women in Puzzles

Women's puzzle names are as diverse as their male counterparts. A graceful name that is rich in vowels seems to fit the bill for this exclusive group of ladies.

First names: Mia, Oona, and Liv

At the top of the list of ladies' names is the versatile "Actress Farrow" (MIA). The only alternate clue for this three-letter entry is the missing word "Mamma — !" Unless you're some latterday Rip Van Winkle, you must be familiar with Mia Farrow's marvelous movies as well as her best-selling autobiography. Even the people in her life belong to the Puzzle Hall of Fame. Perhaps you've read about her peculiar home life with "Director Allen" (WOODY). Or about her long-ago marriage to "Conductor Previn" (ANDRE). I've observed a new clue for her as "Soon-Yi's mom," which borders on the questionable because it touches upon the type of unpleasantness that is banished in the crossword puzzle domain.

First runner-up for lady's first name is "Mrs. Chaplin" or "Eugene's girl," for the one and only OONA. (Eugene refers to the playwright Eugene O'NEILL, whose daughter she was.) Another given name that's graced the grid is LIV as in "Actress Ullmann."

Newly inducted Hall of Fame ingenue LIV Tyler ("Tyler of *Stealing Beauty*") offers a fresh clue.

Last names: Day, Loy, and O'Hara

In the surname category, "Actress Maureen" (O'HARA) is among the screen legends who lives on in clues. O'Hara's contemporary MYRNA LOY, co-star of the *Thin Man* series is a contender as well for every reason. Not only does LOY have two versatile names, but the movie itself is a repeater for its canine co-star ASTA.

Keep your puzzle antennae up for tricky names that read as words. For example "Day, for one." A clue for DORIS, it may easily be mistaken for its ordinary definition as in the 24-hour increment of time. Kinder editors give Day a context in one of two ways, either by offering a modifier such as "Actress Day" or "*Pillow Talk* star" or offering the solver a choice, such as "Day or Lessing," where Lessing refers to the author of *The Golden Notebook*.

Screen Stars Worth Knowing

The names of screen stars form a crossword clique all their own. This gallery of folks includes those who have gained grid fame because they have names that key well into the diagram. On the other hand, many names are familiar to you thanks to publicity agents. As for the others, well, you'll find yourself coming to know how they spell their name — but that's about all you'll know about them.

In a theater near you

Think Cannes Film Festival on the E channel and you're going to be in good shape when it comes to current screen stars in the grid. This is the place to put the spellings (and faces) to the people whose names you're likely to see in the grid these days.

First names

Today's big screen-to-grid hot first names include SLY ("Actor Stallone"), SEAN ("Actor Penn"), and ALEC ("Actor Baldwin") for leading men, and EMMA ("Actress Thompson") and DEMI ("Actress Moore") among women.

A trio of performers named ERIC are vying for grid fame: Bogosian and Robertson, with young Stoltz gaining ground. RENE ("*Get Shorty* star") Russo and UMA ("*Pulp Fiction* star") Thurman are coming up in the female arena. (Constructors rub their hands with glee when new stars with three-letter names like UMA start gaining attention.)

What distinguished company ALEC Baldwin is in, puzzle wise. At this juncture he is taking the mantle from his puzzle predecessors Guinness and Templeton who haunted the diagrams for decades prior to his newly claimed fame. By the way, ALEC Baldwin is married to a very popular KIM — "Actress Basinger."

Keep your puzzle antennae up for famous surnames that may easily be mistaken for everyday words. Examples of names that encourage this pitfall include Actor Jeremy IRONS, entertainer Bob HOPE, British comedian Eric IDLE, and rocker Keith MOON. Deliberately oblique clues like "Hope, for one," "Moon, e.g." or simply "Irons" may frustrate you needlessly. Kinder constructors offer you a choice of two names as a tip off that the entry is a name, as in "Idle or Stoltz."

The versatile ANNA, too, has at least one fresh clue from recent times branching out from the old-time actresses Sten and Magnani. The Crossword Hall of Fame has welcomed "Actress Paquin," the little girl from New Zealand who made her debut on the big screen in *The Piano*.

ANNA is a palindrome, which is a word that reads the same forward and backward. Another famous palindrome is "MADAM I'M ADAM." Not that palindromes have too much to do with crossword puzzles — you may occasionally run into palindromes as a theme to a Sunday puzzle.

Last names

In the surname category four letter men "Actor Richard" GERE and "Actor Alan" ALDA lead, with "Actor Jean Claude — Damme"(VAN) following suit. Neither "Actor Brad" PITT nor "Actor Johnny" DEPP have caught on as repeaters yet, at least insofar as acrossionados are concerned, but "Actor Nick" NOLTE has. "Actress Sharon" has already etched her place in STONE as an entry.

The most frequently-mentioned surname in puzzles is undoubtedly DEE, which is usually clued separately or together as "Sandra" or "Ruby." You may also see DEE alternately clued as "Failing grade" or "River of Scotland."

Lesser knowns

Some stars remain in the collective consciousness thanks more to their uniquely spelled names than to their recent work. For given names look to DYAN ("Actress Cannon"), DINA ("Actress Merrill"), DONNA ("Actress Pescow"), and INGA ("Actress Swenson").

From time to time you encounter the six-letter ELAINE, which answers to "May or Stritch." And there is only one Peggy in puzzles, namely CASS in response to "Auntie Mame actress." NEAL, meanwhile, remains the territory of Patricia NEAL "*The Fountainhead* star."

The top ersatz celeb name is probably ELKE Sommer. Even if you can't recall her blonde Nordic good looks, you can spell her name in answer to the clue "Actress Sommer."

Also on the ersatz horizon are film makers Gus Van SANT and Nicolas ROEG, as well as actress RAE Dawn ("Daughter of Thomas") Chong and Irish actor Stephen REA ("*The Crying Game* actor").

Directors and producers

Behind-the-scenes crossword-wise, Producer OTTO Preminger remains alone in this category as the answer to "Producer Preminger" or simply "Preminger." Top directors include ELIA "Director Kazan" and NORA Ephron, who offers a new spin on that female name described either as "Director Ephron" or "Author Ephron."

The other ELIA is "Famous essayist" or "Lamb."

The LEE family also pops up frequently in puzzles. Young director ANG LEE provides an excellent double opportunity for constructors with his jazzy name. Of course, he joins a distinguished line of LEE clues so widespread in the world of entertainment. From Pinky through Spike, LEE has continued to dominate in the surname department. Additionally, it appears as a given name from "— J. Cobb" to "— Remick."

Film stars of yesteryear

American Movie Classic buffs may have the edge in the grid when the clue calls for a familiarity with screen stars of days gone by.

"Vamp Theda" BARA leads in the surname division followed by "Actress Rita" GAM and "Silver screen star Mary" ASTOR. "Actress EVE" (ARDEN) appears in both positions, with an ambidextrous puzzle name. FAY "Wray of *King Kong*" fame tops the given names. Next in the line up is ELSA "Actress Lanchester," whose namesake is the "Lioness in *Born Free.*"

Quick: Name Fred Astaire's sister. Answer: ADELE Astaire. She has staked out her place in the Hall of Fame pantheon along with the other five letter A girl's name of yore, AGNES, as in "Actress De Mille" or "Actress Moorehead." In the five-letter category is the one and only ILONA "Actress Massey," along with IRENE as in "Actress Dunne." (Parents-to-be searching for unusual girls names would do well to turn to crosswords for the next generation of famous ladies.)

Male stars of yore include legends such as GENE "Actor/dancer Kelly" or NOEL "Playwright Coward," each with a name that offers a lovely balance of vowels and consonants. "*Wizard of Oz* star" BERT LAHR offers two puzzle friendly names, with the puzzle preference going to the first name. "Director Erich — Stroheim" (VON) also offers his title to the Hall of Fame. Other popular grid guys include TAB "Actor Hunter," the VAN contingent — "Actor Johnson" or "Actor Heflin" — and ELI "Actor Wallach." Repeater ELI appears often as "Yale man" after the university founder.

You find a veritable laundry list of R-vowel-consonant names among the celebs of days gone by:

- RAY brings back "Actor Milland" or "Actor Bolger."
- RED answers to the deliberately vague clues "Buttons" or "Skelton," as in the actor and entertainer.
- REX is more often "Actor Harrison" than the deliberately vague "Stout, for one."
- RIP is the one and only "Actor Torn."
- ROD, a dual faceted name, evokes "Actor Steiger" or "Actor Serling" as well as fly fishing equipment.
- ROY tends to be "Cowboy Rogers" before "Campanella."

In the four-letter group Marlene Dietrich's co-star EMIL Jannings (of *Blue Angel* or *Waxworks*) appears as the only puzzle man bearing that German monniker. In its French form as EMILE, the clue becomes "Author Zola."

Crossword's most memorable movie role is NORA, as in the sophisticated couple NICK and NORA Charles of *The Thin Man*. MYRNA LOY played the part, and is firmly entrenched in the Hall of Fame for both names — although she is more often evoked by the role. Despite the fact that her co-star was the suave William Powell, the film's fox terrier ASTA ("Nora's pet" or "Nora's pouch") rates higher in this domain. ASTA is arguably the most popular pup in puzzles, with TOTO (of Oz) and television's RIN-Tin-Tin being the two closest contenders.

If you only keep two movies in mind, make them *The Thin Man* and *The Wizard of Oz* for maximum solving support. The cast of Oz peppers the diagrams — from actors RAY Bolger to BERT LAHR to Dorothy's dog TOTO.

As for the contemporary movie role to remember, Jim Carrey fans take note: ACE Ventura has taken a foothold. Leading actress role goes to Norma RAE. Sally FIELD ("You really like me!") played the union organizer, you may recall.

Puzzle Perennials

Of course, certain talents are legendary and therefore timeless. No one can replicate what they did and they remain forever in a time warp for solvers and nonsolvers alike. I'm speaking about a typical ONER ("Unique person") like "Miss West," or MAE. (She can be disguised by her surname as "West" for an extra challenge.)

RITA Hayworth qualifies as a screen goddess, although she has lost puzzle ground to the more current clue "Singer Coolidge" and "'60s Actress Tushingham." No one has replaced the one and only five letter GRETA Garbo but three-letter blond bombshell KIM Novak is now challenged by "Actress Basinger." Another three letter screen goddess is the incomparable "Miss Gardner" or AVA. Who can possibly take her place?

With their fabulously composed given names, both AVA and author ERLE Stanley Gardner have ensured that their common surname appears among the clues on a regular basis.

What About TV? Stay Tuned!

The same formula applies to TV stars as to all members of the Crossword Hall of Fame: The puzzle favors names with a balance of vowels (heavy on E) connecting common consonants. Popularity is based on the letters of the name rather than prime-time ratings. Most puzzles contain some allusions to television, while *TV Guide* crosswords makes it the main thrust of the entries.

A.M. shows

Kiddie shows are invading puzzles via "*Sesame* —" (STREET or STS, if clued as "Sesame, et al."). The most popular character from that show is ELMO, described as "Ticklish Seasame St. regular." "Puppeteer Lewis" has no competition for her well-balanced first name SHARI with its final I. Children's entertainer Soupy SALES lives on in the squares if not on the tube.

When it comes to adult morning programming, "Talk show host Philbin" is the only REGIS worth remembering.

News personalities

News anchors in the clues include morning newsman MATT Lauer, a welcome addition in the four-letter category. Among the occasional substitutes DAN "Rather, for one," offers a welcome ambiguous surname, while "Anchor Sawyer" offers DIANE.

P.M. shows

Afternoon programming can be summarized in one name: OPRAH. With PHIL Donahue off the air, no other host currently challenges her grid-friendly letters.

As for prime time, TIM Allen of *Home Improvement* is dominating as the prime clue for that nifty name, which is an improvement over Tiny. TV actresses feature MARG Helgenberger, who offers constructors a tricky four-letter option ending with G, and PAM Dawber. Top rated show *Mad About You* has entered the repeater arena as well through the character IRA as well as co-star Helen HUNT.

Ever since SULLIVAN and ASNER, television has been a rich supply of men named Ed. Because the puzzle requires at least three letters per entry, the name Ed almost always appears as the plural EDS. For example, "The Begleys Sr and Jr" or "Mister and McMahon," referring to the prime time horse and Johnny Carson's sidekick.

Emcee ALEX Trebek of *Jeopardy* note is a familiar name to most acrossionados because his show is an excellent practice ground for puzzle skills. He offers a fresh new alternative to the other ALEX, author "— Haley."

Late night

The midnight hour offers a good source of pithy names. Carson's replacement JAY LENO, a double whammy, leads the pack. *Tonight Show* originator, Jack PAAR, with his double A spelling, has insured himself puzzle immortality despite the lack of reruns of the show he started. Letterman gets grid time with his nickname DAVE, while CONAN O'Brien is coming up in the grid and, with any luck, will follow in Paar's footsteps.

Networks

The only channel in puzzles appears to be CBS, with its puzzle-friendly call letters. (Introducing the stations is a recent innovation, because the grid is usually a commercial-free zone.) Among clues, MTV is gaining quite a bit of air time with references to "Home of V.J.'s."

Reruns

Old timers are plentiful in puzzles, beginning with funnyman SID Caesar. His ambiguous name makes for the tricky clue "Caesar" until you start to anticipate his appearance. Comedic stars dominate the entries, from Lucille BALL and DESI Arnaz to BEA Lillie to ART Carney.

From the 1960s clue immortals include Barbara "*I Dream of Genie* star EDEN," LANI O'Grady of *Eight is Enough* and the one and only MARLO "That Girl" Thomas, who may also appear as "Phil's wife" in the sense of "Talk show host Donahue."

Perhaps the most important celeb from television for puzzle lovers around the world is the man who invented *Wheel of Fortune,* namely MERV Griffin.

The most popular television show of yesterday in puzzles seems to be *The Andy Griffith Show.* In addition to ANDY, repeaters from that sitcom include ersatz celeb DON Knotts as well as the role of OPIE, played by the boy who became big-time director RON Howard.

Following Fashion in the Grid

Supermodels have invaded the world of clues. At the top of this esteemed list is ELLE Macpherson, who has given constructors an up-to-date alternative to the dull standard of the past "Female pronoun: Fr." NAOMI Campbell contributes some cameos with her vowel-rich five-letter given name ending in I. And breaking into film, there's Carol ALT.

In the world of crossword fashion, OLEG Cassini never goes out of style, with DIOR a distant second. Cosmetics queen ESTEE Lauder is vying for her rightful place in crosswords (a perfect mix of E's plus two top consonants) with some success.

Author! Author!

Of the eternally popular authors in crosswords, mystery writer ERLE ("Stanley Gardner") rules. If inventing Perry Mason did not buy him eternal fame, the unique spelling of his given name certainly has.

On the simplest level his clue reads "— Stanley Gardner." At the next level of clue challenge, he becomes "Perry's creator." By using Mason's given name in the clue, you understand that the entry is looking for a given name as well. The inventor of the mystery genre, Edgar Allan POE, also ranks as a top puzzle entry.

Writers with odd first names are a tight little clique in the grid with staying power. Here's a short list, in alphabetical order, of the most common of these oddballs:

- **ANAIS** = "Author Nin" or "Diarist Nin"
- **ANYA** = "Author Seton"
- **AYN** = "Author Rand"
- **BRET** = "Author Harte"
- **EDA** = "Author LeShan"
- **EDNA** = "Author Ferber" or "St. Vincent Millay"
- **ELIE** = "Author Wiesel" or "Wiesel of letters"
- **ENID** = "Author Bagnold"
- **EZRA** = "Poet Pound"
- **GORE** = "Author Vidal"
- **IAN** = "Author Fleming"
- **IRA** = "Author Levin"
- **ISAK** = "Author Dinesen"
- **LEN** = "Author Deighton"
- **LIN** = "Author Yutang"
- **RONA** = "Author Jaffe"

As for author surnames, the clue structure may go one of two ways. The obvious clue simply states the given name. The second option describes the author by work. Top honors go to the following names:

- **AGEE** = "Author James" or "Author of *Pal Joey*"
- **AMIS** = "Author Kingsley" or "Author of *Lucky Jim*"
- **BERNE** = "Author Eric" or "Author of *Games People Play*"
- **COOK** = "*Coma* author" or "Writer Robin"
- **DAHL** = "Author Roald" or "*James and the Giant Peach* author"
- **HALEY** = "Author Alex" or "Author of *Roots*"
- **LEE** = "Author Harper" or "Author of *To Kill a Mockingbird*"
- **LOOS** = "Author Anita" or "*Gentlemen Prefer Blondes* author"
- **MAAS** = "Author Peter" or "*Underboss* author"
- **OATES** = "Author Joyce Carol" or "Author of *Cybele*"
- **O'HARA** = "Author John" or "*Butterfield 8* author"
- **RAND** = "Author of *Atlas Shrugged*" or "Author Ayn"
- **ROTH** = "Author Philip" or "Author of *Portnoy's Complaint*"
- **TAN** = "Author Amy" or "*Joy Luck Club* author"
- **URIS** = "Author Leon" or "Author of *Trinity*"

Literature 101

Required reading for crosswords? Herman Melville is unequaled for his contribution of oddly spelled easy-to-key four-letter entries. The white whale MOBY DICK is still his best-known work, with its evil Captain AHAB ruling the grid as top villain. His pair of adventure stories OMOO and its sequel TYPEE are also puzzle perennials.

Two repeater titles in the crossword course are SHE by H. Ryder Haggard and "God's Little —" (ACRE), a standard missing-word clue.

Playwrights abound in the puzzle universe. Some of the more popular entries include the following:

- **INGE** = "Playwright William" or "*Bus Stop* or *Picnic* playwright"
- **O'CASEY** = "Playwright Sean"
- **ODETS** = "Playwright Clifford"

Whether or not you've seen Marilyn Monroe in *Bus Stop* or William Holden in *Picnic,* INGE will brand itself upon your memory as you encounter him from puzzle to puzzle.

Play of the Crossword Year: "A Lesson From —" (ALOES) by South African, Athol Fugard.

The clue "Literary monogram" may indicate either GBS (as in George Bernard Shaw) or RLS (as in Robert Louis Stevenson).

Singers

GRIDLOCK BUSTER

Sometimes constuctors can get devious when it comes to dropping names in the grid. For example, often the clues omit the word "Singer" for superstars such as "Horne" for LENA.

The following names should be music to a solver's ears:

- **ARLO** = "Singer Guthrie" or "Woody's son"
- **BING** = "Crooner Crosby"
- **CAB** = "Calloway"
- **CLEO** = "Singer Laine"
- **EDIE** = "Singer Adams"
- **ELLA** = "Fitzgerald"
- **ERIC** = "Singer Clapton"
- **ETTA** = "Singer James"

- **GLEN** = "Singer Campbell"
- **LENA** = "Horne" or "Horne of Broadway"
- **NAT** = "Singer Cole" or "King Cole" or "Natalie's dad"
- **PATTI** = "Singer Page"
- **REBA** = "Country singer McEntire"
- **RITA** = "Singer Coolidge"
- **TONI** = "Singer Tennille"
- **TRINI** = "Singer Lopez"

As for noted songs, the crossword standards fall into the missing-word category:

- "I — Rhythm" = GOT
- "These — Are Made For Walking" = BOOTS
- "What — For Love" = I DID
- "— Be Cruel" = DON'T
- "— In Love With Amy" = ONCE

Opera has contributed one standard four-letter repeater to crosswords, namely ARIA or "Operatic solo." In more advanced puzzles, a clue by example indicates the name of an aria as in "O, sole mio, e.g." "Diva Kathleen" (BATTLE) and "Diva turned director" (SILLS) offer tricky surnames to the clue mix.

Top crossword composers in the grid include "Composer Thomas" (ARNE) and "Composer Rorem" (NED).

An up-and-coming name in the puzzle is Sir PAUL McCartney ("Former Beatle"), who has been making inroads in the grid.

A number of other rock groups and performers are also slowly making headway as repeaters, including the following noted entertainers:

- **ANT** = "Rock star Adam"
- **BONO** = "Sonny —" or "U2 singer"
- **DAN** = "Steely —"
- **DEE** = "Rocker Kiki"
- **ELTON** = "Rocker John"
- **ENO** = "Rock music producer Brian"
- **ERIC** = "Rock star Clapton"
- **IDOL** = "Rocker star Billy"
- **MAC** = "Fleetwood —"
- **STING** = "Rock star and actor"
- **TINA** = "Rocker Turner"

Sports Pages

Sports figures loom big in puzzles, and they account for my entire exposure to baseball. More specifically, you can spot the following names in the grid, whether it is baseball, basketball, or soccer season:

- **ALOU** = "Baseball family" or "Felipe, Jesus, or Matty"
- **BERRA** = Baseball's Yogi"
- **ENOS** = "Baseball's Slaughter"
- **MAYS** = "Willie of baseball"
- **OMAR** = "Pitcher Daal"
- **OTIS** = "Baseballer Amos"
- **OTT** = "Baseball name of fame" or "Mel of baseball"

In soccer there is only one "Soccer superstar," and that is PELE.

The tennis court has provided a handful of Hall of Famers, namely "Netman Nastase" (ILIE), "Tennis player Rod" (LAVER), "Tennis ace Lendl" (IVAN) and "Tennis great Arthur" (ASHE).

Up-and-coming Hall of Famers include MATS "Netman Wilander," thanks to the easy-to-key letters in his given name ending with a surprise S, and SEVE "Golfer Ballesteros." Wilander gives a fresh spin to the otherwise dull definition clue " Table settings" or "Wrestling equipment."

Vatican and Biblical VIPS

Papal names make excellent entries, especially LEO and PIUS ("Papal name"). The Vatican also introduces a new option to the game: a name that includes a Roman numeral, as in the following names:

- **LEO IV** = "Pope: 847-855"
- **LINUS** = "First Pope"
- **PIUS X** = "Vatican name" or "Pope"

The papal wardrobe also supplies a hoard of repeaters:

- **FANON** = "Papal cape"
- **MITRE** = "Papal hat"
- **ORALE** = "Papal vestment"
- **TIARA** = "Papal headwear"

Hey — when it comes to the Pope, you just can't know enough! Keep your eyes open for the following additonal papal repeaters:

- **BULL** = "Papal edict"
- **CURIA** = "Papal court"
- **ROME** = "Vatican locale"

The Bible provides a rich source of puzzle material beginning with "First man" or "First lady," which leads to ADAM and EVE. The most popular four-letter Biblical figures are ABEL, ENOS, ESAU, and NOAH. Other biblical references that recur include the following:

- **ABEL** = "Biblical brother"
- **ACTS** = "Book of the Bible"
- **AMOS** = "Prophet"
- **ARARAT** = "Biblical mountain"
- **EDEN** = "First garden"
- **EDOM** = "Biblical country"
- **ELI** = "Biblical judge"
- **ENDOR** = "Biblical town" or "Biblical witch's home"
- **ENOS** = "Biblical patriarch"
- **ESAU** = "Biblical brother" or "Biblical twin"
- **HOREB** = "Biblical mountain"
- **LUKE** = "Book of the Bible"
- **MAGI** = "Wise men"
- **NEBO** = "Biblical mount"
- **NOAH** = "Biblical figure"
- **THOU** = "Biblical pronoun"
- **UNTO** = "Biblical word"

The *Dell Crossword Dictionary* has two pages of Bible characters in case you need to go farther a field for a Bible-related entry. (See Chapter 9 for more information on crossword-friendly references.)

Chapter 7
Foreign Languages for Crossword Lovers

In This Chapter

- Discovering popular French words for the crossword
- Conquering crossword Greek
- Getting a handle on crossword Latin
- Mastering crossword Spanish
- Filling in German entries
- Enjoying Italian-language clues

Some people think that you can't be a really successful solver unless you belong to the United Nations and have a working vocabulary of at least ten languages. Not true. Solving crosswords is like visiting foreign lands — you don't necessarily need to speak the native language, although it helps. A phrase book suffices during a brief stay. Acrossionados rely on their phrase book of standard repeaters in foreign tongues to choose the correct entries.

In this chapter, I point out the most popular repeating crossword words in French, Greek, Latin, and Spanish, which are the four languages you're most likely to encounter in your puzzle travels.

Parlez-Vous Crosswordese?

A passing knowledge of any Romance language (those based on Latin) helps in the solving process, and you can get by with a small, select vocabulary. Even the smallest exposure to French shows you how the French people use vowels differently. For example, if you have ever eaten apple pie "— mode," you already know the answer to a clue asking you to supply the missing words: A LA.

You may have noticed that I have a French name, and you may suspect that I know some French. Although you get extra credit for this observation, my extensive background in the language (a B.A. and M.A. coursework) convinces me even more that whether you speak the language has no bearing on spelling the handful of short French words you need for crossword puzzles.

To be or . . . to be

If you don't speak any French, then all French words probably appear odd to you. A good place to start is with ETRE because E is such a popular crossword letter (even in French).

Constructors often clue the French word ETRE as any of the following:

- "To be: Fr."
- "French I verb"
- "To be, in Paris"

After you build your vocabulary, many French terms will occur to you without any conscious effort at all. In fact, you may realize how many French words permeate your everyday life and provide you with a "Raison d'—" (Answer: ETRE).

Take heart that French articles (*le, la, l', les, un,* and *une*), required in the spoken word, are omitted from the grid; the clue only calls for the noun itself. For example, where you see a clue like "French friend" the answer is simply AMI and not UN AMI or L'AMI.

Don't even think about the accent marks that appear in French. First of all, you never use accent marks (even in French) when spelling in capital letters. Secondly, accent marks are not part of the game.

Next stop: South of France

Words containing the letter E rule in the puzzle universe because this letter appears to be the most crossword compatible. French offers a wealth of three-letter E words that constructors can't keep their hands off of. For example, ETE, which means summer, is one such succulent word for the constructor.

ETE may prove to be the one French E repeater that you want in your pocket. Vacationers and constructors have one thing in common: a fondness for summertime in France.

The constructor most often clues ETE as either of the following:

- "Summer: Fr."
- "French season"

Sometimes, the clue implies the language of the entry by a reference either to a location in that country or to an easily identifiable local name. Don't let this tactic throw you; just translate the clue for the correct entry. For France, constructors use several cities, primarily Paris, as touchstones, while Pierre mainly serves as the local name. Consequently, the clue "Summer, to Pierre" takes you to the same three-letter E word. (Because constructors are such a creative bunch, they also like to use alliteration in these clues, such as "Summer on the Seine" and "Friend to FiFi" for AMI.)

With the recent popularity of Peter Mayle's books about the French region of Provence, a clue for the entry ETE may read "High season in Provence."

The clue "Nice season" proves the trickiest clue of all for ETE, bordering on overuse. The clue is completely accurate if you read it correctly. You're not in Kansas any more: Don't read Nice in English. Think France — the French town of Nice lies on the Riviera. Because constructors think of France as having only one season, ETE proves the correct entry.

The language of love

When exploring the vagaries of the "French soul" (AME), you discover a host of helpful words in the grid and, perhaps, in the world.

In my years of puzzle experience, I've noted that French entries seem to revolve around the subject of love. If you think about *toujours l'amour*, the following vocabulary list becomes a little more fun:

- **AMOUR** = "Love, to Pierre"
- **AMI** = "French friend"
- **AMIE** = "Girlfriend, to Pierre"
- **CHOU** = "French endearment"
- **CHERI** = "French endearment"

Constructors sometimes clue CHERI as "Colette novel"; CHERI is Colette's tale of a young gigolo.

Say you, say MOI

Of course, the tendency in a country so closely associated with love is to become jealous. Key French possessive terms to know include the following:

- **A LUI** = "His: Fr." or "French possessive"
- **A MOI** = "Mine: Fr." or "French possessive"
- **SES** = "French plural possessive"

Two words may run together in the grid without a black square between them. You read and understand the phrase as two words but fill it in as one. For example, the answer to the clue "Mine: Fr." is A MOI, which is two words, except in the grid, where you write it as "AMOI."

Royalty still counts

Marie Antoinette may be history, but where else can you capture the romance of French royalty in a few letters, except in crosswords? You can ace your French history lesson in the crossword by remembering the following clues and entries:

- **REINE** = "Queen: Fr." or "French queen" or "Marie Antoinette, e.g."
- **ROI** = "King: Fr." or "French king" or "Louis XIV, e.g."

The abbreviation e.g. is Latin for *exempli gratia,* which means for example. (Check out Chapter 5 for more information on common crossword abbreviations.)

Sometimes you may see the clue "Louis XIV, *par exemple*." A foreign word in the clue, which is almost always italicized, often tips you off to a foreign-language entry (ROI in this case). Likewise, the English entry KING corresponds to the English language clue "Louis XIV, for example."

At the café — French locales

Puzzles like locations; keeping the following French locations in mind can help you break through the crossword language barrier:

- **ARLES** = "Rhone city"
- **CAEN** = "French city"
- **CAFE** = "Coffeeshop: Fr." or "Pierre's coffeeshop" or "— de la Paix (Paris landmark)"
- **ICI** = "Here: Fr." or "— on parle francais (store sign in Paris)"
- **ILE** = "Isle: Fr." or "— de la Cite"
- **LYON** = "French city" or "City on the Rhone"
- **MANS** = "Le — (racing town)"
- **NICE** = "Riviera town"
- **NIMES** = "French city" or "Ancient French city"
- **ORLY** = "French airport" or "Parisian airport"
- **PARC** = "Park: Fr." or "Bois de Boulogne, e.g."
- **PARIS** = "Fashion capital"
- **SEINE** = "French river" or "Parisian river"

An alternate clue to "Parisian river" for SEINE is "Fisherman's net."

Paying the price

When you have to pay at the crossword CAFE, you reach for either of the following two entries.

- **FRANC** = "French money" or "French coin" or "French monetary unit." For alliteration, "Moolah in Metz"
- **SOU** = "Old French coin" or "Worthless French coin"

GRIDLOCK BUSTER

Discontinued by the French government, the ECU lives in crosswords as the answer to "Old French coin." In the future, you may see ECU as "Currency to Pierre."

Touché!

In an earlier ERA — to borrow a repeater — jealous French lovers dueled over a desirable lover. Luckily, dueling is no longer the norm. However, heraldic terms live on in the grid as repeaters. (Things "heraldic" refer to *heralds,* those messengers of yesteryear who made proclamations that began "Hear ye! Hear ye!") The basic kit for the crossword fencer includes the following French entries:

- **APPEL** = "Fencing move" or "Fencing ploy"
- **EN GARDE** = "En — (fencer's cry)"
- **ENTE** = "Heraldic term"

- **EPEE** = “Fencer’s sword” or “Fencer’s foil”
- **ORLE** = “Heraldic wreath”
- **SEME** = “Heraldic design”

Another weapon in the crossword arsenal is SNEE as in “Snick’s partner,” a type of dagger. (The French borrowed SNEE from from the Dutch word *Snickersnee.)*

Terms of address

Ready to meet your French family? Prepare yourself for working the puzzle — and attending a French family reunion — by keeping the following clues and entries in mind:

- **ADIEU** = “French farewell” or “Farewell to Pierre”
- **MERCI** = “Thank you: Fr” or “Thanks, to Pierre”
- **MERE** = “Mother: Fr.” or “French mother”
- **MLLE** = “French Miss” for short
- **MME** = “French Mrs.”
- **NEE** = “Wedding page word”
- **PERE** = “Father: Fr.” or “French father” or “French cleric” or “— Goriot (Balzac)”
- **S’IL** = “— vous plait”

The word NEE connects a woman’s married name to her maiden name, as in “Hillary Clinton, NEE Rodham.”

MME sometimes appears as the plural, MMES.

Bon appetit

Food takes on a new flavor in the Land of Crossword French. Thanks to the current boom of coffee shops and the efforts of Julia Child, most of these French food terms have become part of the English vernacular familiar to the average solver:

- **BABA** = “— au rhum”
- **BRIE** = “French cheese”
- **CAFE**= “Morning beverage in Paris”
- **CREPE** = “French pancake”
- **EAU** = “Water: Fr.”
- **HORS** = “— d’oeuvres”
- **LAIT** = “Milk: Fr.” or “Café au —”
- **OEUF** = “Egg: Fr.”
- **PAIN** = “French bread”
- **PATE** = “French spread”
- **ROUGE** = “Red: Fr.”

- **SALUT** = "French toast"
- **SEL** = "Salt: Fr." or "French seasoning"
- **TARTE** = "French pastry"
- **TASSE** = "French cup" or "Word after demi"
- **THE** = "Tea, to Pierre"
- **VIN** = "Wine, in Paris"

Other common crossword French

When all else fails, see if any of the following French words fit into the space you need to fill on your grid:

- **AVEC** = "French preposition" or "— *plaisir*" or "With, to Pierre"
- **BETE** = "— *noire* (bugbear)"
- **DOS** = "Back, in Paris"
- **ECOLE** = "French school" or "Place for *eleves*"
- **ELEVE** = "French student"
- **ELLE** = "French pronoun" or "French fashion magazine"
- **ETAT** = "French state" or "Coup d'— "
- **IDEE** = "French idea" or "French notion" or "Brainstorm in Paris"
- **LYCEE** = "French school"
- **MAI** = "Springtime in Paris"
- **MATIN** = "Morning in Metz"
- **MER** = "French sea" or "Debussy opus with La"
- **MOT** = "French word" or "Le — juste"
- **NEZ** = "French nose"
- **NOM** = "French name" or "Pierre, *par exemple*"
- **NON** = "French negative"
- **NUIT** = "Parisian night"
- **ONDE** = "French wave" or "Wave on *la mer*"
- **PAS** = "Step, to Pierre" or "N'est-ce —?" or "Word with *faux*"
- **SANS** = "Without: Fr."
- **SEC** = "Like some French wine"
- **VIN** = "Wine, in Paris" or "French wine"

It's (Not) Greek to Me

How can a language like Greek, with a completely different alphabet, benefit crosswords? Curiously, the different alphabet makes the Greek language *useful* to puzzles. Greek offers a treasure trove of puzzle-friendly letters spelled out phonetically in the English alphabet. For example, a clue like "Greek R" becomes RHO.

The Greek alphabet consists of only 24 letters; yet over half of them repeat in crosswords. Solvers owe a great debt to this ancient culture for spicing up the grid with its array of letters ending in vowels.

In your journey through crossword Greece, HOMER, who is often clued as "Odyssey author" or "Iliad author," may guide you. If you see a clue such as "Music hall to Homer," you know that the constructor wants you to pencil in a Greek word (ODEUM). The capital, Athens, in a clue may also indicate a Greek entry, as in "Marketplace in Athens" for AGORA.

The ALPHA bit

You may find that when you see the vague clue "Greek letter" or the tricky clue "Letter from Greece," you may need to go through the process of elimination to arrive at the correct answer. Try any of the following Greek letters on for size (I list the letters in the order that they appear in the Greek alphabet):

- **ALPHA** = "Greek letter" or "First Greek letter" or "Macho man, perhaps"
- **BETA** = "Second Greek letter" or "Phi — Kappa"
- **GAMMA** = "Greek letter" or "Type of ray"
- **DELTA** = "Greek letter" or "D, to Homer"
- **ZETA** = "Greek letter"
- **ETA** = "Greek letter" or "Greek vowel" or "Letter on a sweater" or "Greek H"
- **THETA** = "Greek letter"
- **IOTA** = "I, to Homer"
- **KAPPA** = "Greek K"
- **LAMBDA** = "Greek L"
- **RHO** = "Greek consonant"
- **SIGMA** = "Greek consonant" or "Greek S" or "Frat letter"
- **TAU** = "Greek letter" or "Greek T"
- **PHI** = "Fraternity letter" or "Part of frat trio"
- **CHI** = "Greek letter" or "Sweetheart of Sigma"
- **PSI** = "Greek letter"
- **OMEGA** = "Greek letter" or "Last Greek letter"

Yes, you find an equivalent of U in Greek: UPSILON. Greek also includes another E (EPSILON) and a second O (OMICRON). But because these words run seven letters apiece, you won't bump into them too often. Ten to one you run into these longer Greek letters more often on a college campus than in the grid.

Alpha is the Greek A, while Omega is the Z. Put them together and you have "the alpha and omega," meaning the entire Greek alphabet, from soup to nuts.

Two Greek consonants — GAMMA and DELTA ("G and D, to Homer") — have assumed completely new identities with definitions that leave their origins behind. Thanks to modern science, GAMMA also answers the clue "Word with globulin." Technically, GAMMA is now defined as a "Chemical substance." DELTA has joined the vernacular and has the dictionary definition "River plain" as its clue.

Alternately, DELTA answers the clue "Actress Burke" of television note ("Designing woman").

Although ALPHA, ETA, IOTA, and OMEGA answer to the clue "Greek vowel," each one has a cliché definition outside the alphabet. Between ETA and IOTA, it's a toss up as to which has done more grid time. ETA answers "Airport abbr." — the letters represent airline lingo for Estimated Time of Arrival. IOTA has also left its original meaning in the dust. More often, constructors clue IOTA as a small speck, as in "Bit" or "Trace." ALPHA may clue as "Beginning" and OMEGA as "End."

Hanging out on Mt. Olympus

Anyone who's seen Disney's 1997 animated movie *Hercules* has a good background for the repeaters that hail from Mt. Olympus:

- **ARES** = "Greek god" or "God of war"
- **ATE** = "Greek goddess" or "Goddess of infatuation"
- **EOS** = "Goddess of the dawn"
- **ERATO** = "Greek muse of poetry"
- **ERIS** = "Goddess of discord"
- **EROS** = "Greek god" or "God of love"
- **HADES** = "Greek god" or "Mythical underworld god"
- **HERA** = "Greek goddess" or "Greek Juno"
- **HERMES** = "Greek god" or "Olympian messenger" or "Mercury"
- **HORAE** = "Greek goddess of the seasons"
- **GAEA** or **GAIA** = "Greek earth goddess" or "Mother Earth"
- **NIKE** = "Greek goddess of victory"
- **ZEUS** = "Top Olympian" or "Greek Jove"

NIKE started out as "Greek goddess" before transforming into "Running shoe."

Pillars of the grid

When visiting Greece, you have to visit the ruins of the Acropolis. This ancient structure has a lot to offer crosswords. The most striking thing about the Acropolis, of course, is its graceful columns, which, depending on design, come in three five-letter crossword styles ending in -IC:

- **DORIC**
- **EOLIC** (also known as AEOLIC)
- **IONIC**

All three column types answer most commonly to the clue "Greek column."

Does it matter if you can tell one from another? Only if you want to. DORIC columns are the simplest of the three, with the least ornamentation. IONIC have the ram's horn design at the top (or they look like the letter I). The EOLIC style developed from a Greek tribe that settled ancient Thessaly, Boeotia, Lesbos, and Asia Minor.

Speaking of pillars, that old standby clue "Inscribed slab or pillar" for that B.C. ancestor of the crossword grid, namely STELE, completes the list.

Miscellaneous popular Greek words

While sightseeing in crossword Greece, you need to know the following additional words:

- **AGORA** = "Greek marketplace"
- **AMPHORA** = "Greek jar"
- **DRACHMA** = "Greek money"
- **EPIC** = "The Iliad"
- **ILIAD** = "Greek epic, with The"
- **LEPTON** = "Money in Athens"
- **OBOL** or **OBOLI** = "Greek coin" or "Greek weights"
- **ODEUM** or **ODEA** = "Greek music hall"/"Greek music halls" or "Greek theater"/"Greek theaters"
- **OLPE** = "Greek flask"
- **STOA** = "Greek portico"

Famous Greek nationals

Whether you think of modern or ancient Greece, you have a choice of the most famous native. In modern times, you can guess the most famous name, even if the clue only mentions the surname "Onassis." What is the three-letter nickname for the mogul who married Jackie Kennedy and turned her into Jackie O? ARI. The modern actress IRENE PAPAS also offers two crossword-compatible names.

From ancient Greece, the pantheon of great talents includes many familiar crossword repeaters:

- **AESOP** = "Greek fabulist"
- **GALEN** = "Greek physician"
- **HOMER** = "Greek poet" or "Greek epic poet"
- **PINDAR** = "Greek poet"
- **PLATO** = "Greek statesman" or "*Republic* author" or "Socrates' pupil"
- **ZENO** = "Stoic"

Latin for Solvers

Latin offers special vowel combinations that open up new vistas in the diagram. Constructors enjoy using Latin in the grid because many Latin words end in the unusual vowel combination "AE," such as ALGAE. Latin also gives constructors a good excuse to introduce the letter Q into the grid. And in the universe of crosswords, that could mean QUID PRO QUO (which most commonly answers "Tit for tat").

To expand the crossword vocabulary, constructors consider all languages fair game. After constructors realized how variety could provide spice in a solver's life, non-English entries began to invade the repeaters in order to liven up the solving challenge without bogging down the grid with boring and obscure terms. You should do fine with the few Latin words I present in this section.

CAESAR and other noted Romans

Keep in mind that, in the crossword, clues imply foreign entries by including a common name from that culture. For example, AVIS could clue as "Bird, to Ovid." In clues that refer to Latin, you may see any of the following names:

- **CAESAR** = "Cleopatra's beloved" or "Julius —" or "Salad order"
- **CICERO** = "Roman orator"
- **NERO** = "Roman emperor" or "Noted Roman" or "Famed fiddler"
- **OTHO** = "Roman emperor" or "Roman emperor 69 A.D."
- **OVID** = "Roman poet" or "*Metamorphoses* author"
- **REMUS** = "Romulus and —" or "Brother of Romulus" or "Co-founder of Rome"

Caesar uttered the immortal sentence that lives on in four-letter-entry puzzle infamy: VENI, VIDI, VICI, which translates into "I came, I saw, I conquered." The whole quote is way too long to appear too often in puzzles, and so a clue relating to this quote usually refers to just one of the words — such as "I came, to Caesar" (VENI). When you see the clue "Caesar's words" the entry becomes ET TU, as in, "Et tu, Brute?"

When speaking Latin, you pronounce the letter V as W, because no W exists in the Roman alphabet. Of course, pronounciation plays absolutely no role in solving a crossword puzzle — I'm just telling you this so that you can impress your friends at cocktail parties when the subject turns to Latin.

Everything begins with ARS

All those statues and buildings still standing from Caesar's time testify to the value that Roman culture put on art. "Art, to Caesar," that is. Answer: ARS. (Three letters with a final S on a nonplural entry — what a neat little entry.) You may occasionally see ARS as a missing-word clue "— Antiqua" (musical term) or "— Nova" (musical term). But most often you see *"— gratia artis,"* which means art for art's sake (which also is the MGM motto).

As a missing-word clue, ARS appears in the saying "Vita brevis, — longa." Translation: "Life is short, art is forever."

See you in court!

Today's legalese yields many top Latin repeaters and potential missing-word clues that have become part of the vernacular, such as "— bono" (PRO).

"Legal matter" or "In medias —" asks for the entry RES. In addition, you may come across the following legal terms:

- **ACTA** = "Recorded proceedings"

  Depending on the composition of a word, plural forms are different in ancient Rome. The letter A at the end of a word may indicate the plural of a word ending in UM. For example, ACTA in its singular form is ACTUM.

- **DIES** = "— juridicus"

  Don't mistake a Latin word for English. For example, when you see the clue "Dies —," you may interpret the clue as something to do with dying. However, typically, the correct entry for the clue is DIES IRAE. Latin allows constructors to use an otherwise unpleasant English word, to the constructor's great relief.

- **ET ALIA** and **ET ALII** = "Et —"
- **IN RE** = "Concerning"
- **IPSE DIXIT** = "— dixit" or "ipse —"
- **IPSO FACTO** = "— facto"
- **NON** = "Persona — grata"

Words beginning with the letter Q for $100, Alex

Q is always the exception rather than the rule in puzzles, because the letter Q doesn't fit well with many words and requires a U to follow it in almost every case. Certainly, in the realm of repeaters, the list of Q entries is limited, dominated by Latin phrases.

In crosswords, solvers and constructors welcome all combinations of three letters that produce universally understood abbreviations. To Caesar, one entry provides such an abbreviation: QED, which stands for *Quod Erat Demonstratum*, a geometry term. For lawyers, QED is part of building a case. For constructors, QED offers a great three-letter Q entry without a U.

As a rule, when you see the clue "Part of QED," the answer is not QUOD. "Part of QED" or "QED word" more often leads to ERAT. Experienced acrossionados choose the E word over the Q word every time.

Another Q puzzle perennial is the "Sine-non link." Answer: QUA, as in *sine qua non*, meaning essential. By itself QUA may answer the clue "In the capacity of."

Alternately SINE answers the dictionary definition clue "Trigonometry term."

Finally, the phrase QUID PRO QUO means an exchange of favors, as in "tit for tat." "Quid pro quo" may appear as a missing-word clue with any of the three words appearing as the blank.

Letters = numbers = dates

Caesar used Roman numerals when keeping his appointment book. Luckily, he used puzzle-friendly letters when entering his appointments.

Constructors sometimes use Roman numerals to ask for historical dates. For example, you may come across a clue such as "Elizabethan date." When you talk about Queen Elizabeth I, you reach back to her reign in the 1600s. For Caesar, that means combining M with D and C, and perhaps a few more letters, depending on the year and the number of squares you need to fill. Sometimes, just to make things interesting, constructors compose mini-arithmetic problems using Roman numerals, such as "XV x II" to get XXX.

Roman numerals have the following numeric equivalents:

- **I** = 1
- **V** = 5
- **X** = 10
- **L** = 50
- **C** = 100
- **D** = 500
- **M** = 1,000

To compose a date (or any number) with Roman numerals, you string together the various letters. For example, "Roman 2001," to use an upcoming date, requires two M's and one I for MMI. Try a smaller number as in "52 in old Rome," which combines one L and two I's for LII.

When faced with a three- or four-"letter" year, don't panic. Because most puzzle years postdate the year 1000, you can lightly pencil M in the first box of the entry, and D usually appears in the second box. Then, check the entries crossing that word in the other direction for the specific year, which may be a mix of I with V, X, or L. When you're just dealing with Roman numerals rather than dates, lean toward C or D in first box.

Because puzzle entries require a minimum of three letters, the smallest value is III (3), as in "mid-afternoon on a sundial."

As for the year, the standard clue "Part of AD" yields ANNO. (The complete phrase is *Anno Domini.*)

It's Cicero's parrot! It's a Hertz rival!

In the land of crossword Latin, you only have to worry about one animal, the bird. You may spot any of the following bird-related entries flying by in the crossword:

- **ALAE** = "Wings: Lat."
- **ALAR** = "Winglike"
- **AVIS** = "Bird: Latin" or "Rara —"

With the introduction of brand names into the clues in recent times, constructors now alternately clue AVIS as "Hertz rival."

By Jove! Roman gods

The gods of crossword Latin live within the grid:

- **AMOR** = "God of love"
- **CERES** = "Goddess of agriculture" or "Harvest goddess" or "Goddess of grain"
- **CUPID** = "God of love"
- **DEI** = "Gods: Lat." or "Latin gods"
- **DEUS** = "God: Lat." or "Latin god" or "God to Caesar"
- **JOVE** = "Roman Zeus" or "Jupiter"
- **JUNO** = "Goddess" or "Roman Hera"
- **MARS** = "God of war"

Catch all phrases

To round out the important Latin words, the Romans gave modern language a few short ways of saying "and so forth and so on," which include the following:

- **ET AL** = "Common catch all: abbr."
- **ET ALII** = "Common catch all"
- **ETC** = "Common catch all: abbr."

Depending on whether the catch all has three or four letters, you can make a determination about the correct entry.

You see i.e. (that is) and e.g. (for example) in clues all the time; constructors puts these abbreviations in clues that use examples for the entry. For TREE, you may see a clue like "Ash, e.g." Solvers could never do without the Latin abbreviations i.e. (id est) and e.g. (exempli gratia).

Miscellaneous Latin phrases

Crossword constructors love the words that peppered Ancient Rome, including the following:

- **AMAS** = "Latin lesson word"
- **AMAT** = "He loves, in Latin "
- **AMO** = "I love, in Latin" or "Word on a Latin valentine"
- **AVE** = "Hello, to Caesar" or "— atque vale" or "— Maria"
- **IDES** = "Fateful day for Caesar"
- **ID EST** = "That is, to Tiberius"
- **ITER** = "Roman road"
- **NONES** = "Roman date" or "Date preceding the ides"

- **NOVA** = "New star"
- **OSTIA** = "Seaport town near Rome"
- **PUER** = "Latin boy"
- **STOLA** = "Roman matron's wear"
- **TOGA** = "Roman garb" or "Forum wear"

Mi Puzzle Spanish Es Su Puzzle Spanish

Most crosswords embrace short words rich in vowels. However, if the solving process becomes too predictable because of a limited vocabulary, the game suffers. Spanish comes to the rescue by enriching the list of possible entries.

Constructors often use a common name or location to imply a foreign entry. For Spanish, you see the commonly used JUAN or PEDRO to indicate a Spanish-language entry. For example, VAMOS may clue as "Let's go, to Juan" or even "Let's go, Juan." Constructors normally use MADRID as the touchstone city, leading to clues such as "House, in Madrid" for the entry CASA.

Spanish solving starts at home

Research shows that crossword Spanish begins in the home, which is rich in four-letter words ending in A. Look to any of the following entries when the clue calls for a Spanish word related to the home:

- **CASA** = "House: Sp." or "Spanish residence" or "Home, to Juan"
- **OLLA** = "Pot: Sp." or "Spanish pot" or "Earthenware jar" or "— podrida"
- **SALA** = "Room: Sp." or "Room in a casa" or "Room to Juan"
- **SIESTA** = "Nap to Pedro" or "Nap in Nayarit"

The welcome-wagon Spanish saying, *Mi casa es su casa*, invites you to make yourself at home. The phrase also serves as a potential missing-word clue with ES SU omitted, as in "Mi casa — casa."

Say HOLA ("Spanish Greeting") to a top Spanish crossword repeater

The Spanish repeater, OLLA, has spawned one of the all-time top crossword repeaters, OLIO, which answers "Spanish hodge-podge." Technically, OLIO is a form of OLLA, applying the word *stew* to mean hash or jumble.

Articles: You can leave home without them

In crossword Spanish, you don't have to worry about articles. No reason to worry about if the word is masculine or feminine and whether it needs EL or LA.

You encounter articles only as part of geographical-location entries, such as LAS or LOS. Because they commonly answer missing-word clues, you don't need to concern yourself with an intimate knowledge of articles here either. For example, you may run across the clues "— Vegas" and "— Angeles," which do involve articles, but only in the context of commonly known place names.

Forms of address

You must have good manners when traveling abroad and through the grid. The following terms should help you address any situation when in Spain (or in the crossword):

- **DON** = "Spanish nobleman" or "Spanish title" or "— Juan"
- **DONA** = "Spanish noblewoman" or "— *Flor and Her Two Husbands*"
- **SENOR** = "Spanish gentleman"
- **SRA** = "Mrs: Sp." or "Spanish Mrs."
- **SRTA** = "Miss: Sp. Abbr." or "Spanish miss: abbr."

In puzzle politics, the modern English female term MS is too short for a clue to answer and doesn't appear in plural. Apologies to Crossword Hall of Famer GLORIA Steinem.

Meeting the family

You get to know many family members among the Spanish repeaters, including the following relations:

- **MADRE** = "Mother: Sp." or "Sierra —"
- **NINA** = "Girl: Sp." or "Spanish girl"
- **NINO** = "Boy: Sp." or "Spanish boy" or "El —"
- **PADRE** = "Father: Sp." or "Spanish cleric"
- **TIA** = "Aunt: Sp." or "Spanish aunt" or "Aunt, to Juan"
- **TIO** = "Uncle: Sp." or "Spanish uncle"

Constructors may clue NINA as a proper name, as in "Folksinger Simone" or "Ship for Columbus."

Bull fighting: the sport of crossword choice

As an armchair traveler, you venture into arenas that you may not normally approach. While many solvers may not have attended a bullfight, every acrossionado becomes familiar with a few terms involved in the sport. If all you retain from crossword Spanish are the entries related to this national pastime, you're ahead of the game:

- **BOLERO** = "Bullfighter's jacket"
- **CORRIDA** = "Bullring"
- **MATADOR** = "Bullfighter"
- **OLE** = "Bullfighting cheer"
- **PICADOR** = "Bullfighter"
- **TOREADOR** = "Bullfighter"
- **TORERO** = "Bullfighter"
- **TORO** = "Spanish bull"

Alternately, BOLERO also answers "Ravel opus." Most folks are familiar with this musical piece by Hall of Famer "French composer Maurice" that appears in the soundtrack of the "Dudley Moore movie hit" TEN.

Coin of the realm

When buying your ticket to a bullfight, it depends whether you're attending a show in Spain or Mexico. As a result, one of the following units of currency should fit the bill:

- **PESETA** = "Spanish money" or "Money in Madrid"
- **PESO** = "Money in Monterey" or "Cash, in Cancun"
- **PESOS** = "Coins in Cancun"

The most famous Spaniards

Remember the following Spanish heroes as you work through Spanish-language clues in the grid:

- **EL CID** = "Spanish hero" or "Charlton Heston role"
- **DALI** = "Spanish surrealist"
- **GOYA** = "Spanish portraitist"
- **LEON** = "Ponce de —"
- **MIRO** = "Artist Joan"
- **PABLO** = "Picasso"

Miscellaneous popular Spanish crosswords

Keep the following repeaters in mind as you travel through crossword Spain:

- **ADIOS** = "Goodbye in Avila"
- **AGUA** = "Water: Sp."
- **ANO** = "Year in Spain"
- **DIAS** = "Buenas —"

- **ENERO** = "January: Sp." or "Spanish month" or "January to Juan" or "Month after Deciembre"
- **ISLA** = "Spanish island" or "— de Mujeres"
- **ORO** = "Spanish treasure"
- **RIO** = "Spanish river"
- **SI SI** = "Spanish words of encouragement"
- **TACO** = "Spanish dish" or "Mexican dish"
- **TOLEDO** = "Spanish city" or "Holy — !" (Goodness!) or "View of —" (El Greco painting) or "Ohio town"

German for the Grid

For puzzle purposes, any G-rated words that fit into the grid and interlock well with other crossing words are potential entries. That includes foreign languages, and German is no exception. Crosswords don't travel very far into the language of Germany, though, because the words tend to be too long for crossword dimensions. But you still find a few German repeaters that make the cut.

When an entry requires crossword German, the clue may state the language clearly as in "Gentleman: Ger." Or, the clue may imply the language through reference to a German city, such as "Gentleman in Berlin." While clues attached to foreign entries in other languages tend to use a man's name to identify the country (Pierre = French, Juan = Spain), when it comes to German, constructors use city or town names to reference the language, including the following German *burgs*:

- Berlin
- Bonn
- Koln
- Munich
- Ulm

Forms of address

You can add the following German-language forms of address to your crossword lexicon:

- **FRAU** = "German wife" or "Herr's partner"
- **GRAF** = "German count" or "German nobleman"
- **HERR** = "German gentleman" or "Mister in Munich"
- **VON** = "German title"

German grammar

Although you don't need to know how to use them, a few German articles do appear regularly in the grid, including the following:

- **DAS** = "German article" or "— Rheingold"
- **DER** = "German article" or "— Alte (Adenauer)"
- **EIN** = "German article" or "Article in Berlin"

The former German Chancellor, Konrad Adenauer, often appears by his nickname as the missing-word clue "— Alte (the old man)."

Tourist destinations

When it comes to German locations in the puzzles, you almost always return to one of the following three-, four-, or five-letter places:

- **BADEN** = "German spa"
- **EMS** = "German spa"
- **ESSEN** = "German industrial area"
- **RUHR** = "German river" or "German valley"
- **SAAR** = "German region"

German VIP's

Crossword constructors call on the following famous Germans when they need an entry that combines vowels and consonants in a way not usually found in English:

- **DURER** = "German artist Albrecht"
- **HEGEL** = "German philosopher Georg"
- **HEINE** = "German poet"
- **KANT** = "German philosopher"
- **SPEE** = "German Count von —"

Other German words

When you need just ein Bißchen more help to fill in a German-language entry, try out one of the following repeaters to see if it fits your needs:

- **ACH** = "German expletive" or "Alas in Bonn"
- **DANKE** = "German thank you" or "Thank you, in Ulm"
- **DREI** = "German three" or "German number" or "Three in Ulm"
- **NEIN** = "German negative" or "No in Bonn"
- **VIER** = "German four" or "German number"

Now That's Italian Crosswordese

Italy has blessed the world with many fine artists and statesmen through history, and constructors frequently take advantage of the opportunity to cite an Italian-language entry in the grid.

Constructors usually mention the cities Rome or Milano in a clue to indicate that the entry is in Italian.

Music, Italian style

Italian provides puzzles with several heavy music-related entries.

Many of these entries are considered part of the English language now, and so constructors may not indicate the language of origin in the clue.

- **ALLE** = "— breve: music"
- **ASSAI** = "Very: music" or "Musical direction"
- **CODA** = "Musical ending" or "Musical epilogue" or "Finale"
- **LARGO** = "Musical direction"
- **LENTO** = "Musical direction" or "Slow: music"
- **RONDO** = "Musical composition"
- **SOTTO** = "— voce (softly)"

Opera is the favored musical form with Italian composers and their works are prominent in puzzles. Get your pencil ready to fill in any of the following entries when you hear opera referred to in a clue:

- **AIDA** = "Opera heroine"
- **ARIA** = "Operatic solo"
- **BOHEME** = "Puccini opera with "La""
- **MIMI** =" Opera heroine" or ""La Boheme" role"
- **NORMA** = "Opera by Bellini"
- **OTELLO** = "Opera by Verdi"
- **TELL** = "William —" (Rossini opera)

Accepted currency (lira)

When buying your ticket to an opera in Milan at La Scala, the world famous opera house, bring along the local money, the one and only LIRA, which you see clued as the following:

- "Italian coin"
- "Money in Milano"

Note that constructors favor alliteration in clues where possible so that M in "money" is echoed in "Milano."

Familiar tourist traps

A crossword tour of Italy arrives at the following same stops time and again:

- **ASTI** = "Italian commune" or "Italian wine district"
- **ATRI** = "Italian bell town"
- **BARI** = "Adriatic port" or "Italian university town"
- **ESTE** = "Villa d'—"
- **ETNA** = "Italian peak"
- **LIDO** = "Italian resort"
- **MILAN/MILANO** = "Northern Italian city"
- **PISA** = "Leaning tower city"
- **ROMA** = "Italian capital"
- **TURIN** = "City on the Po"

Italian VIP's

Famous names in Italian cover a wide gamut of talents. You won't have to search too far for a puzzle that calls on one of the following Italian noted personalities:

- **AMATI** = "Italian violin maker"
- **ECO** = "Italian author Umberto"
- **LOREN** = "Italy's Sophia"

Other Italian words to remember

In a pinch, these entries may help you answer a clue that calls for an Italian-language entry:

- **BENE** = "Okay, in Roma"
- **CARA** = "Dear: Italian" or "Sweetheart in Siena"
- **GRAZIE** = "Thank you in Turin"
- **OGGI** = "Today, in Turin" or "Italian news magazine"
- **SIGNOR** = "Italian gentleman"
- **SIGNORA** = "Italian lady"
- **STRADA** = "Road in Roma" or "Fellini film with "La""

Chapter 8

Mapping Out Your Crossword Geography

In This Chapter

- Getting your bearings on the crossword map
- Recognizing the mountains
- Crossing the rivers
- Hopping from island to island
- Saluting the United States in the puzzle

Location, location, location! In the puzzle sense, this old saw means locations that meet the repeater requirement: words of three to five letters. Good acrossionados anticipate these special destinations that they visit time and again (in the puzzle).

You have to think globally for puzzles. You see the 50 states of the U.S. in various forms, and entries from all over the world appear very often. Get out your compass, because you're about to travel SSW, SSE, NNE, and NNW (ESE, WSW, ENE, and WNW, too).

In this chapter, I deal only with the repeaters — those locations that you visit most often in the universe of crossword clues. Plenty of out-of-the-way great places turn up in the grid from time to time, but the more popular ones are easy to spell — like ROME ("Where the Tiber flows"), and TARA ("Home of Scarlett O'Hara"). Plus, not every three- to five-letter location contains crossword-compatible letters. I just don't want you to be sad if you never spot your home town in the grid.

When it comes to finding your way around the crossword map, having an atlas handy can really help. I recommend a standard atlas with a comprehensive index, such as *Around the World: An Atlas of Maps and Pictures,* Gary Hincks, and Steve Noon (Rand McNally and Company, $14.95).

The Highs: Mountain Ranges of Note

Everything about mountains becomes puzzle fodder. From "Mountain ridge" (ARETE) to "Mountain lake" (TARN) to "Glacial snow" (NEVE), entries abound in this setting. Even "Mountain goat" (IBEX) repeats often.

Although the most mentioned country in crosswords is EIRE — also known as ERIN or "Land of Joyce" — you won't find mountains on the Emerald Isle. Grid-wise, the higher altitudes take acrossionados most often to Switzerland, Russia, and Greece.

While on the puzzle trail, you may come across the Gaelic three-letter repeater TOR — clued as "Rocky hill" or "Craggy peak." Once, when hiking in the countryside of Great Britain, I happened upon a TOR or two and was thrilled to see the word in action outside of the grid.

For clue purposes, mountains come packaged as a "range." For example, you may see the clue "Swiss range," which leads to ALPS.

Land of the cuckoo: Switzerland

The best-known ALP on the crossword map is MONT Blanc, which usually answers the missing-word clue "— Blanc." (You can also buy a pen of that name, but to date that has not become a common clue.)

Although most location entries conform to their English spellings, constructors take the occasional liberty of borrowing from the language of the region. Check for guide names in the clue that hint at a foreign response. In the case of ALPS, the constructor may use the clue "Swiss range, to Pierre" to indicate the French spelling of the answer: ALPES. Clearly, the introduction of the additional E in ALPS offers a five-letter opportunity to the grid without obscuring the original entry.

The other five-letter range beginning with A and ending in S: ANDES or "South American range."

Land of Beluga caviar: Russia

Because the USSR disbanded, constructors had to alter its clue to reflect history, as in "Russia, once." Luckily, names of the "Russian ranges" remain untouched. They include two five-letter puzzle perennials: the URALS and ALTAI.

ARAL answers "Russian lake" and URAL answers "Russian range." Even if you mix them up, you're ahead of the game if you fill in R-A-L in the final three squares.

Land of Homer: Greece

Constructors often use a recent innovation called rhyme-scheme phrasing to liven up a dull dictionary-definition type of clue. For example, you may see "Tot's cot," which leads to CRIB. In geography, the catchy "Greek peak" refers to mountains in Greece.

As an answer to "Greek peak," you find these two repeaters:

- **MT IDA** (Either a five-letter entry including both parts or in three letters just IDA)
- **OSSA** (Usually a four-letter entry excluding MT)

The best-known Greek peak, although not a repeater, is MT OLYMPUS or "Home to Zeus." More often, Olympus appears in the clue "His home is Mt. Olympus" for ZEUS.

Top volcano

Yes, I know — a volcano is technically a mountain, but puzzles aren't an exact science either.

Which word has four letters, starts with E, and ends with A? This universally known volcano makes the ideal entry. Hint: "Italian volcano." Because VESUVIUS won't fit, the answer must be ETNA (other common clues for this mountain include "Sicilian spouter" and "Sicilian smoker"). Another word that offers the grid a four-letter entry for "Volcano output" is LAVA.

Remember this alternate clue for ETNA: "Lab burner," or a cone-shaped device that heats liquids.

The Lows: Rivers to Ford

Names of rivers and other water formations are standbys in the universe of repeaters. Even as a missing word, RIVER fills in the blank for "Up the —" or "Down the —."

In Spanish, RIVER becomes RIO, as in the implied missing word "Grande, e.g." RIO is two letters away from the English repeater RILL, clued as "Brook" or "Streamlet."

An acrossionado needs to know only one part of a river: LEVEE or "Embankment."

The entry NILE answers the clue "Longest river in the world."

My personal favorite in this category is "Tuscan river": the ARNO. Not only is it located in a beautiful part of the world, but it's pronounced like my surname.

Top puzzle river: starts with Y (or I)

Acrossionados see a lot of the river that flows from France into Belgium and its homonyms. Clue: "Belgian river." Three sound-alike river entries flow in the grid:

- **ISER** = "Czech river"
- **ISERE** = "French river" or "River into the Rhone" or "River in Grenoble"
- **YSER** = "River in Belgium" or "Belgian waterway" or "River into the North Sea"

Don't worry about French accent marks; you don't use them in puzzle entries.

French rivers

As repeaters, rivers flow all over the French countryside. The most popular "French river" entries consist of five letters ending in E:

- **LOIRE** = "France's longest river" or "River at Orleans"
- **MARNE** = "River SE of Paris"
- **RHONE** = "Isere connection"
- **SEINE** = "River in Paris" or "Left Bank sight"
- **SOMME** = "River at Amiens"

Constructors delight in the letters A before O of the trickiest French river, the SAONE ("River to the Rhone"). Solvers can easily confuse the SAONE with the better-known "Parisian river," the SEINE.

SEINE alternately clues as "Fisherman's net."

Navigating the United Kingdom

England proves a great source of three-letter rivers, comprised of puzzle-friendly letters. All may answer the clue "English river":

- **CAM** = "River in E. England"
- **DEE** = "River in Solway Firth" or "Scottish river"
- **EXE** = "River in Devon" or "Channel feeder"
- **URE** = "River in Yorkshire"
- **WYE** = "River of eastern Wales"

In some river-related clues, you see the location mentioned, as in "Stratford upon —" for AVON.

In the four-letter category, England contributes another series of river repeaters:

- **AIRE** = "River in Yorkshire"
- **AVON** = "River at Bath" or "River to the Severn"
- **OUSE** = "River in NE England" or "Yorkshire river" or "River to the Wash"
- **TEES** = "River in N. England"
- **TYNE** = "English river"

The British spell their river OUSE; the French spell theirs OISE.

Island Hopping

When going to a desert island, I'd pack a puzzle or two. Repeaters describing small isolated land masses show up often in crosswords.

The obvious four-letter entry ISLE answers well-known clues like "Capri, for one" or "Wight, e.g."

If you come across a clue like "Isle, to Pierre," then fill in ILE. To Napoleon who ended his days on ELBA, it may be "Island of exile."

Keep your puzzle antennae up for the tricky clue for ISLE: "Man, for one." After touring the Irish Sea, you'd see it as a reference to the Isle of Man, not to the human race.

Other strange little entries pop up in the water. When you see "Islet" you have three possible correct entries in the three letter category: AIT, CAY, or KEY. (This last one may also clue as "— Largo.") In four letters, the entry is EYOT. In five letters, ATOLL answers "Coral island."

The most important crossword island — "Emerald Isle" — reveals ERIN, which is how acrossionados refer to Ireland. In the Irish Sea lies the ISLE of note: MAN (a tricky double entendre). Where you're looking for ISLES or "Irish isles," the answer is ARAN, a group of islands.

You may have heard of these glorious Greek ISLES in the Mediterranean:

- **CRETE** = "Mediterranean island"
- **DELOS** = "Greek isle"
- **IOS** = "Greek isle" or "Cyclades island" or "Aegean island"
- **PAROS** = "Greek isle"
- **SAMOS** = "Greek isle" or "Aegean island"
- **TENOS** = "Aegean island"
- **THIRA** = "Santorim"

O Say Can You Spell: The United States

In crosswords, Hawaii serves as the main source of some welcome repeaters. When landing in Honolulu, you first hear the "Hawaiian greeting" ALOHA. Then, someone drapes a LEI, the traditional "Hawaiian neckwear," around your neck.

Begin your tour of Hawaii with "Hawaiian island," which clue any of the following:

- **OAHU**
- **LANAI**
- **MAUI**

Hawaii also has the other two crossword volcanos: MAUNA LOA, which usually shows up as a missing-word clue with LOA omitted, and MAUNA KEA, which usually appears with the KEA missing.

Many four- and five-letter repeaters from Hawaii include the following:

- **AWA** = "Kava"
- **HILO** = "Hawaii Island port" or "Hawaiian city" or "Hawaiian seaport"
- **HULA**= "Hawaiian dance"
- **KAVA** = "Pepper shrub" or "Root" or "Gum resin"
- **LANAI** = "Hawaiian patio" or "Hawaiian porch" or "Hawaiian veranda"
- **LUAU**= "Hawaiian cookout" or "Hawaiian feast"
- **NENE** = "Hawaiian goose" or "Hawaiian state bird"
- **PELE** = "Hawaiian goddess of fire"
- **POI** = "Hawaiian taro paste" or "Hawaiian dish"
- **TARO** = "Poi source"

For greater flexibility, the United States mostly appear in the grid as abbreviations. Because an entry requires at least three letters in most cases (two-letter words are becoming extinct), the possibilities become limited. You may see many clues cite the nearest state, as in "Neighbor of R.I." for MASS. Here are the most popular state abbreviations:

- **ALA**
- **CAL**
- **DEL**
- **N. DAK**
- **N. MEX**
- **S. DAK**

Spelling, not location, is on the test

You need to remember how to spell geographical locations that appear in the crossword, not how to identify them on a map. Puzzles test your recall of specific words that fit into a grid and interweave as legible entries. At the same time, they tickle your funny bone with amusing phrases like "Hilo hello" for ALOHA, or they try to deceive you with duplicitous clues like "Man, for one" to elicit ISLE. In addition to improving your spelling, you may retain the location of some of these exotic locales — just like how you recall an address after you write it several times.

Puzzles may make you appreciate how much you know and help you revisit subjects you left behind. As you progress, you'll find greater challenges within the universe of crosswords. Challenges always bring rewards to the enterprising solver, and the game's appeal depends on the endless process of discovery.

Chapter 9

The Tools of the Puzzle Trade

In This Chapter

- Scanning the shelves in the puzzler's library
- Shopping for word finders
- Looking things up in crossword puzzle dictionaries
- Discovering other resource books for puzzlers

Given the title of this chapter, you may be surprised to hear that one of the great things about crosswords is that you don't need any "tools" to play the game — all you really need is brain power, a puzzle, and a writing utensil. To get the answers, you can use your noodle, or you can impose yourself upon others within earshot to make them use their noodles — they love it when they can supply an answer.

Yet I know from experience that solvers are an acquisitive bunch. Just like any other hobby, after you find out about solving aids and you see the array of printed material designed to help — despite the fact that you don't *have* to get any of these items, they tempt you. Besides, everyone who knows that you're into puzzles starts giving you stuff for your birthday like sweatshirts and toilet paper printed up with crossword grids. I know — I've received them all on various occasions. And if you have a hankering for that fabric-covered board with a slot for your puzzle magazine so that you can carry it around the house, go for it!

If you're just starting out with crosswords, you may actually find reference materials very helpful. Until you have practiced enough to develop at least a limited vocabulary of those odd little words known as *crosswordese* in the puzzle universe, keeping a couple of reference books handy is smart. In trying to make crosswords seem difficult and mysterious, acrossionados are loathe to share the secret words. By the same token, a *tyro solver* (beginner or novice) may be too shy to ask. Luckily, puzzle editors are generous in sharing the knowledge.

In this chapter, I tell you about basic reference guides for the confirmed and novice acrossionado.

Tracking Down the Answer in a Word Finder

Crosswordese is a funny language. You don't have to know the meaning of the words in order to solve a puzzle — you just need to know how to spell the words. Therefore, you don't necessarily need a standard dictionary. In fact, many solvers use a *word finder* instead of a dictionary.

A word finder provides combinations of letters that supply the missing letters to an entry you are trying to complete. The word finder lists partially completed entries alphabetically by number of letters per word, ranging from two to seven letters. When you open a word finder, you see incomplete word fragments joined by blanks. For each fragment, the word finder lists all the possibilities that use the letters you know.

You reach for a word finder when you hit the wall — that terrible state when you need just one or two letters of a word to complete an entry, and you can't think of the missing letters to save your life. For example, say that you're having trouble with the final letter of a four-letter word that looks like BIL* (the asterisk represents the missing letter). With a word finder, you can look under B to find out what your options are — BILE, BILK, BILL. One of these choices should give you the correct entry and get you over the wall.

Some crossword dictionaries include an abridged word finder in an appendix, which can be extremely helpful; you can read more about crossword dictionaries in "Looking Up Answers in a Crossword Dictionary" in this chapter.

If you feel flush due to a windfall, go for the ultimate word finder called *The Crossword Answer Book* by Stan Newman and Daniel Stark, published by Times Books ($27.95). This ambitious tome simply lists every possible configuration of puzzle entry that you may ever encounter. If you have an unfinished entry that looks like *H*F* (with each * representing a missing letter), the *Answer Book* is the place to find every possible answer. I recommend this book for the following reasons:

- It contains 650,000 entries (no clues) in alphabetical order by number of letters, making the book very comprehensive and easy to use. The *Answer Book* lists three- to seven-letter entries, arranged by word length and sorted by two given letters per category.
- The *Answer Book* includes not only common two-word phrases but also full names, such as ED ASNER and KEY WEST.

Clueing In to the Crossword Key

When you have no idea what the answer to a clue may be, and you don't have even a single connecting letter to inspire you, consider heading to the shelf for a crossword key.

A *crossword key* matches common entries with common crossword clues. Typically, a crossword key offers one entry per clue, which you find organized by clues.

For example, if you come across a clue like "Brit. weapon" and the four-letter entry escapes you, you may find the answer by looking up the clue in the key, looking under B. The key gives you the entry, which is STEN.

Looking Up Answers in a Crossword Dictionary

A crossword dictionary doesn't explain what a word means or how to use it. A *crossword dictionary* matches parts of common clues with typical entries listed by number of letters. You look up a word in the clue that's stumping you and find a list sorted by number of letters per entry. For example, if you look up a typical clue like "Flower part," you find a series of entries, beginning with four letters at STEM and escalating through AMENT and COROLLA. You can then select the one that best suits your grid.

A traditional dictionary may still come in handy

Everyone should have access to a *Webster's Unabridged New International Dictionary* or some other unabridged dictionary. Even though understanding the meanings of the words that you scribble into the grid doesn't matter, you may want to find out the definition to some cool-sounding word at some point.

Among puzzle constructors, the Second Edition is the preferred edition, although I use and recommend the Third Edition, which is more readily available. Of course, not everyone has space or money for the unabridged version, which is available at most public libraries. A good desk version is fine for everyday purposes (but not for constructors).

By the way, Webster's officially added *crossword puzzle* to the English language in 1934. The name appeared in the "New Words" section of the 1927 edition in hyphenated form as *cross-word*. In light of the way the puzzle industry revived dictionary sales, I suggest that the dictionary editors give away pencils with every dictionary sold.

Many times, the editors of the crossword publications that you find in the bookstore compile crossword dictionaries. Your best bet is to buy the companion dictionary to the crossword publication you buy, because then your clues and definitions are drawn from the same database. In other words, if you're a Dell Puzzle Magazines fan, you may want to invest in the *Dell Crossword Dictionary,* which hasn't gone out of print since its debut in 1950.

If you're looking for a comprehensive crossword dictionary, here's a list of recommended ones:

- *A to Z Crossword Dictionary* by Edy Garcia Schaffer (Putnam, $21.95; Avon, $5.99): An alphabetical listing of 225,000 clue words and their possible entries.
- *Andrew Swanfeldt Crossword Puzzle Dictionary,* 6th Edition (Harper Books, $15): An alphabetical listing of clues with possible entries presented by number of letters.
- *The Master Crossword Puzzle Dictionary* by Herbert Baus (Doubleday, $24.95): Highly regarded by industry insiders, this one includes 200,000 clue words and one million answer words arranged alphabetically and by length.
- *New York Times Dictionary,* edited by Tom Pulliam and Clare Grundman (Times Books, $27.50; paperback, $17): Includes multiword entries and shaded boxes that highlight geographical clues and entries.
- *Random House Crossword Puzzle Dictionary* (Random House, $23; Ivy Books, $5.99): An alphabetical listing of 700,000 clues and answers that features geographical locations in shaded boxes.
- *USA Today Crossword Dictionary,* edited by Charles Preston and Barbara Ann Kipfer (Hyperion, $12.95): A compilation of clues from the pages of the newspaper with emphasis on names and nouns, organized by main subjects with related subgroups.
- *Webster's New World Dictionary,* edited by Jane Shaw Whitfield (Macmillan, $20; paperback, $12.95): In addition to the alphabetical listing, a special feature of Tables in the back of the book highlights topics of puzzle interest by section (Bible, chemistry, Supreme Court, and so on).
- *Webster's New World Easy Crossword Key,* edited by James H. Capps (Simon and Schuster, $10.95): Includes 155,000 puzzle clues matched with entries, as well as helpful supplements that list missing-word clues and clues that begin with numerals.

If you'd rather have a crossword dictionary that you can carry around with you (some of the more comprehensive guides are rather large and heavy), consider one of the following handy pocket crossword dictionaries:

Choosing between a word finder and a crossword dictionary

If you have to choose between buying a crossword dictionary and a word finder, your selection depends on your solving needs. Answer the following questions to determine what kind of solver you are and, consequently, what type of reference you should choose:

Do you need to see the entire entry? Until you have a basic knowledge of the lingo of crosswords, you may be more comfortable relying on a crossword dictionary. This type of reference book contains an alphabetical listing of common clues. You look up the clue word, and the possible entries follow, sorted by number of letters. Seeing all the possible words in their entirety can give you a tremendous boost if you're a novice solver.

For example, say that the clue is "German river" in four letters. You turn to "Germany" in *USA Today Crossword Puzzle Dictionary* (edited by Charles Preston and Barbara Kipper) and find a laundry list of German items from *authors* to *seas. Rivers* is a rich subset, with four listed in the four-letter category: ELBE, MAIN, ODER, and RUHR. Surely you can connect one of the words in this group with some interlocking clues and find the right answer.

Are you the kind of solver who is always searching for that final letter to complete an entry? Then you'll do better with the type of reference that categorizes words by number of letters and then offers you the possible combinations in a word finder. Rather than spelling out the entire word, you find combinations of letters in alphabetical order.

For example, you may find yourself against a wall with a clue for "German river." You have EL*E, and you need that one middle letter. In the finder system, you can search for the missing letter by looking up EL*E, where all the combinations are listed: ELBE, ELLE, ELSE. You can take it from there.

- *Crossword Busters* by James Dykes (Berkley, $5.99): A compact reference sorted by categories from alphabets to zodiac signs.
- *The New York Times Concise Crossword Dictionary* by Tom Pulliam, Clare Grundman, and Gorton Carruth (Warner Books, $5.99): A portable, abridged version of the book listed previously by the same authors.
- *Random House Concise Crossword Puzzle Dictionary* (Warner Books, $6.99): An abridged version of the comprehensive volume.

Some dictionaries sort the entries by number of letters so that finding exactly what you need for the puzzle at hand becomes easier. For example, if you have a clue like "Divvy" with a seven-letter entry, you can turn to D in the dictionary and find Divvy, which shows you a list of all the possible entries, organized by length: the five-letter entry is SHARE; the six-letter entry is DIVIDE; and the seven-letter entry (the one you need in this particular case) is PORTION.

Combining Word Finders and Dictionaries

If you're not sure which type of solver you are, then you may benefit from a combination dictionary/word finder. Here are two good ones:

- *Dell Crossword Dictionary,* revised by Wayne Robert Williams (Dell Books, $5.99): A combination reference that includes three sections: clues and their definitions in alphabetical order, special sections on topics of crossword interest (sports teams, a name finder, and more), and a word finder for three- and four-letter words. Updated in 1994, it's pocket-sized and convenient to carry.

- *New American Puzzle Dictionary,* edited by Albert and Loy Morehead (Signet, $5.99): A "classic" reference from the man who introduced the Puns and Anagrams-style puzzle. This book offers more than 150,000 words divided into three sections: clues and their definitions in alphabetical order, special sections on topics of interest, and a word locator (same thing as a word finder) for words of two to four letters. The Moreheads also include tips on solving cryptic crossword puzzles; you can read more about cryptic puzzles in Chapter 13.

Other Helpful References

A puzzle editor's job is to offer you enough information on the page to help you through the grid on your own steam. On the other hand, part of the fun of solving is refreshing your memory on certain subjects.

Reference books beyond dictionaries or word finders round out a puzzler's library. I find the following "other" references to be especially helpful:

- *Benet's Reader's Encyclopedia* by William Rose Benet and Bruce Murphy (Harpercollins, $35): Many people consider this book to be the most comprehensive guide to world literature on the market.
- *The Billboard Book of Top 40 Hits,* by Joel Whitburn (Billboard Directories, $19.95): In addition to the great photographs provided throughout the book, you can find all kinds of popular music trivia in this reference.
- *Information Please Almanac* (Houghton Mifflin, $10.95): An almanac is a handy guide when you're grasping at straws on topics relating to celebrities, current events, or even geography. The 1997 edition features a special crossword puzzle section called "First Aid to Crossword Puzzlers." Highlights include common crosswordese as well as key names from the Bible and ancient mythology. (I prefer an up-to-date edition of *Information Please* as a reference to current celebrities because I'm forever forgetting whether Liv Ullmann spells her surname with one or two Ns.)
- *Leonard Maltin's Movie and Video Guide* (Signet, $7.99): No matter how often you see a film or hear a name, you need to check spelling from time to time. Maltin includes a movie-title index for stars and directors. Besides, you need a source to help with those clues that refer to the Oscars.
- *Total Television: The Comprehensive Guide to Programming from 1948 to the Present* by Alex McNeil (Penguin USA, $29.95): If you think that descriptions of 5,400 series and their major participants from 1948 to 1995 may help you in your solving, then pick up this book. Besides, it makes interesting light reading.
- *The World Almanac* (St. Martin's Press, $9.95): The standard almanac everyone's used since school days. It works!

The World Wide Web: Your global reference

Those of you who are lucky enough to be connected to the World Wide Web already have access to just about any reference material a puzzler could need — for free! Even if you aren't a Web head, you may have already heard about the wealth of information available out there in Cyberspace; you can find out what you need to know about the most obscure topics you can imagine, including aliens, recipes for fish stew, and video games. Most important to the puzzler is that you can search the World Wide Web and Web sites to find very specific information. For example, if you come across a clue that's really stumping you, you can fire up your browser, plug in the key words from the clue, and surf until you find an answer. (If you need a little help on your Web-searching skills, pick up a copy of *World Wide Web Searching For Dummies* by Brad Hill, published by IDG Books Worldwide, Inc.)

Part III
Building Your Sunday Puzzle Power

"No wonder the glacier was able to overtake him."

In this part . . .

Some people think of the Sunday-size puzzle as a terrible monster, an unconquerable foe — a kind of daily-size crossword puzzle gone crazy on steroids. If you're one of these people, I want you to know that you are not alone. Many people look at the larger size of the Sunday puzzle and freak out. That is, until they read this part of the book, which takes the terror out of the Sunday puzzle, reducing it to a doable (and fun) challenge.

I also show you how to work the other kinds of puzzles commonly found on the Sunday puzzle page, including the diagramless and the acrostic puzzles. As a bonus, this part also covers some other advanced puzzle types (even though they are rarely, if ever found on the Sunday puzzle page) — these include the Puns and Anagrams and cryptic-style puzzles.

Chapter 10
Always on a Sunday

In This Chapter

- Looking at the differences between daily and Sunday crosswords
- Examining Sunday puzzle themes
- Planning your approach to the Sunday puzzle
- Recognizing patterns in Sunday puzzles

According to data from *In One Day: Things Americans Do* by Tom Parker, published by Houghton Mifflin, Americans fill in about 50 acres of crossword puzzles in a day. And they wash them down with 17 million gallons of coffee. That's on the average work day. Then there's the Sunday culture.

Mastering the daily pocket-size crossword is the province of travelers, insomniacs, and other people with time to kill (no offense). But the Sunday crossword is the place for swashbuckling acrossionados. Solving a daily crossword involves an understanding of basic tactics, some familiarity with *repeaters* (clues that come up again and again in puzzles), and the ability to put those two things together. Working a Sunday crossword requires a wider knowledge of clever wordplay. That's why the Sunday puzzle requires more than a lunch hour to get through.

However, as I always remind anyone who seeks my advice, good Sunday-puzzle solving comes from experience — experience that you gain after navigating the daily-size puzzles for a while.

Setting Sunday Puzzle Standards

Sunday crosswords appear in the magazine section of most major newspapers, usually in the back pages. Regardless of where you find the puzzle, each one adheres to certain basic elements that were established in the very first Sunday puzzle that appeared in *The New York Times* in 1942.

The following features make the Sunday puzzle the bigger, smarter sibling of the daily crossword:

- **Larger grids:** The Sunday puzzle can range from 19 x 19 to 23 x 23 squares, making the Sunday puzzle significantly larger than the daily (your daily dose is usually only 15 squares across).

  Of course, a bigger grid means more clues — the average Sunday puzzle may measure 21 x 21 squares with 140 to 144 clues. (The number of words per puzzle is limited. Too many words indicates an excess both of short — probably repeater — entries and black squares. Maximum word counts are 168 for a 23 x 23 grid and 144 for a 21 x 21 grid. Exceptions are made for unusual themes that warrant a few extra entries.)
- **Titles:** Sunday puzzles have names with personality, such as "Name Shuffling," "Strike Three!" "You Can Say That Again!" and "Off With Their Heads."

- **Themes:** With more grid space, the constructor can work a theme (topic) into the squares that is captured in a title above the grid. Topical entries recur in symmetrical places within the grid and usually involve six extended answers in each direction. Taking the example of "Strike Three!" by longtime constructor Louis Sabin, the first across theme clue reads "Deprived ai?" The question mark tips you off to some funny business in the entry, which refers to the title. It implies that the solver must "strike" (cross out) three letters from the entry. A peek in the dictionary defines ai as "three-toed sloth." The entry, then, becomes TOED SLOTH.

  The addition of themes to a puzzle limits the constructor when he or she composes the puzzle's grid. Big blocks of "cheater" black squares just to make a theme work are unacceptable. (This last rule is up to the judgement of the individual editor. If a theme warrants the addition of a few more black squares, some editors are known to break the rule.)

- **Bylines:** Traditionally part of the pay for a Sunday puzzle constructor is getting to see his or her name at the top of the page. (In recent times, daily puzzles have begun to include constructor bylines, although less prominently.)
- **More work:** Sunday puzzles are more work to create, and they require more time to solve. After all, you have to solve in two stages: You've got a theme and twice as many clues to decode. If you have trouble decoding the theme, Sunday solving will be harder. But after you catch on, you'll reap twice the fun.

World War II and *The New York Times* turned Sunday into "Solvingday"

The universe of acrossionados owes this weekend ritual to the ingenious grande dame of the crossword, Margaret Farrar. The tradition that she began was introduced at the height of WW II. *The New York Times* publisher, Arthur Hays Sulzberger, a solver himself, approached Mrs. Farrar with a request to introduce a Sunday puzzle to liven up the paper's somber pages. Sulzberger was also responding to a growing demand for puzzles from GIs who worked crosswords to fight boredom during long watches.

Even a new feature as seemingly innocuous as a puzzle had to be fashioned to fit in with the tone of the newspaper that was traditionally referred to as the "Gray Lady." (In fall of 1997, color was finally introduced to the paper's pages.) Mrs. Farrar was instructed to opt for the solemn issues of the day over the typically frivolous fun subjects associated with crosswords. Luckily, Margaret (as she allowed herself to be called) came up with just the right formula to please both management and acrossionados.

When the Sunday puzzle page made its debut on February 15, 1942, a short editorial note explained the split page format that the paper continues to follow to this day: "Beginning today, *The New York Times* inaugurates a puzzle page. There will be two puzzles each Sunday — one with a flavor of current events and general information, and one varied in theme, ranging from puzzles in a lighter vein, like today's smaller one, to diagramless puzzles of a general nature."

On the top half of the page appeared a crossword (maximum size — 23 x 23 square) by Charles Erlenkotter with the appropriately staid title "Headlines and Footnotes." Clearly, the title confirmed to any reader that here was a puzzle with a serious range of subjects. What's more, it was familiar in its presentation and completely recognizable to the average solver.

Since that Sunday in February 1942, the crossword has assumed its place in the newspaper (and in the American routine) as the main solving attraction. In over 50 years, it hasn't budged an inch from that role.

The newsy tone of the first Sunday puzzle established new inroads for acceptable material within the puzzle grid. Proper names and locations became common fodder for the entries. The constructors' informal "Hall of Fame" began to actively recruit celebrity names with the vowel/consonant combinations typical of repeaters that are a mainstay of the modern crossword. Names also give constructors different letter combinations not available in everyday crosswordese.

Only the Shadow knows: Constructors without names

Constructors of daily-size newspaper puzzles remained nameless until recent times. When Will Shortz assumed Eugene Maleska's mantle at *The New York Times* in 1993, he started a new policy of publishing a byline with the daily crossword. Granted, the daily byline isn't as prominent as the Sunday byline at the top of the page: On a daily, the name is listed in reduced type below the lower-left corner of the grid. While the byline is a bonus for the constructor, who now earns top dollar in the field for a daily effort at $75, it offers solvers the opportunity to identify the author of the work.

Although certain key differences separate the daily from the Sunday puzzle, some parameters apply to both the daily- and Sunday-size crosswords that can help your solving abilities:

- **No entry is repeated in the same puzzle (not even in its plural form).**
- **Overall interlock always applies, so each letter works both across and down.**
- **Black-and-white grid patterns are symmetrical (in all puzzles, theme entries appear in symmetrical rows across and down).**
- **Entries are always validated through common reference books.**
- **Fewer black squares in a diagram means a greater solving challenge.**

Sunday-size puzzles are intended to require more solving time. The assumption is that you have the extra time to lavish on the puzzle by the time Sunday rolls around. Of course, how much time you spend with any puzzle depends upon your skill level. You always hear about the acrossionado who can polish off a Sunday crossword in 10 or 15 minutes. Solving a Sunday puzzle that fast can be done, if fast is your goal. The extra zip of Sunday solving is the promise that you're on the trail of a wittier type of wordplay. Because a Sunday puzzle involves more entries, the constructor has an opportunity to dazzle you with clever turns. Whether it's the Sunday *Times* or any other Sunday puzzle, you know that the Sunday puzzle tells a story, and getting to the bottom of it is supremely satisfying.

There's More! The Second Half of the Sunday Page

Many Sunday puzzle pages include more than just the Sunday-size crossword; some newspapers offer other types of puzzles on the lower half of the page.

The Sunday puzzle page of *The New York Times* shows how two great puzzles on the same page can add up to twice the fun on Sunday. If you consider the Sunday-size crossword the main attraction, then the lower half of the *Times* puzzle page is the sideshow.

While the top half of the *Times* puzzle page is firmly entrenched in the Sunday crossword culture, the bottom half is somewhat more flexible. On any given Sunday, you could find one of the following types of puzzles on the bottom half of the page:

- Puns and anagrams
- Diagramlesses
- Cryptics
- Double Crostic

Most solvers haven't had the pleasure of entering the less-charted territory at the bottom of the page, mostly because they're not sure how those other puzzles work. And until someone shows you how they work, the other types of puzzles appear inscrutable. Don't worry — I show you everything you need to get started with diagramlesses, cryptics, and double acrostics in Chapter 11, and in Chapter 12 you can read all about the wordplay that makes up a Puns and Anagrams puzzle.

If You Don't Get The New York Times . . .

While *The New York Times* may have started the Sunday Puzzle tradition, almost every newspaper offers a Sunday puzzle. You have the same wide variety of puzzle sources on any given Sunday that you have during the week — depending on which syndicate your newspaper chooses. Even if you do get *The New York Times,* consider trying the Sunday puzzle in any of the following newspapers for a change of pace:

- *The Boston Globe:* Medium to difficult
- *King Features Syndicate:* Easy to medium
- The *Los Angeles Times:* Medium to difficult
- *Creator's Syndicate:* Medium to difficult
- Tribune Media Services: Medium to difficult
- *The Washington Post:* Medium to difficult

The format and presentation of the Sunday puzzle in these papers adheres to the standards set by *The New York Times.* The puzzles differ in level of difficulty — I note my assessment, based on discussions with the sources, in the preceding bulleted list. The puzzles also differ in attitude or spirit; each editor has a different set of guidelines that gives their puzzles a distinctive tone.

Acrossionados who travel internationally can quench their thirst for solving with the *International Herald Tribune.* The *Tribune* reprints the Sunday puzzle from *The New York Times* (and the daily, too).

Miss Anna Gram starts a puzzle trend

For its debut in *The New York Times* in 1942, the "sideshow" Sunday puzzle featured a more fanciful creation entitled "Riddle Me This" with an author by the name of Anna Gram. (Anna was actually a pair of male collaborators, Albert Morehead and Jack Luzzatto.) Accompanying the puzzle was this brief blurb: "Here are puns and persiflage, anagrams and homonyms, all fair game for the amateur sleuth."

In March 1943, a story in the *New York Times* magazine section speculated whether wartime insanity was to blame for the instant popularity of the Puns and Anagrams puzzle. Unlike the straightforward American crossword, designed as a vocabulary quiz to be solved in the hallowed halls of a library, this breed of crossword became a party game. The puzzle's popularity was largely due to fun clues such as "Faculty member becomes tender (7 letters)." (The answer is PROFFER; PROF = faculty member and OFFER = tender, as in the legal variety.)

It's All in the Theme

A crossword *theme* is a subject that works its way into the clues. The theme emerges through a limited number of the longer entries — in a typical Sunday puzzle, up to 12 of the longer entries can be related to the puzzle's theme.

If a daily puzzle features a theme, typically three or four of the entries are related to the theme.

Theme entries are often composed of a clever phrase, or you may find a theme as simple as a series of double entendres using crossword compatible words. Sometimes the clues are everyday phrases, but misleading.

Themes may develop through the repetition of a word throughout the grid. Whereas you don't see an entry repeated under normal circumstances, the exception is made for a theme. For example, you may see a common element repeat, such as a color (GREEN THUMB, GREENHORN, GREEN GODDESS) or related words (GREEN THUMB, BLUE MOON, RED CARPET).

A theme may also be as far-fetched as a combination of dissimilar elements such as KEVIN BACON OMELET in response to "Star breakfast dish?" You read the answer in two elements with the central word overlapping: Star = Kevin Bacon; Breakfast = Bacon Omelet.

Sometimes a theme is more than a set of related phrases. A quotation may be broken into smaller elements that read consecutively as you solve to convey a message. Like a staircase, the quote begins in the top left corner and reads at right angles down to the right bottom corner. A sample quote from an actual puzzle reads: "NOTHING SO NEEDS REFORMING AS OTHER PEOPLES HABITS." Clues give you the section of the quote with the first clue telling you "Start of an eight-word quote descending in stairstep fashion."

Eugene Maleska, the third *New York Times* puzzle editor and Will Shortz' predecessor, devised the *Stepquote,* which made its debut in *The New York Times* in 1964.

Mommy, where do themes come from?

Any G-rated material that is familiar to the average solver is potential fodder for a theme. To give you an idea of the range, here are some umbrella topics that I've come across in my career as solver and editor:

- **The arts:** music, literature, art, film ("Music Lesson" and "Colorful Airs")
- **The home:** food, cooking ("Around the House" and "Fit to Be Dyed")
- **The world:** countries, cultures, sports, travel destinations ("In the Old Sod" and "Literal World")
- **Contemporary subjects:** outer space, slang ("Out Yonder" and "Space Madness")

Everything under the sun is fair game — provided that it belongs to the popular lexicon.

Obviously, the publication that prints a puzzle influences the types of themes you see in its puzzles. You expect to find plenty of television references in the *TV Guide* crossword, for example. Elsewhere, you expect TV to serve as one of several sources of repeaters. You won't find a theme about a specialized topic such as vintage wines in a Sunday-size puzzle unless you're working a crossword in the pages of a food and wine magazine.

Themes be praised!

In his classic book *How to Solve Crossword Puzzles,* Norman Hill heralds the crossword theme (along with the introduction of the multiple-word entry) as the salvation of the crossword. After years of filling crosswords with the same old dictionary definitions, themes offered constructors new, exciting possibilities. For the solver, themes introduced an additional element of challenge and fun.

Some subjects have been universally rejected by the Sunday crossword community, no matter how helpful they may be to the puzzle. Don't expect to see words related to taboo subjects, such as RAPE, in your Sunday crossword.

According to *The New York Times* specifications, themes are to be narrowly defined and consistent. Freshness is a factor as well. Obscurity is out. You don't want to have a stale theme from yesteryear unless you happen to be solving a vintage crossword. Besides a timelessness, the other characteristic that themes may have in common is a sense of humor. They are designed to elicit a grin — or a groan — once solved.

You're entitled to some help

Granted, crossword themes can definitely test your puzzle prowess. To make things a little easier for you, constructors offer help on the theme of the puzzle. The title of a Sunday-size crossword puzzle provides a giant-size hint about the puzzle's theme.

By reading the title before you fill in the first repeater, you are tipped off as to the subject of the theme you're about to encounter. More often than not, the title gives you a head start on the solving process by giving you some direction. Usually composed of a short phrase, such as "Headlines and Footnotes," "Pound for Pound," or "Family Ties," titles offer some insight about the wordplay involved in the theme-related entries. For example, in the case of "Off With Their Heads," don't expect the puzzle to have anything to do with guillotines. The title is crossword code for "off with the first letter of the entry." "Name Shuffling" involves entries that are anagrams; "Strike Three!" removes the number three from a common phrase in the entry; "You Can Say That Again" combines homonyms in the entries.

Some Sunday puzzles even include blurbs that give you further insight into the fun ahead. The blurb that accompanies "Pound for Pound," for example, tells you: "Dieting can be a lonely chore. Maybe this will keep you company." Now that's food for thought.

The ambiguity created by these tricks raises the level of decision-making into a test of your solving sense. Tournament winners always follow a plan that helps them decipher the clues and unravel the entries. But much of their technique relies on practice, as well as shorthand tricks that speed up the writing process.

Repetition underlies the concept of crossword themes: A word may reappear and tie together the theme entries or, less often, the theme clues. Any time you don't know where to turn in a crossword grid, just tell yourself to check for repeaters. Focus on a small part of the grid and decide to complete that corner rather than looking at the whole grid.

No Place to Hide: Digging for the Theme Clues and Entries

When solving a puzzle, you deliberately seek out theme clues as a step toward cracking the code. If there's a title, you want to see how it relates to the theme clues. You can easily spot a theme entry in a puzzle by looking for the following items:

- **Theme clues occasionally end in a question mark (?).** If you don't see any question marks in the Sunday puzzle clue list, then scan the grid for the longest entries.
- **Theme entries appear in symmetrical parts of the grid.** As a rule, you find theme entries as mirror images within the diagram. So if you come upon a theme entry two rows from the top, you know that its match belongs in the entry two rows from the bottom at the opposite side.
- **Theme entries must be the longest entries in the grid.** Non-theme entries are always shorter than theme entries. Sometimes the only way you know whether a clue refers to the theme is by measuring the length of the entry.

For example, in Puzzle 10-1, you can spot the theme in five Across clues and three Down clues (Across at 21, 36, 55, 76, and 94 and Down at 15, 30, and 55.) Each theme clue ranges between 10 to 15 squares long, and no unrelated entry outnumbers them.

Cracking the Sunday Puzzle Code

Technically, you could approach the Sunday puzzle using the same strategy that you use to work the daily-size puzzle (see Chapter 1 for my nearly foolproof strategy for working the daily-size puzzle). After all, the Sunday puzzle is just a larger version of the daily puzzle — a kind of daily puzzle on steroids, right? Well, I guess you could look at it that way, but if you apply the daily approach to the Sunday puzzle, you don't take advantage of some key information that the constructor has kindly provided you with. Read on, and all will be revealed.

Sluggers hit the squares before hitting the diamond

Many baseball players like to work crosswords before a game to insure mental alertness. First baseman Keith Hernandez is said to be among those players. Although Keith grew up with an acrossionado father, he didn't develop a taste for the crossword until the 1980s. After he acquired the lingo of crosswordese, he felt more at home in the squares. Subsequently, he turned into a Sunday solver — since relocating to New York City; Hernandez remarked that receiving the *Times* pushed him into the habit. A typical team player, he knows that he's not alone if he needs a solving hand.

Forming a strategy

A few generalizations can be made about Sunday crosswords as long as you understand that a wrong interpretation of the clues may lead you astray. (Of course, this sage piece of advice applies to a puzzle of any size.) In general, you can use this plan of attack for starting out with the Sunday puzzle:

1. **Look at the title.**

   Deep down, the constructor and the editor are your friends. They want to give you as much information as you need to lead you to a complete solution. The title of the puzzle is your first step toward figuring out the theme of the puzzle. Read the title and consider each word from every angle. If the title is "Phil in the Blank" don't assume that each of the theme clues is a simple missing-word clue. The "misspelling" of "Fill" indicates that the theme clues probably have something to do with famous guys named Phil.

   Sometimes you see a descriptive blurb under the title of the puzzle. Editors weave extra hints about the title and theme clues into these blurbs. Personally, I rarely "get" any of the hints provided in these blurbs right off the bat. For most solvers, the blurbs usually just provide an extra chuckle at the end of the solving process after I've figured out the theme and can see what the editor was trying to "tell" me in the blurb.

   Some acrossionados advocate reading the theme clues early in the game. Although you may not get the answers to the theme clues instantly, you put your subconscious on the case. According to this school of solving, the sooner you enter the "data" into your mind, the faster you can begin the solving process. While this approach may be okay for the intermediate or expert-level solver (you know who you are), I think it's too fast for novice crossworders. (When you can unravel the theme entries before getting any of the crossing clues, you have arrived.)

2. **Find your comfort level by looking for missing-word clues.**

   If you've already visited Chapter 1, you know that this is the first step I advocate for puzzles of all sizes. You should look for missing-word clues first because they are usually the easiest clues to solve, and you want to find and solve an easy clue in order to gain a toehold into the grid. Of course, everyone likes different types of clues; after reading all about the different types of clues in Chapter 2, you may decide to start by looking for another type of clue.

   Solving experience is the best way to acquire an eye for figuring out what the constructor is trying to tell you in the clues. Crosswords are not a game that you can easily reduce to the simple sum of its parts. You may understand each element separately yet still struggle to fill in the entire grid. In any case, you must be able to judge a clue correctly (or at least competently) before you can hope to decipher the code. If you can't interpret the clues of a crossword, you end up aimlessly sticking isolated letters in remote squares without getting any interlocking entries. Solvers who fall into this category become pencil pushers who soon give up. Read Chapter 2 (which is all about clues) to avoid becoming one of these hopeless pencil pushers.

3. **Focus on a corner of the puzzle (especially the corner in which you've filled the most missing-word clues).**

   The Sunday grid appears daunting at first. If you concentrate on a cozy corner, you may find yourself filling it in without distracting yourself with the rest of the grid. In fact, you may want to take a swipe at each corner before moving into the center of the grid.

4. **Find the repeaters.**

   Filling in the repeaters gives you a nice head start toward the longer entries. (The chapters in Part II clue you in on the most common repeaters.)

5. **Locate and consider each theme-related clue.**

   You should now be in a pretty good position to address the theme clues, meaning that your work on intersecting clues has provided some of the letters already for the theme clues.

   The theme is your friend. Because the theme entries are longer, solving them allows you to make major headway on the grid very quickly.

   Theme clues may end in a question mark (?), making it easy to spot them in the clue list.

6. **Rinse and repeat.**

   Puzzles are a cumulative process. You may need to run through these steps several times before you finish. Just remember to enjoy your escalating pleasure as filling in one clue allows you to figure out the entry for another clue.

Don't hesitate to erase: When something looks impossibly weird, such as JZLM, you can't force the interlock to work. Decide which entries have to go and try other ones. And don't forget to cheat when necessary. Consult a crossword dictionary or word finder (see Chapter 9 for more information on essential reference books for solvers). When you get stuck, taking a peek is okay if you're working with a publication that prints the answers in the back of the book. How else are you going to improve your game?

Getting some practice

Hey, I'm not going to throw you out into the world of Sunday solving without a short walk through to get you ultra-comfortable with the whole thing. I invite you to investigate a few of the clues in Puzzle 10-1.

I don't want to spoil the whole puzzle for you, and so I just discuss a few of the clues here — and in fact, if you don't want any help, you should stop reading this section now. You can find the answers to the puzzle in Appendix A.

Interpreting the title is your first step on the road to success. The title contains the key to unlocking the code of the theme within the grid. In the case of Puzzle 10-1, the title "Pound for Pound" could have something to do with weights, dieting, or poets. The blurb accompanying the title confirms that you're dealing with a weighty theme.

Don't shy away from the theme clues. Just because the entries take up more grid space doesn't necessarily mean that they are more difficult to decipher than any other clue. In fact, after you get the "trick" of a theme, you can make greater headway into filling in the grid with theme entries because they're longer. In fact, theme crosswords may be quicker to solve in the final analysis, because the clues tie in with each other and provide extra hints about the theme entries.

In Puzzle 10-1, you jump right in by examining the first Across theme clue up close. I put the number of letters per entry in parentheses right after the clue just for your information; in reality, the Sunday puzzle isn't as helpful!

21 What some people get when they study the scales (12 letters)

Right off the bat, you know that you're dealing with tongue-in-cheek wording: The title of the puzzle and the accompanying blurb explain that the puzzle is about weight, so you can rule out a musical interpretation for "studying the scales." The clue is too vague to decipher by itself. You have to work on some crossing clues first.

Puzzle 10-1: Pound For Pound

(Dieting can be a lonely chore. Maybe this will help keep you company.)

Across

1 Punish with a fine
7 Swung around
12 Neckwear decor
18 One 's life work
19 New Orleans' Vieux
20 Of no difference
21 What some people get when they study the scales
23 Mortar's partner
24 Road curve
25 River in France
26 Seance noises
28 Showed the way
29 Miss Doone
30 Certain contract
32 River islands
33 Burns's sweet river
36 Food for people who like to cram things
39 Desserts
40 Cake frosting ornament
42 Miss Davis
45 Dance
47 Pronoun
48 Put on —, as a baseball player
50 Echoed
52 Complete
54 New York canal
55 Places in a store where rich foods are sold
59 U.S. publisher
61 Famed jockey
62 Virginia willow
63 Rood and tau
65 Mountain of Crete
67 Airline board listing
72 Kitchen gadget
73 Capacity
75 Verne captain
76 A boaster's potbelly, in a way
79 Ahead
80 Social group
82 Musical work
83 Cuckoopints
86 Indefinite degree
87 Adjective suffix
88 Vacant
89 Fattening beverage
92 Eat like —

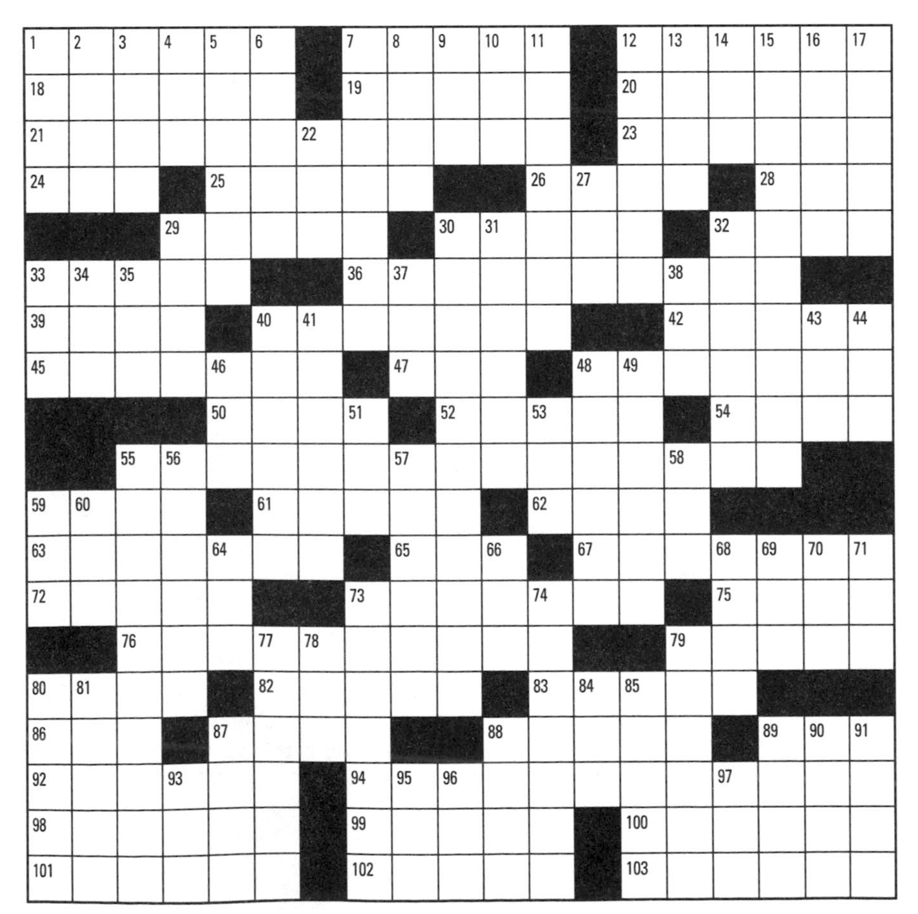

94 Generalized scale readings for the overweight
98 Child's garment
99 Problem for a vet
100 Flair
101 Spots
102 Old chariot
103 Lawyer's concern

Down

1 Head or heart ailment
2 Miss West and others
3 Geological times
4 Gun up the engine
5 Island off India
6 Mistake
7 Egyptian images
8 Put on cargo
9 Swiss canton
10 Seabird
11 Bring into dishonor
12 Machine lever
13 French islands
14 City transport lines
15 Overtight belts of fat men, so to speak
16 Waterway
17 Requires
22 German article
27 Domestic beast
29 Dieter's triumph
30 What two overweight people might say and then go on
31 — excess
32 Run — (be ill)
33 Army address
34 Five-spot
35 Golf-ball perch
37 Defendants, in Roman law
38 Where, to Caesar
40 Tranquillity
41 *Salome* and *Aida*
43 Numerical prefix
44 Compass reading
46 Indian cymbals
48 Attacked
49 Main road
51 Clamor
53 Black bird of New Zealand
55 Sounds that bode ill for the scales
56 Declare
57 Nondieter's favorite kind of thing
58 Attention
59 Month: abbr.
60 Shout: Fr.
64 Sign for a hit show
66 Jolson and others
68 Stopping places
69 Fido's M.D.
70 —, amas, amat
71 Trim
73 "—, the deluge"
74 Like a solitaire game
77 Earth pigments
78 U.S. money unit: abbr.
79 Greek letters
80 Trap
81 Habits of a group
84 British heroes of WWII
85 Merge
87 "— a man in your future"
88 U.S. playwright
89 Length times width
90 Seasonal time
91 Italian family
93 Campus in Troy, N.Y.: abbr.
95 Western group: abbr.
96 Us: Ger.
97 Business letter abbr.

A quick glance at 1 through 4 Down reveals some accessible repeaters (for more information on types of clues, see Chapter 2): An implied missing-word clue and a Hall of Famer, followed by two repeaters:

1 Head or heart ailment (4 letters) = ACHE

2 Miss West and others (4 letters) = MAES

3 Geological times (4 letters) = ERAS

4 Gun the engine (3 letters) = REV

Now you're really rolling. You can fill in the first four letters of the theme entry: HEAV plus eight blank squares. You know that the subject involves weight, which leads you to guess that the fifth letter may be Y, as in HEAVY. HEAVY looks okay in the third square of 5 Down, "Island off India." (Hint: Sri Lanka, at one time.)

Move on to the three final Down clues, which include a dictionary definition, a geographical reference, and a repeater from the crossword birdcage:

8 Put on cargo (4 letters) = LADE

9 Swiss canton (3 letters) = URI

10 Seabird (3 letters) = ERN

You're making progress with the first theme clue: You now have HEAVY (3 blanks) DIN (1 blank).

Although I don't usually advocate inserting ING before you have a leg to stand on, in this case you can go for the final G after DIN. ING is a standard English suffix, and unless you're looking at a plural, G is the most likely last letter in a word that ends with IN (blank).

Plow on by having a look at 22 Down, "German article." The German language plays a minor role in the lexicon of crosswordese (Chapter 7 provides an in-depth look at the foreign languages that commonly surface in the crossword). When a constructor uses German in a clue, he or she is asking you to search your memory banks for random German words; you don't have to go too far back in history to remember John F. Kennedy's famous quote "Ich bin ein Berliner" at the Berlin Wall in 1961. Check to see what you get when you add the E from EIN to the theme clue: You get HEAVY (blank) E (blank) ING.

You have only two Down clues left to check, both dictionary definitions, one of which is a repeater:

6 Mistake (6 letters) = ERROR

7 Egyptian images (7 letters) = SCARABS

Presto, change-o! The completed entry spells HEAVY READING. Your hard work on the intersecting clue pays off by allowing you to unlock the first theme clue. Now that you have the first theme clue under your belt, you also have an inkling about how the other theme clues may work out.

In a marriage of his two careers as a lyricist and a constructor, Richard Maltby *(Harper's Magazine)* wrote a song called "Crossword Puzzles" in which a woman reminisces over the Sunday puzzle. If only she hadn't been a better solver than her ex-boyfriend, she laments, perhaps she'd be listening to "wedding chimes instead of doing the crossword puzzle in *The New York Times*." The lyricist's special humor strikes a chord as the jilted solver mulls over 38 Across: "She carries a torch . . . the Statue of Liberty, of course."

When you find yourself completely at a loss with any sort of puzzle, follow a piece of advice I picked up from the crossword master Margaret Farrar: Try another puzzle. As she wrote in the introduction of the first published puzzle collection, "Inspiration sometimes waits for a return engagement."

Getting Guidance from Your Best Teacher

You can increase your comfort level with the Sunday puzzle with any of the following activities:

- Look at the answers and then unravel the connection between the theme clues and entries.
- Watch a seasoned acrossionado solve the Sunday puzzle. Sometimes seeing someone else work the puzzle can underscore the fact that it is possible to conquer these puzzles.
- Attend a competition and watch the tournament players in action. Brilliance is inspirational.

But the best way to discover how to navigate the grid is to try it yourself. Over time, you figure out what works and what doesn't and what kinds of tricks the constructors try to pull.

Chapter 11

The Bottom of the Sunday Puzzle Page

In This Chapter

- Expanding your puzzle routine
- Attempting the diagramless
- Unraveling the acrostic

Many newspapers feature two puzzles on the Sunday puzzle page; *The New York Times,* the originator of the Sunday puzzle page, always offers both a Sunday-size crossword, and either a diagramless or an acrostic puzzle or some other unique creation (consult Chapter 10 for tips and hints on working the Sunday-size crossword).

Of course, your opportunities to work diagramless or acrostic puzzles are not strictly limited to Sundays — many puzzle books and magazines offer these puzzles, and even some newspapers run an occasional diagramless during the week.

Crosswords at the acrostic and diagramless level require patience, intense concentration, and more tools than the average solver needs. Both of these puzzle types require an extra step in the solving process. For the acrostic solver, the extra step involves filling in a word list. For the diagramless solver, the extra step lies in figuring out the diagram.

Because these puzzles require some extra effort, think of them as a treat rather than regular daily fare — a filet mignon versus a burger.

Caution! Grid under Construction: The Diagramless

In a diagramless puzzle, you get a list of Across and Down clues, but no grid to fill in with the entries. Your job is to sketch out a grid (according to the dimensions shown at the top of the puzzle) by using the answers to the clues.

When working a conventional crossword, you don't need any special equipment. As long as you have a writing utensil, you can play. When you tackle the diagramless puzzle, however, you need some additional equipment, including the following:

- **Graph paper:** You may see an empty grid right next to the list of clues, but when you start out with the diagramless, you should think of this grid as a place to sketch in the entire puzzle after you have solved it. While you are actually solving the puzzle, you should do your work in a separate space.

  The blocks on graph paper lend themselves well to constructing a grid. You can easily count off the number of squares in the dimension supplied by the puzzle. The paper should also be of sufficient quality to withstand repeated erasing. P.S.: Working a diagramless puzzle is not the time to get stingy. Go ahead and treat yourself to the extra organization afforded by graph paper instead of trying to work the diagramless on blank paper or on the back of an envelope.

  Try to keep at least two sheets of graph paper handy while solving a diagramless puzzle. With the extra sheet(s), you have the opportunity to experiment as you try to uncover the grid's pattern.

- **A really good eraser:** Unless you're clairvoyant, you are not attempting the diagramless with a pen, so I assume that you can erase your false moves. This type of puzzle requires a lot of trial and error, so get over any bad feelings you may associate with penciling in the wrong answer. You will be erasing — frequently.

An eraser is a terrible thing to waste. Do yourself a favor and pencil entries into the grid very softly. You can always go over your entries again with a heavier hand after you become more certain about them.

Preparing for the diagramless: A lesson in puzzle anatomy

The key to success lies in correctly numbering the appropriate squares. To understand how a diagramless works, study a crossword diagram closely. Note these basics about how the black and white squares make up a crossword's diagram and where the numbers appear:

- There is always a number in the first square of every entry.
- The first letter of every Across entry has a black square (or left-hand border frame) to its left.
- The last letter of every Across entry is followed by a black square (or right-hand border frame).
- Each Down entry has a black square (or top border frame) above it.
- The first letter of a Down entry has a number in the square.
- The last letter of a Down entry is followed by a black square (or bottom border frame).
- When one square is the first letter of both an Across and Down word, two clues will have the same number with one in each column.

Fill in a black square to the left of and above each number that appears in both Across and Down columns.

Necessity was the mother of a new puzzle

A happy editorial oversight caused the development of the diagramless, or so Margaret Farrar, longtime puzzle editor at *The New York Times,* told me. The seed of this puzzle style sprouted at a luncheon in 1925 over a stack of crosswords. Margaret was convening with her collaborators, Prosper Buranelli and F. Gregory Hartswick, the trio responsible for the very first crossword puzzle collection, to review material for a future edition. When they found that a grid was missing from the manuscript, Hartswick sketched out a blank one on the back of a menu. By following the clues, they realized that they'd come upon a new angle on solving the standard crossword. They aptly dubbed their creation the diagramless.

Your first steps

Discovering the shape: that's what solving a diagramless is all about. Because this is the primary challenge of this puzzle, the constructors make the clues as straightforward as possible.

Because you don't have a black-and-white grid pattern to look at, the first step in attempting the diagramless is to refer to the dimensions indicated at the top of the puzzle. The dimensions look like a math formula, as in "15 x 15." (Puzzle grids always measure an odd number of squares, such as 15 x 15 or 21 x 21.)

Advanced diagramless patterns don't always conform to the typical square patterns of crosswords that have fewer black squares. Instead, more black squares are used to create symmetrical patterns, such as a windmill or snowflake. Sometimes the grid for a diagramless is oblong or rectangular rather than square, as in 15 x 17 or 17 x 21. If the diagram isn't a square, the first number indicates the number of squares across, and the second number represents the number of squares down. Designs emerge with familiar patterns, like Mickey Mouse's face, for example.

After you figure out how many squares you need, go ahead and sketch them out on your graph paper. For a 15 x 15 puzzle, draw a frame that measures 15 squares across and down on your graph paper to help you focus on the emerging pattern.

The grid patterns are mostly, but not always, symmetrical. Symmetry can help you as you uncover the pattern of the diagram. After you solve a block of words in the top part of the grid, for example, you can safely transfer that pattern to its corresponding area in the bottom corner.

Besides the dimensions of the grid, you need to look for another important piece of information. Very often, the puzzle tells you where the first Across square should appear — without this hint, the diagramless would be almost impossible to solve. A sample "hint" could read: "1 Across begins at the top line two squares in." Go ahead and write in the number one in the upper left-hand corner of the square where the first Across entry begins.

Armed with the dimensions of the grid and the location of the first square across, you are ready to dig into the clues.

Diagramless advice from someone who should know

Mrs. Farrar recommended a clever way of practicing diagramlesses by working a regular crossword without the grid. Instead, use a blank sheet of graph paper. By trying this approach, you're guaranteed a 15 x 15 grid with a standard pattern, and you can get the hang of how the numbers fall in the squares.

Feel free to turn any crossword in this book into a diagramless by folding over the page so you don't see the grid, or by covering it with a piece of paper.

Scanning the clues

Even before you proceed with the first Across entry, I recommend jotting down any answers that pop out at you next to their clues.

Scanning all the way through the Across and Down clues and writing down as many entries as you can beside the clues is helpful. Islands of answers may emerge this way. Sometimes you can solve separate parts of the puzzle and unite them later.

Only confirmed acrossionados try to discern the pattern before working the clues. The fun of the diagramless lies in coordinating the two as you solve.

Don't worry about the clues: Diagramless clues are simpler than those of the average crossword because the constructor doesn't want to compound the handicap of working without a diagram. The challenge here is deciding where the answers go.

Determining the length of the first entry

Unlike a crossword, you want to approach the diagramless from 1 Across for best results. Solving a diagramless is more than just answering the clues: Your goal is to get the numbers in the right squares. Without a grid, you don't have that visual reference to how many letters are in each word. Instead, you follow two steps to determine how many letters appear in the 1 Across entry:

- **Look at the number of the second clue Across.** (Not to be confused with 2 Across, which could never exist because that would limit 1 Across to a single letter.) The second Across clue borders the length of the first Across clue. If the number of the second Across clue is 6, for example, then you can surmise that the entry for 1 Across contains five letters.
- **Check that the Down clues with the numbers between the first and second Across clues don't have an Across function.** This is really just an act of confirmation. If the second Across clue is 6 Across, you know that the first word consists of five letters. The five Down clues, from 1 through 5, that don't have an Across function confirm your assumption.

Working off the first Across entry

What distinguishes 1 Across from every other Across clue is that the solver can be certain that each letter of its entry serves as the first letter of a Down entry.

After you solve 1 Across, you can blacken the square after the last letter of the entry. If the first entry is five letters long, for example, insert the numbers 1 through 5 in the appropriate squares and try to solve as many of the first few Down clues as you can.

Before long, you create a block of answers that sets the puzzle on its path.

Determining the location of the second Across entry

In the standard crossword, the second entry Across appears following a black square directly to the right of the first Across entry in the grid. But the diagramless makes an exception. In the diagramless, the second Across entry can appear in the following additional places:

- One line down and to the left of 1 Across
- Directly under 1 Across
- To the right of 1 Across, but separated by more than one black square

Whether the second Across clue appears in the Down column or not determines your next solving move:

- **If it doesn't:** What if the second Across clue number doesn't appear in the Down column? For example, if 6 Across doesn't have a 6 Down clue, you know that the second Across answer appears directly *below* 1 Across. Chances are that the answer to 6 Across may begin to emerge after you fill in some of the first five Down entries.
- **If it does:** If the second Across number also appears in the Down column, and if more than two numbers after 6 Down are all Down clues only (such as 7 and 8), then that entry most likely appears to the right of 1 Across, following the typical crossword format. For example, the entry for 6 Across consists of the first letters of 6, 7, and 8 Down.

  If the second Across number also appears in the Down column and if one or two numbers after 6 Down are Down clues only, then you fill it in below 1 Across, at least one square to the left of where 1 Across begins. Often, the next Down clue begins in the square below and to the right of where 1 Across ends.

The diagramless puzzle offers many challenges and many rewards

I believe that the extra effort of acquiring a supply of graph paper and sketching out the diagram discourages many acrossionados from going on to the diagramless. After all, the last thing you need when you're looking for solving satisfaction is a worn out eraser or a wastepaper basket full of crumpled graph paper.

As one wit remarked famously, "Diagramless puzzles are for people who are unable to leave the house."

Certainly, this specialized puzzle has a much narrower following than the widely popular crossword — which is really a shame, because the diagramless clues are actually simpler. What's more, taking on a new crossword challenge has its rewards when you return to the standard game because working the diagramless gives you a greater understanding of how the squares are put together.

Looking in the mirror

After you see a black-and-white pattern start to emerge at the top part of your graph, you can safely turn your grid upside down and sketch in the mirror image of the developing pattern in the bottom of the grid.

Of course, if you find the entries easier to solve at the bottom of the grid, you may want to try a bold move and approach the diagramless from the bottom.

Working some sample puzzles

In puzzle 11-1, I give you a chance to put your diagramless skills to the test. Don't worry — I'll stick with you long enough to get you well on your way to solving the grid. Of course, if you'd rather try the puzzle on your own, please feel free to totally ignore this section of the book. I won't feel hurt, I promise.

Stick with me as I start you out on Puzzle 11-1:

1. **Check out the dimensions of the puzzle.**

   This one measures 13 x 13.

2. **Consult the editorial "hint" that tells you in which square 1 Across begins, and insert the number 1 in that square. (It's always on the top row.)**

   Here it begins three squares in.

3. **Read the clue for 1 Across.**

   In this case, the clue is "How — can you go?"

   Unlike a traditional crossword, you must approach the diagramless from 1 Across for best results.

4. **Determine the length of the first Across entry.**

   The length of the first entry is measured by the number of the second clue. The number associated with the second entry, therefore, tells you how long the first entry is. For example, the second Across clue in Puzzle 11-1 is 4 Across; you know that the first entry consists of three letters.

   The word missing from the common phrase in 1 Across is LOW, which you can fill in immediately.

5. **Start solving the Down clues that start at 1 Across.**

Please also feel free to enjoy Puzzle 11-2, a diagramless by Frank Longo.

Only for the strong at heart

In the *Puzzlemaker's Handbook*, authors and puzzle experts Mel Rosen and Stan Kurzban offer a truly crackpot approach to the diagramless. This one is for seasoned solvers only (and you know who you are).

Rather than starting off at the top or bottom, you start from the center, at what the authors term the *waist* of the puzzle. Your objective is to identify which Across clue falls in the middle of the puzzle.

Where you have an odd number of Across clues, the center clue is easy to find — if you have 75 Across clues, for example, 38 is in the center row. Where you have an even number of Across clues, say 76, the center contains two entries — 38 and the one following it.

Puzzle 11-1: 13 x 13 Squares

The first Across entry starts two squares in.

Across

1 "How — can you go?"
4 Architect I.M.
7 Evil god of Norse myth
8 "Mikado" trio
10 See-through kitchen wrap
11 Fisherman
13 Japanese royal flower
16 Dander
17 Rendezvous
18 " — Little Teapot"
19 Robin Cook book
20 Period
21 Unemotional
23 Wicker-work
25 Lean and sinewy
26 Book before Obadiah
27 Past
28 Silents actress Normand
30 Soon-Yi's mom
33 West Virginia flowers
36 Ghost
37 Greek letters
38 Instep covers, once
39 Smooth out
40 Method: abbr.
41 Soak, as flax

Down

1 *M* star
2 Approve
3 Neville's successor
4 Huffs
5 Skating figure
6 Between jobs
7 Cowardly Lion portrayer
8 Singer Tucker
9 Mideastern native
10 Bill Nye's subj.
12 Gossip item
14 Host
15 Treasure hunter's aid
19 Coquettish
20 Kinswoman, for short
21 Venice's Bridge of —
22 Companies
23 Portent
24 Certain ant or termite
25 Kids' card game
26 Helps hoods
28 Type of eel
29 Mine entrances
30 Musical format
31 — instant (shortly)
32 Foolish sort
34 Plunges
35 Wander

Puzzle 11-2: 17 x 17 Squares

The first across entry starts three squares in, and 4 Across follows after eight squares.

Across

1 School grp.
4 Employment
7 Is a dud
9 "Venerable" saint
10 With 1 Down, piece of the profits
12 Shaw of swing
13 A trapshooter takes it
14 Prior to, in poesy
15 Type size just smaller than nonpareil
16 Fraternity candidates
18 — *Syndrome* (1987 action flick)
19 Impolite sound at a lecture
20 Give — (call)
21 Tiny 10 Across
24 Member of a Swift race
25 Half a popular TV duo
26 Manicure site
27 Getting one's piece of the profits
32 Prepared a turkey, in a way
33 Prepare cheese
35 Rorschach tests, essentially
36 *Language and Silence* author George
38 Proportional share
39 Rainbow, e.g.
40 Exclamation of disapprobation
41 Arroyo
42 Piece of the profits
44 After 21 Across a dairy offering
45 Sucker
46 D.J.'s collection
47 Official O.K.

Down

1 See 10 Across
2 — Maria
3 Brisk in tempo
4 Golf alternative
5 Garfield's housemate
6 Apiarist's specimen
7 Keeps from succeeding
8 *The River Wild* star
9 Civil War general Braxton
10 Salt-N-Pepa's style
11 "Without a doubt!"
12 One who's known for 27 Across
15 Kind of acid
17 — Jones
18 They may get licked after dinner
20 In pain
22 Where one's shadow may be seen?
23 Harass
25 Does an autumn chore
26 Father Christmas
27 It may be extracted
28 Star-shaped
29 Investigate
30 Watch-stopping Geller
31 Decuple
32 Ice unit
34 More than exalt
35 Jordan's team
36 Patriotic men's org.
37 Make calls
38 Tobacco plug
41 Auto industry inits.
43 "Telephone Line" band, familiarly

Do you just like crosswords — or are you obsessed?

Years ago, I clipped an article from *The Washington Post* by author Bill Maxwell in which he made the distinction between the Inveterate Crossword Puzzler (ICP) and the Occasional Crossword Puzzler (OCP). By comparing characteristics of the two, I think you can determine whether you're ready to expand your solving routine.

An ICP:

- Prefers ink
- Answers the clue "Terra — (5 letters)" = FIRMA
- Recognizes the "Home of the brave" (6 letters) = WIGWAM

An OCP:

- Uses pencil
- Answers the clue "Terra — (5 letters)" = COTTA
- Believes the "Home of the Brave" (7 letters) = ATLANTA

One Giant Step: The Acrostic (The Double Crostic)

"The Double Crostic is to crosswords what chess is to checkers."

— Norman Cousins, author and longtime editor of the *Saturday Review*

When there's a "message" involved in a puzzle, as with a crossword theme, you get an extra kick from solving. That's the solver's thrill. When you solve an acrostic puzzle, you can be 100 percent sure the puzzle contains a message because the grid contains an entertaining quotation from a book.

The king of acrostics

For all intents and purposes, Thomas H. Middleton represents the top brand name in acrostics in the latter half of the 20th century. Middleton has become synonymous with the acrostic since the late 1960s when he assumed the responsibility for the *Saturday Review* Double Crostic.

Acrossionado Laura Z. Hobson hand-picked Middleton, a former actor, in 1967 when she was on a campaign to shore up the *Saturday Review's* puzzle standards. Marriage to Norman Cousins' sister made Middleton all the more amenable to this position. Subsequently, he has become an institution in the puzzle field. His byline has become familiar through his long-term association with *The New York Times* acrostic as well as the acrostic series for Simon and Schuster.

Mr. Crossword, meet Miss Acrostic

The acrostic is designed very differently from a crossword, despite the common elements of the grid and clues. The main differences between the two types of puzzles include the following:

- **Entries:** Rather than a random selection of words, the grid contains an excerpt from a written work. The words in the quote are separated by black squares. The end of the word is indicated by the black square and not the frame of the grid.

  Although familiar words mainly comprise the acrostic answers, the occasional oddball obscure word does intrude. Elizabeth Kingsley, the creator of the acrostic, wrote to a correspondent: "Do you realize that "h's" are the bane of my existence, being as common as they are, and that 'h's' predominate in Greek, Hebrew, Hindu, and other Oriental words? If you were constructing a puzzle and had letters left over and they made a Vedic deity, what would you do?"

- **Grid:** The grid is rectangular, as opposed to the block grid associated with the garden variety crossword puzzle.
- **Orientation:** The words only read across, not down.
- **Clues:** Instead of clues, you have a "word list" organized by the letters of the alphabet from A to V or W, sometimes as far as Z. The letters in each answer word are assigned a number that indicates where they appear in the grid.

  Clues fall into two categories:

  - **Straightforward definitions:** For example, the clue "Worthy; meritorious" followed by nine dashes is answered by the straightforward answer DESERVING.
  - **Missing words:** For example, the clue "The actual enemy is the —" followed by seven dashes is answered by UNKNOWN.

- **Grid numbers:** Every single square contains a number in sequence followed by a letter — for example, "1 C." The letter refers to the word list, described in the preceding bullet. For example, "1 C" means that the letter for the first square appears in Word C. Look for the number in the dashes next to clue C.
- **Word list:** Additionally, when you read the initial letters of the answer words in your word list from top to bottom (or A through W), they spell out the author and title of the work that is quoted in the grid.

Puzzle 11-3 shows off the finer aspects of the acrostic puzzle.

What's in a name?

What's the difference between an acrostic and a Double Crostic? Nothing except copyright. The acrostic goes by a number of names, including the *Double Crostic, anacrostic, wordagram,* and *quoteword.* The name just depends upon which publication you're solving in. At this time, *The Nation* magazine owns the D-C (as it's known). Meanwhile, *Games* publishes them as Double Cross, and *Dell* magazines publish anacrostics, while most other publications refer to this puzzle as an acrostic.

Puzzle 11-3

A Having many columns

44 5 81 131 77 43 121 57 68

B Previous; bygone

65 19 32 7 79 103 74 25 136

C Dolly Varden, the salmon's relative

3 72 126 90 144

D Written agreement deposited with a third person

143 112 67 146 158 100

E City in SW Virginia

134 40 110 63 89 142 50

F Cover; Pervade; flood

38 133 59 35 161 157 168

G Pranksters; show-offs

162 6 119 106 10 17

H Aromatic herb of the mint family

145 88 135 70 116 169

I Undulating; tremulous; unsteady

140 9 75 108

J Omission of one or more words from a construction

62 24 166 36 130 52 86 29

K Strip, free from; sell off

91 101 73 14 61 125

L Seaport in NW Israel

96 155 46 87 170

M Resembling humans

23 164 171 150 51 105 11 160 173 154

N Ideas; whims

172 132 33 97 26 42 16

O Waterproof footwear

124 163 137 94 27 8

P Hateful; causing animosity

80 93 22 58 118 54 31 71 47

Q Food; the study of food material

117 18 176 107 2 37 41 84 123

R Retreats; withdraws (2 wds)

149 12 20 129 165 53 141 104

S Right away (3 wds)

21 13 139 1 122 98 127

T Book of the Old Testament

66 148 30 113 167 111 15

U "Why persecute we him, seeing — the matter is found in me?" (3 wds Job 19:28)

95 56 114 45 92 34 151 78 138

V Sweethearts; darlings; pips; beauts

4 147 49 153 83 69

W "Sees Helen's beauty in a brow of —" ("A Midsummer-Night's Dream" V, 1)

60 174 156 39 64

X About

120 48 85 99 175 82 159

Y Canines

76 115 109 102 28 128 55 152

■	1S	2Q	3C	4V	5A	6G	7B	■	8O	9I	10G	11M	12R	13S	14K	15T	16N	■	17G	18Q	19B	20R	21S	22P	23M	24J
■	25B	26N	27O	28Y	29J	■	30T	31P	32B	33N	■	34U	35F	■	36J	37Q	38F	■	39W	40E	41Q	42N	43A	■	44A	45U
46L	47P	48X	49V	50E	51M	52J	■	53R	54P	55Y	56U	■	57A	58P	59F	60W	■	61K	62J	63E	64W	65B	66T	67D	68A	69V
■	70H	71P	72C	73K	74B	75I	76Y	■	77A	78U	■	79B	80P	81A	82X	■	83V	84Q	85X	■	86J	87L	■	88H	89E	90C
■	91K	92U	■	93P	94O	95U	96L	97N	98S	99X	■	100D	101K	102Y	103B	■	104R	105M	106G	107Q	■	108I	109Y	110E	111T	112D
■	113T	114U	115Y	116H	117Q	118P	■	119G	120X	121A	122S	123Q	124O	■	125K	126C	■	127S	128X	129R	130J	■	131A	132N	133F	134E
135H	136B	137O	138U	■	139S	140I	141R	142E	143D	■	144C	145H	146D	147V	148T	149R	150M	■	151U	152Y	153V	■	154M	155L	156W	■
157F	158D	■	159X	160M	161F	■	162G	163O	164M	■	165R	166J	167T	168F	169H	■	170L	171M	■	172N	173M	174W	175X	176Q	■	■

Eyeballing the grid

The empty grid can give you some helpful hints about the way the sentence unfolds:

- **Single-letter words:** When you see a white square between two black squares, the two obvious choices in the English language are A and I. (On the rare occasion, you may come across an initial, as in "J.D." Salinger where J and D are separated by a black square.) If multiple single-letter words appear in the grid, odds are that the excerpt is in the first person, and you can start by trying I in each place.
- **Three-letter words:** Most often, you're looking at THE or AND.

Hunkering down to a puzzle

Technically, the double aspect of the acrostic describes the way the two basic elements of the puzzle interact. You work with the same two variables of the crossword — the grid and clues — but in a new way. You use the following multi-step solving process for an acrostic:

1. **First, scan the definitions in the word list.**

   Often the clues are wordier than in the average crossword. In fact, the constructor doesn't disguise the entries at all and offers you tags where the answer contains more than one word.

   For example, you may see "Release (2 wds)" with five dashes after it for the answer LET GO. In fact, the acrostic constructor may cite a source for a word that is part of a title or quotation for easy reference, such as "For as he thinketh — so is he" (3 wds, Proverbs 23:7). Instead of numbers, you find the word list (about two dozen words) sorted by letters from A through W, most often. Each letter is represented by a dash with a number under it. That number is its assigned place in the grid.

2. **Fill in the dashes for the answers you know.**

   Read the word list from top to bottom and answer as many words as you can. Of the 22 or 24 words, chances are you can answer about one-quarter. If you don't know the answer easily, you may consult the standard dictionary without any pangs of conscience. A clue like "More beautiful" followed by eight dashes may elude you until the word "lovely" in the dictionary jogs your memory that the correct word is LOVELIER.

3. **Transfer the letters you have so far from the word list into their assigned squares in the grid.**

   Every single letter serves in a word in the grid as well as in an answer on the word list. As you fill in the word list, you note a number under each letter that indicates its placement in the grid. Put the letters in their assigned grid squares. At first, it may look a bit sketchy with stray letters sprinkled around the grid. That's how the fun starts.

   Words in the quotation may run from one row into the next. The beginning of a word may appear on one line at the upper-right corner, while the final letters appear in the next line below to the far left. That split includes words of one syllable, as in TH on the top line and ERE on the next line, below and to the left, to read as THERE. Only a black square indicates the end of the word, not the outside frame of the grid, as in the standard crossword.

4. **Try to complete words in the grid.**

   As you transfer the letters from the word list into the grid, you begin to create the words in the quotation.

At some point, you may notice a three-letter word that looks like TH(blank) in the grid. Now work from the grid back to the word list by guessing that the third letter is E. Track the E to its word on the word list by using the letter in that square. Doing so gives you a fast way to locate the number and helps you figure out the definition of that word. Look for as many words as you can complete in the grid before returning back to the word list. Some of your guesses may be wrong, but that's the way you play the game.

5. **Keep your eye on the initial letters of the word list.**

   The initial letters of each answer in the word list spell out the name of the author and title of the work quoted in the grid. As you define the words, you have another approach in closing in on the answers.

   If you see that the first three letters down read CHA with a blank followed by LE, you may guess that the first name of the author is CHARLES. Fill in the R and S in the proper places, which may help you complete those two words.

6. **Review the grid as you fill in words.**

   As the grid begins to fill in, you begin to see connections between articles and nouns and verbs and objects, and you may see a theme or topic emerge. After you fill in every square, a quotation of about 25 words emerges as you read the grid from left to right.

When you undertake the acrostic, throw away everything you know about crossword clues. Crosswordese and repeaters have no place in this special subset of the crossword. The word list consists of synonyms and fill-in-the-blanks, while the grid contains a sentence, which includes just about any G-rated word.

Elizabeth Kingsley: Creator of a newer, harder puzzle

The Double Crostic made its debut in the pages of the *Saturday Review of Literature* (later known as the *Saturday Review*) in March 1934. This innovative puzzle format was the brainchild of a former English teacher from Brooklyn.

During a college reunion at Wellesley, Elizabeth Kingsley had an epiphany about how to improve the crossword puzzle. Dismayed by the popularity on campus of modern writers such as James Joyce and Gertrude Stein, Kingsley put her mind on keeping the classics alive. By working literary excerpts into the grids, she recognized a way to realize her goal.

For clues, she turned to her anagram letters (which are much like Scrabble tiles). By spelling out the quotation with the anagram letters, she could then scramble the letters together and rearrange them. To create the clues, she selected the letters in the author's name and the title of the work and set them in first place down the line of the word list.

In her original instructions, Kingsley underscored that "Up and down the letters mean nothing! The black squares indicate ends of words; therefore, words do not necessarily end at the right side of the diagram."

Shortly after the Double Crostic made a splash at the *Saturday Review,* the publishers Simon and Schuster launched the book series, which Thomas Middleton continues to create to this day. After retiring from the magazine at the end of 1952, the *Saturday Review* hailed Mrs. Kingsley as "Her D-C Majesty" (also known as "Our Queen Elizabeth") and credited her with having "resuscitated more poets and essayists lost through the centuries than all the English I classes in the U.S.A. combined." She passed the baton over to Doris Nash Wortman. Since the 1960s, the byline associated with the acrostic is Thomas H. Middleton.

Chapter 12

The Insider's Guide to Puzzle Wordplay

In This Chapter

- Attempting puns and anagrams
- Interpreting tricky clues
- Getting puzzle humor

"No puzzle constructor does his job unless he includes the element of wit in his work."

— Norman Cousins, author and editor

If you solve enough crosswords, eventually you run into some clues that seem to operate under a different set of rules. Rather than relying on the dictionary, these clues are based on *wordplay,* which introduces word games into the clue structure. When clues start to look like mini sentences instead of straightforward dictionary-type definitions, you've entered wordplay territory.

You're more apt to encounter this sort of clue slipped into a Sunday puzzle rather than a daily puzzle, although some daily puzzles do include wordplay. Wordplay clues also pop up more frequently in the clue list of a so-called *New Wave* crossword puzzle in your weekend newspaper. (What to make of a clue like "It may be over your head" with a four letter entry? The answer, HAIR, elicits a chuckle.)

Eventually, you may encounter a crossword where all the clues contain wordplay. The grids look familiar, but the clues don't match anything you can look up in your puzzle dictionary or word finder. Where to find the ten-letter entry that answers the clue "Et, et, et, et, et, et, et, et, et, et"? (Hint: Count the number of "ets" to get to TENETS.) Chances are, upon closer inspection, you find yourself staring at a Puns and Anagrams style puzzle. The name of the puzzle tells you a little about what you're getting into.

Unfortunately, I haven't found an expeditious way to compile a crossword word finder for wordplay clues because such clues never repeat. Each tricky clue is the unique creation (and property) of a constructor's amazing turn of mind. Knowing that these tricky clues exist and how they work may not help you against drawing a blank occasionally, but you can at least approach them with an air of authority. And for some acrossionados, knowing what to expect is almost as good as getting every clue right off the bat.

In this chapter, I discuss these special, seemingly senseless, wordplay style clues that may confuse you at first. I also get you acquainted with the Puns and Anagrams style puzzle.

Punny Clues are the Puzzler's Whodunit

A pun plays with a word in a humorous way that may not be immediately obvious. Take the clue "It may be over your head" as an example. At first reading, "it" seems to refer to a subject that may be "over your head," which usually means "beyond your comprehension," which is the way people usually use that phrase. In the clue, however, the phrase is intended literally, pointing to something on top of your head. Although the entry is a simple everyday word, HAIR, you solve the clue in a circuitous way. It's a two-step solving process: First, you interpret the clue, and then you guess the entry.

Think of these clues as double entendres, which are quips that you can interpret in one of two ways: literally, or as the implied double meaning. The second aspect is typically rooted in the humor of insult or *malapropism* (the amusing replacement of one word with another that sounds like it — for example, *celibacy* for *kielbasi*) .

My dad was a pro at creating double entendres. One of my all-time favorites is the way he referred to the scion of a milk fortune as the *Dairy Heir,* pronounced to sound like *derriere,* French for *hindquarters.* While the title was grammatically accurate in English, he gave the term new meaning with where he placed the accent. His joke is just the type of flight of fancy that you find in puns and anagrams clues.

Puns and Anagrams Puzzles

When you see these puzzles in *The New York Times* Sunday magazine they are known as Puns and Anagrams, and elsewhere, as in Dell puzzle magazines, under the title of Punanagram Puzzles.

Puns and Anagrams puzzles test a different aspect of your solving skills altogether. They appear normal in presentation — typically two columns of clues, Across and Down, usually accompanied by a grid of 15 x 15 squares. That's where you leave chartered crossword puzzle territory.

The clues

While the grid is completely familiar in presentation, the Puns and Anagrams clue structure is completely different. Gone are the missing words, dictionary definitions, and crossword celebrities that frequent the squares in the everyday American crossword.

Wordplay bridges the gap

Wordplay clues are derived from the British cryptic crossword, which you can read more about in Chapter 13. In essence, wordplay clues replace dictionary definitions with clever word game disguises. Instead of a straightforward clue you'll find that clues read like brain teasers. Wordplay clues add another step to the crossword solving process since you have to solve the clue in order to get to the answer. With a little practice, you'll understand how to decipher these fun exercises.

Who thought of this stuff, any way?

The Puns and Anagrams style crossword is said to be the brainchild of Albert Morehead, a bridge columnist at *The New York Times* in the 1940s. Morehead became mesmerized by the British-style cryptic crossword while attending a bridge tournament on the "Other side of the pond, for short" (ENG). Why not inject more wordplay into the standard American crossword, he asked himself.

He immediately set to work on devising a hybrid. By co-opting the American diagram and adapting the clue structure with a heavy dose of puns, he came up with a winning combination. In cahoots with collaborator Jack Luzzatto, Morehead submitted *Puns and Anagrams* for publication to *Redbook* magazine in 1942. Soon after, this style of puzzle took a regular slot below the standard crossword on the Sunday puzzle page every fourth week in *The New York Times. Judge,* a popular magazine of the day, lauded these nonconformist clues as "ambidextrous and witty."

The constructor gives you clues in either of two formats:

- **Puns:** Your basic play on words. You solve a kind of riddle to get the answer.
- **Anagrams:** These require you to scramble letters within the clue to form the entry.

Sometimes the clues include a parenthetical reference to the number of letters involved in the entry, at the end of the clue such as "(6)." If they don't indicate the number of letters, then it behooves you to count the number of squares in the entry yourself.

Wordplay dominates the clues, which turns solving into a two step process. First, you've got to determine which format the clue implies. Once deciphered, you fill the entries into the grid in the ordinary way.

Margaret Farrar, the grande dame of crosswords, offered the most sage advice to those attempting the P&A: Do exactly as you're told. She meant that the solver must read the clue and follow it literally. Read on to see what Margaret means.

The grid

The grids of Puns and Anagrams puzzles sometimes look different in two subtle ways:

- **The grid may contain fewer black squares.** Editors require a lower word count in a 15 x 15, with a maximum of 72, as opposed to 78 or 80. (Longer words mean more white squares.)
- **The grid doesn't contain a theme.** Without a theme, the constructor is free to use entries that don't relate at all. You don't find the familiar pattern of parallel entries that herald a theme. Instead, each entry stands alone.

Answering anagrams

The majority of clues in a Puns and Anagram puzzle fall into the anagram mode.

Keep your solving antennae up for a word or words in the clue that may belong to the anagram. Any of the following words indicate that the clue is an anagram clue:

- Break
- Rip
- Tear

By "breaking" the letters of a word or phrase, you find that it serves as the anagram for the correct entry.

But just as often, you won't find an indicator word to give you a hint in the clue. For example, take the clue "He trips." Checking the grid, the entry requires 7 letters. Hey, that matches the number of letters in the clue! A little unscrambling gets you to the entry HIPSTER.

To decode an anagram clue, take the following steps:

1. **Check how many letters appear in the entry.**
2. **Identify which adjacent words or single word within the clue match that number of letters.**

   Sometimes the whole clue belongs to the anagram.

   If you don't find a match of letters, then you may be looking at a pun, which you can read more about later in this chapter. Any words qualify, as long as the number of letters corresponds to the answer.
3. **Rearrange the letters to come up with the correct answer to the rest of the clue.**

   This step is much like solving a jumble (see Chapter 4 for more information on the jumble).

For example, a clue such as "Fashions seen in the sly set (6)," directs you to SLY SET, which has a total of six letters. You can "see fashions" by unscrambling those two words, SLY and SET, to give STYLES.

Every clue has a synonym lurking in it. In some sneaky way, the constructor usually provides you with a straightforward definition. It's somewhere within the sentence of the clue, and you have to sniff it out. Here's an example:

A tense body in Washington (6)

At first glance, the sentence seems to refer to a stressed-out person, but don't read the clue for sense. First, check how long the entry is by reading the parenthetical number. Second, look for six letters in the clue that can be recombined: A + TENSE. (BODY + IN is another candidate, but the letters are less crossword compatible.) Next, rearrange the letters to come up with the straightforward definition for: "Body in Washington." Think Washington, DC. Next, unscramble A+TENSE for SENATE.

Beware tags, those appendages following a colon in a typical clue. They do not play the same role as in the conventional crossword. For example, in the clue "Those with a worker's role: Sp.," first check the number of letters in the entry: six letters. Don't read the clue as you would outside of a wordplay arena. In this case, SP is part of the anagram in combination with ROLE. Together, they yield PROLES, which "defines workers."

When identifying the words that contain the anagram, you always use complete words unless instructed otherwise. You must look for indicators to decide whether a partial word is implied. If just part of the word is involved, you see signal verbs such as "leave," "export," or "lose." Look at the next example:

Dan leaves jading dance (3)

The clue tells you that the letters in DAN are "leaving" (being omitted). First, check the number of letters in the entry. Then, decide where to eliminate the letters for DAN. You have two options: JADING and DANCE. If you cross out A, D, and N in JADING, you're left with JIG. The final word of the clue serves as the synonym of this three-letter word.

Any word within the clue may potentially belong to the anagram, including proper names. Take a look at this example:

Fancy duds in NY Fire (6)

First, identify six available letters. NY + FIRE qualify. Second, read the balance of the clue for a synonym: fancy duds. Next, unscramble NYFIRE for FINERY.

Numbers in clues also play a different role than in the standard crossword. They may indicate letters in a clue word that the entry requires. For example, take the entry WNW, which American puzzles clue as "Vane direction." Mel Rosen and Stan Kurzban cite the Puns and Anagrams clue "Direction 242 swine headed" for this entry. The numbers refer to the second and fourth letters of SWINE, which give you the literal reply to "Direction headed."

Crossword puns

In a crossword pun, the clue conveys the wordplay on the meaning or sound of the entry. The contrast between the meanings of the similar-sounding words gives the pun its kick.

When you see a question mark at the end of a clue, you can expect to find that the entry contains a form of wordplay or in-joke. The question means that something about the entry is tongue-in-cheek. After you see the question mark and feel sure that you're looking at a pun clue, you need to follow these steps to arrive at the entry:

1. **Check how many letters are in the entry.**
2. **Resist the temptation to interpret the sentence as a straightforward thought.**
3. **Read each word of the clue separately, thinking of alternate meaning for each word.**
4. **Look for hidden elements in the words of the clue.**

Here's an example of how a crossword pun works:

Rather run-down? (5)

First, check the number of letters in the entry: five. Next, don't take the clue as a reference to health. Third, look at each word separately: Rather, run, and down. The answer, RECAP, is a reference to an on-air run-down by the newscaster Dan Rather.

You come across clues for parts of words in devious ways. For example, consider the clue "Kind of urgent." Your first reaction may be to interpret this clue to mean ASAP. But the entry measures only three letters. In fact, the answer, INS, combines with urgent as a prefix to create insurgent.

Some diabolical constructors may fashion a clue to look like a pun when actually it's a straightforward definition. To paraphrase Freud's observation about cigars, sometimes a question mark is just a question mark.

The New Wave Makes a Splash in Puzzles

On the threshold of the 1980s, a rambunctious new crop of acrossionados came on the puzzle scene. This intrepid group made its mark in 1977 with the launch of *Games* magazine, edited by Will Shortz , which set the stage for pumping new blood into the puzzle universe.

Games became a showcase for the new talent of young constructors such as Henry Hook, Merl Reagle, and Mike Shenk. After decades of serious, high-minded crosswords that stressed the educational value of the game, the new generation of constructors introduced an irreverence bordering on rebellion. This crossword movement came to be known as the *New Wave* to distinguish it from the *Old Guard* (my term).

New Wave constructors dedicate themselves to exterminating crosswordese. These constructors are avid proponents of wordplay clues, including puns and anagrams. They want to give solvers something to talk about, and they think that puzzles should reveal how amazing language is.

Secondly, New Wave constructors keep an eye on design. Master constructor Merl Reagle calls crosswords "word tapestries" and likes to create designs with a sense of movement. "You wouldn't weave a regular tapestry that didn't look good," as he says (not too grammatically).

You know the guy . . .

He's the one who's always standing around the watercooler, waiting for an innocent victim to come along so that he can spring his new really bad pun. That guy and his friends nearly drove the pun to extinction.

About 15 years ago, a movement evolved to preserve the pun. The Toronto-based International Save the Pun Foundation has been promoted through a newsletter, The Pundit, under the guidance of champion and chairman John S. Crosbie.

Here's a few of the type of winning puns that helped bring the pun back into favor:

- In a small European village, one family had a longtime monopoly on making church bells. Finally, the mayor was the only member left of that family. He decreed that only wedding bells from his factory could be played, earning himself the nickname of the wedding *bell tsar*.
- A big-game hunter in Africa agreed to teach a young man his trade. After a long trek, the young man hesitated atop the last, small hill. "Come on!" the hunter urged. "This is no place for a *knoll coward!"*

Self-described "crossword crusader" Stan Newman has championed the New Wave movement toward modernization of entries. Where "survival of the fittest pastime" is concerned, crosswords have a tough row to hoe in the face of MTV and video games, he maintains. His influence is being felt through the dozens of collections that his division publishes annually.

When you're in the mood for laughing out loud while solving, pick up any of these books, which are heavily influenced by New Wave constructors and their attitude towards wordplay:

- *The Boston Globe Sunday Puzzles* by Henry Hook, Emily Cox, & Henry Rathvon (Times Books, $9)
- *Maura Jacobson's New York Magazine Crossword Puzzles* (Story Press, $9.99)
- *Merl Reagle's Sunday Crosswords* (The PuzzleWorks, $7.95)
- *Masterpiece Crosswords* (Times Books, $16)

When solving a crossword by a member of the New Wave constructors, you can't take any clue at face value because nothing is what it seems to be. A clue such as "Cook book" with a four-letter entry turns out to be COMA, a novel by best-selling author Robin Cook. Without a question mark, you may have a judgment call on whether the clue is a double entendre. When you see a clue such as "Low I-Q group?" (five letters), you have been forewarned that the entry is funny, so you won't be astonished when DENSA emerges. (Both these clues are by a master of the double entendre, Henry Hook.)

The question mark at the end of a clue tips you off to a potential giggle. Here are some examples for your solving pleasure from a typical *Boston Globe* Sunday puzzle by Emily Cox and Henry Rathvon:

- "Hip entertainment?" = HULA HOOPS
- "One of the bunch?" = BANANA
- "Sin city?" = SODOM
- "Noted accomplishment?" = MUSIC
- "Be bullish?" = GORE

New Wave crosswords often carry a title that gives you a big hint as to the trick within the grid for the theme entries. Don't let the first meaning throw you off course; keep your puzzle antennae up for the second meaning. It may be something as straightforward as "Hogging the Stage" by Merl Reagle, featuring celebrities who are hams or have *ham* in their names — MuHAMmad Ali, George HAMilton, Marvin HAMlisch, Billy GraHAM. Or it may tip you off to something a little trickier. Take, for example, an ingenious puzzle by Maura Jacobson from the 1986 *Games*/Merriam Webster First USA Open Championship, NYU campus, entitled "Drop Me A Letter." Rather than its literal meaning, as in "mail me a postcard," the title tells you to omit a letter from each theme entry. On closer inspection of two clues, you can get the joke:

- "Cold actor" = RAYMOND BRR
- "Actress who needs penicillin" = MERYL STREP

Chapter 13

Deciphering the Cryptic Crossword

In This Chapter

- Understanding the basics of the cryptic
- Navigating the design of the cryptic
- Recognizing the nine styles of clues
- Reviewing the cryptic lingo

I was a confirmed acrossionado for decades before I dared to undertake the *cryptic,* which is a British-style crossword puzzle. Please don't fall into the same trap I did — don't wait for years to try these exciting puzzles.

A crossword in America is one beast, and in England, it's a completely different animal. The American version is based on a grid that contains a symmetrical diagram. In American crosswords, the clues are essentially definitions, presented in various formats (see Chapter 2 for more information about the clues in American crosswords). In the British-style crossword puzzle, you find symmetry is less important in the grid, and clues have nothing to do with the American style of presentation.

Before you get started with the cryptic puzzle, though, I want to tell you the good and the bad news about these puzzles. The bad news about cryptics is that being able to read English isn't enough to solve these mind twisters. Despite the fact that the puzzles are written in English, cryptic clues make absolutely no sense to the uninitiated solver. Nothing is what it seems to be at first. Education and knowledge are of little help here. Your skill at wordplay is what counts.

The good news is that unlike the clues in the traditional American crossword puzzle, which don't come with instructions, the cryptic has clear-cut rules about clue structure. In this chapter, I initiate you into the world of cryptic clues and cryptic solving.

Working with puns and anagrams is an excellent way to prepare for the cryptic puzzle. Turn to Chapter 12 for more information on the puns and anagrams.

Passing Your Cryptic O Levels

The crossword style that originally developed in Britain has become widely known as the *cryptic*. No matter what the country of origin, crosswords consist of two basic elements: clues and grids. But depending on which side of the ocean you find them, these two components relate to each other in completely different ways.

Cryptic puzzles remind me of the way I feel when I'm handling British money: I understand how the money works, but I can't handle it in the same automatic way that I do American money. Think of solving a cryptic puzzle like the exchange rate between the dollar and the pound: Until you achieve the same level of comfort that you have with the American crossword, you have to keep the "exchange rate" in mind when solving a British crossword.

What are the advantages to solving cryptic crosswords? I can name at least six:

- Cryptics contain more varied entries.
- Cryptics eliminate crosswordese.
- Each clue presents a test of your wits.
- You (the solver) get to approach language in a new way.
- Peeking at the answers is acceptable while you get your bearings.
- You can solve these crosswords in ink with greater confidence.

Sir John Gielgud, master of the British stage, can complete a British-style puzzle in the time it takes a cab to get from his residence to the theater — or so the rumor goes. (Upon closer inspection, however, you may discover that Sir John simply fills in the squares with nonsense letters.)

Taking a look at the British crossword grid

The British version of the crossword grid has more variety than the American grid style. Right off the bat, you may notice the following distinctive differences between the American and British grid:

- Nearly half the letters in the grid are unchecked, which means they read in one direction only and do not cross with another word from which you can get some help.
- Cryptic grid patterns aren't always symmetrical.
- Most 15 x 15 cryptics contain two or more horizontal entries that span the width of the grid.
- The grid may do away with black squares altogether. Instead, some grids indicate the end of an entry with heavy black bars.

Puzzle 13-1 allows you to get acquainted with the finer points of the cryptic grid. You can find the answers to Puzzle 13-1 in Appendix A.

Crosswords cross the Big Pond and come back as cryptic puzzles

Perhaps cryptic puzzles are a case of something being gained in the translation. After crosswords reached the shores of Great Britain in the 1920s, they took a turn for the more complicated, thanks to the ingenuity of one Englishman, who happened to be a literary critic and translator, known to solvers only by his byline *Torquemada.* (Torquemada was Edward Powys Mather. He assumed this disguise from the original Torquemada, who was the Spanish grand inquisitor. That pseudonym gives you an idea of the way he intended solvers to remember him!) He established the tradition among British "compilers" (as constructors call themselves in Britain) to adopt similar arcane noms de plume.

Synonym matching, which is the root of the traditional crossword puzzle, just didn't grab the British solving public of the Roaring Twenties, and so this ingenious puzzle creator adapted the crossword to fit his British audience.

Even then Prime Minister Baldwin welcomed the first American crossword when it made its debut in Great Britain. In January 1925 he held a press conference in which he pronounced that "I as prime minister and you as journalists are engaged in the common work of trying to elevate the people of this country. And you are doing it today through that marvelous medium, the crossword puzzle." Already, compilers were at work adapting the crossword for the British audience. Soon after, the venerable British weekly, *The Spectator,* observed that "without one's realizing it, the virus was spreading through one's veins."

Puzzle 13-1

Across

1 Gather no fire (7)
6 Curtail the use of Southern slang (5)
10 Tied up, TV horse is eating eggs (6)
11 Sluggard ordinarily is without this! (5)
12 Topic is abstract and absorbing — sectional by its very nature (4, 5)
13 Boxes crowded with house money, maybe (6)
15 "Look . . . turn around" (4)
16 Go to a prom about five (7)
17 Reportedly arrest a disease (7)
22 Salts at sea see a lot (7)
23 Earlier, give off energy; nitrogen and oxygen are left (3, 4)
24 High-school math test initially more than half right (4)
28 Creep entrapped by spies' bug (7)
29 Congenial exotic dancers (5, 4)
30 Bird that is a character on *Sesame Street* (5)
31 Cowboy's mostly coarse loop (6)
32 Counter bar for party (5)
33 Junior has motivation to be a doctor (7)

Down

1 Drive "Demon Train" (5)
2 Smell enveloping one kind of pollution (5)
3 Jimmy is supporting bigwig writer (5, 4)
4 Lies about puzzles (7)
5 Sort of round hole — empty and completely bottomless (7)
6 Secure the borders of Santa Fe (4)
7 Tie one on Tuesday, supporting endless desire (6)
8 See? It's not nice to be uncovered (6)
9 Wipes dry, stores last of power tools (7)
14 Under Devil Incarnate (2, 1, 6)
17 First of Crusade's heroic clashes is comparatively special (7)
18 Spacey Mr. Sulu has no twin (7)
19 Class remains confused (7)
20 Discussed broadcasting *Platoon* again (6)
21 Egoist's foul cigar (6)
25 Foreign aid backing Ohio State (5)
26 Talk about African land (5)
27 Scot fractured a leg (4)

1	2	3		4		5	6	7		8	9
10							11				
			12								
13									14		
15					16						
17					18		19				
	20		21		22						
23								24		25	26
				27		28					
29											
30						31					
32					33						

Putting British clues under the microscope

Cryptic crossword clues are always divided into two categories: Across and Down. The clue numbers refer to numbers in the grid where the entry begins. That's where the resemblance to American crosswords ends.

Cryptic clues diverge from the American standard in the following ways:

- **Fewer per puzzle:** There are generally fewer clues in the cryptic, about 60 combined in the average 15 x 15, where American crosswords have closer to 78 in grids of the same size. This is because the grid contains so many unchecked letters that only appear in one word.
- **Wordier:** Unlike the American clue, which is usually only one or two words long, the British clue is wordy. On the surface, the British clue looks and reads like a sentence. Each clue (sentence) functions as a puzzle within the puzzle, adding a step to the solving process.
- **Categorized by type of wordplay:** With nine standard types to choose from, each clue is a carefully constructed minipuzzle composed of a straight definition and a form of wordplay. There is no formula as to how many of each the constructor must use per puzzle. The types of clues you encounter change from puzzle to puzzle.
- **Numbers at the end of clues:** Following the clue, you see a number in parentheses. This represents the number of letters in the entry. If the answer is a multiple word entry, this is indicated in parentheses by breaking down the words as in (2,4) meaning a two-letter word and a four-letter word. You may even see three words in parentheses as (3,3,4) indicating two three-letter words followed by a four-letter word.

The cryptic clue contains two separate parts which contribute to the pseudo-sentence:

- A straightforward definition
- A form of wordplay to help you reach the answer in a different way.

Your job as solver is to distinguish which part is which.

Checking out the entries

As long as you're solving in the English language, you always encounter the typical vowel/consonant patterns in the entries. For example, you don't find JZXL as an entry in either American crosswords or cryptics — that's the territory of the cryptogram code (see Chapter 2 for more information on the cryptogram). You still find the same typical suffixes (-ING and -TION) and the standard past participle (-ED) in cryptics as you do in American crosswords.

You may, however, notice the following differences when you write the entries into the grid:

- You may find some spelling variations from the British lexicon, such as an additional U in words using O (GLAMOUR).
- Each entry has at least one letter that is surrounded by black squares and doesn't interlock with the other entries. (At least half the letters in an entry must interlock with other entries.) Therefore, some letters read in only one direction.

  According to experts Mel Rosen and Stan Kurzban, a letter that doesn't connect to any other entries is known as an *unch* (short for "unchecked letter") among cryptic acrossionados.

- The typical minimum letter count per entry is four. (Some editors may accept three-letter words.)
- The entries may not pertain to a theme.

Where the Fun Is: The Nine Classic Clue Styles

The essence of solving a cryptic puzzle is in figuring out the complex clues. Because the clues are more complex, you have fewer of them to deal with. Because the entries don't necessarily interlock, and they aren't usually part of a theme, you can jump into the clue list anywhere you wish, including at 1 Across.

Each cryptic clue consists of two parts: the straight definition and the wordplay part, not necessarily in that order.

The wordplay portion of the clue may take any of the nine forms that I list in this section, starting with the easiest form and working my way up to the most challenging.

Except for the double definition and charade style clues, every style of clue has "indicator" words that signal what kind of clue you're looking at. The indicator shows you where to find the wordplay. To solve the entry, you bisect the clue into two parts, dividing the straightforward part from wordplay. Then you decipher the code, so that you interpret how the definition is also expressed as wordplay.

Until you get used to deciphering a cryptic clue, you may experience some frustration, because the cryptic clue "sentence" isn't what it seems at all. Although the clue contains a straightforward definition, it's camouflaged in a clever way that may not be immediately clear to you. In fact, the compiler may try to fool you deliberately. Just stick with it, and you'll come out on top of the grid.

Unlike American-style clues, cryptic clues are precise: Only one answer per clue is possible. You don't see vague one-word clues such as "Penelope" (the '60s model and daughter of Marietta) or "Evergreen" (as in fir) for the entry TREE. The cryptic clue formula is so specific that after you decipher the answer, you can go for your pen and jot the entry in the grid in ink!

Punctuation in cryptic puzzle clues is meaningless at best, devious at worst, so watch where you put the emphasis. These clues aren't meant to be read as they appear. In fact, reading the clues straightforwardly leads you astray, as in the example of "Hear prohibited musicians (4)." The entry, BAND, has nothing to do with bootlegged recordings or any unauthorized activity regarding prohibited musicians according to normal logic. Instead, you have to examine each word individually. You "hear" a word that means "prohibited" (banned) in order to get to the entry. The key to solving success is not to read the cryptic clue as a sentence but to break it down into smaller parts. Always weigh each word separately. When I'm really lost, sometimes I find that by inserting slashes between words I can get a grasp on what the clue is trying to tell me, as in "Hear prohibited/musicians." Giving a well-disguised "surface meaning" to a clue distinguishes an adept constructor from a hack.

Double definitions

In the double definitions clue, the constructor combines two different meanings of the entry word to create what reads like a sentence. This relatively straightforward category is most like the familiar American-style dictionary-type clue.

No indicator words tip you off to a double definition clue. However, you can usually recognize a double definition clue because it's typically shorter than the average cryptic clue (two to four words).

To decode the clue, you first dissect the clue into two parts, and then you establish the connection between the two parts.

The two meanings in the double definition clue don't have to belong to the same class of word. One part of the double definition may be a verb, and one part may be a noun.

For example, you may run across the clue "Avoid American car (5)." You begin solving the clue by breaking the sentence into two components, which gives you "Avoid" and "American car." Then you try to establish a five-letter connection between those two concepts. With a little luck (and thought), you come up with DODGE. The first definition is the verb form and the second is the noun — which is acceptable in the cryptic crossword format.

Anagrams

Anagrams are one or more words that rearrange letter order to make one or more different words. For example, you can rearrange the letters in DAME to spell MADE. Both are real words and use the same letters.

A cryptic anagram clue contains a straightforward definition and the entry in a scrambled form, plus instructions to anagram it. The letters of the entry are provided right in the clue.

You can identify an anagram clue by the indicator words associated with anagrams. (An *indicator* is a constructor's way of telling you what kind of clue you're working on.) For anagrams, indicator words imply confusion and chaos. When you get the idea that something is "strange," "in bad shape," or just "bad," chances are the word that follows or precedes the indicator word(s) is an anagram for the entry.

If you suspect an anagram clue, count the number of letters in the word before or after the indicator and compare the count to the parenthetical number. If they match up, then you've located the word you need to anagram in order to form the entry.

Some common indicators for anagram clues include the following words and phrases:

- At sea
- Bent
- Broken
- Confused
- Contrived
- Disrupted
- Eccentric
- Mixed up
- Oddly
- Out of order
- Out of sorts
- Somehow

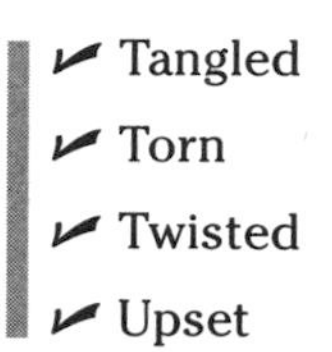

- Tangled
- Torn
- Twisted
- Upset

As with all cryptic clues, to solve you first need to identify the two parts of the clue: the straightforward definition and wordplay. Begin with the straight definition. With an anagram, you have the indicator words that help the identification process because it tips you off as to where the wordplay lies.

The nice thing about the anagram clue is that the entry letters are right there on the page. But they're in disguise, jumbled in anagram form for you to find and rearrange. For example, you may come across the clue "Summarizes awful scrape (6)." The two parts of the clue are "Summarizes" and "awful scrape." Right away, the word *awful* serves as the indicator that *scrape* is the anagram. *Summarizes* is, therefore, the direct part of the clue that defines the entry. Anagram scrape to get to RECAPS, which defines *summarizes.*

You always know how many letters the entry requires by looking at the parenthetical number, which will, of course, match the number of blanks in the grid. Your best bet is to identify a word that matches the number count you need. Sometimes the anagram requires mixing two words together. Then take a stab at rearranging the letters by separating the vowels from the consonants to create the entry.

Concealed words (hidden words)

The concealed-word type of clue is a relative of the hidden word puzzle that I describe in Chapter 4. In both types of puzzles, you're seeking out a word that is hidden in the text. In this case, the entry letters are right in the clue, and they appear in the correct order — if you can find them by attaching letters between words.

You know how many letters the concealed word has by looking at the parenthetical number at the end of the clue. The challenge is to pick the right letters out of the sentence and loop them together.

In is the classic indicator for a concealed-word clue. For example, "Pearl's home in viceroy's territory (6)" may be the clue for OYSTER (joining the end of *viceroys* with the beginning of *territory*). Other typical indicator words include the following:

- Concealing
- Has
- Inside
- Showing
- Within

You can train your eye for concealed-word clues by reading any text in a way that overlooks breaks and joins parts of adjacent words. I've practiced this technique at many a dull business meeting.

A great example of a concealed-word clue is "Dior chided for displaying a bloomer (6)." The two parts of the "sentence" break down as "Dior chided" and "displaying a bloomer." If you interpret *bloomer* as *flower,* you may then notice that when joined, *Dior-chided* conceals ORCHID.

Container clues

Like the concealed word, in container clues, the entry appears on the page. Instead of lurking between words, though, the entry is an "inside word" entirely planted within the letters of a longer clue word or a combination of words. The solver may have to take a word in the clue and insert it into another word to make the entry.

You can expect a container clue when you see any of the following indicator words or phrases:

- About
- Amid
- Around
- At the heart of
- Embraced
- Grasped by
- Holding
- In
- Inside
- Surrounding
- Within
- Without

For example, you can suspect a container clue when you see the word *in* in the clue "City that suits Ron in toto (7)." The first part of the clue is "City." The second part *suits* (or encases) "Ron in toto." By inserting *Ron* in the word *toto,* you get the city of TO-RON-TO.

Some container clues may break the entry into two words: the inside "container" and the word formed by the outside letters. The solving process mimics a charade-style clue, which I describe later in this chapter. For example, take the clue "Around a thousand reporters campus girl is restrained (10)." To solve this clue, begin with the word "around," which alerts you that you're working with a container clue. "A thousand reporters" translates into M (Roman numeral for 1,000) plus *reporters* or PRESS. "Campus girl" implies a female student or COED. Place COED around MPRESS to create COMPRESSED, the answer to *restrained.* (Container clues obviously give constructors a great way to clue ordinary words.)

Reversals

A *reversal* is a hidden word that reads from right to left: The answer is the backward spelling of an entry word within the clue. First, read the clue to identify the straightforward part from the wordplay element. Next, look for an indicator word. For a reversal, you may see an indicator like "returning" attached to a phrase.

You know that you're staring at a reversal clue when you see any of the following indicator words:

- *Backward, return,* or *retreat* for Across entries (also *heading west*)
- *Upward* or *looks up* for Down entries (also *heading north* or *rising*)
- *The wrong way*

Take, for example, the Mike Miller clue "Return infant's item to get reimbursed (6)." First, look for the straightforward part of the clue, which is "to get reimbursed." The word "return" indicates that the word play involves "infant's item." In six letters you need a word that reads in one direction as "reimbursed" and becomes "infant's item" when spelled in the "return." How about DIAPER? In the "return" mode, it becomes REPAID.

The indicator word always appears beside the word to be reversed, not next to the direct definition. For example, Albert Morehead (the man who invented Puns and Anagrams; see Chapter 12 for more information on Puns and Anagrams) cites one neat reversal in the appendix of his classic reference, *The New American Crossword Puzzle Dictionary* (Signet): "Take your pay from the right drawer (6)." The clue divides into "your pay" (the direct definition) and "drawer," six letters which, when read "from the right," give you REWARD. Think of the clue as broken by the slashes I insert: "Take your pay/from the right/drawer."

Sometimes the reversal clue requires one extra solving step by not including the word to be reversed in the clue. Here's an example for a Down clue: "Name of tree the French author looks up (5)." The two parts of the clue are "Name of tree" and "French author." In five letters, you may come up with SUMAC for the entry, which reads as CAMUS "looking up" or reading from the bottom to top.

Homophones

A homophone clue relies on the basic pun and works with the phonetic aspect of an entry: It plays with two words that sound exactly alike but are spelled differently and have different meanings. The clue includes the definition of the homophone sound-alike word. As with any cryptic clue, you must divide the clue into two parts: the straightforward definition and wordplay. Homophone indicators will help you identify the wordplay part.

The following indicator words and phrases tip you off to a homophone clue. They all relate to the sense of hearing:

- Aloud
- I hear
- It's said
- Oral
- Outspoken
- Reportedly
- Sounds
- Sounds like
- They say
- To the audience
- We hear

The clue "Spooky sounding lake (4)" provides a good example of a homophone clue. This clue is easy to bisect: you just break it down into "Spooky sounding" and "lake." In four letters, a word that describes both must be ERIE, the lake that sounds spooky or *eerie*.

This clue style is all about making puns and mistaking one word for another. Sometimes, as in the clues of the Puns and Anagrams crossword (which you can read more about in Chapter 12), the homophone clue is phrased as a question to indicate that it is a riddle.

Charades (buildups)

The charade clue style derives from pantomime, which relies on acting out small components of the total answer in sequence, as in the popular parlor game Charades. Broken into smaller segments, you ultimately connect the smaller segments in the order given in the clue to complete the entry.

When solving a cryptic clue, you begin by separating the direct definition from the wordplay part. For the charade, you may sometimes note an indicator word that identifies it as a charade, but not always.

When parts of the entry are presented out of order, then an indicator will be given. Any of the following indicator words or phrases let you know that you may be facing a charade clue:

- After
- By
- Follows
- Gets
- Goes before
- Leads
- Made from
- To

Unlike the parlor game, in charade clues the entry word may be divided anywhere — not ever by the obvious measure of a syllable. In fact, you can bet your bottom dollar that the setter presents the charade in a most unusual way. For example, I personally get a kick out of this clue by Mike Miller for the entry THINKING: "Slim monarch is cogitating (8)." You've got a THIN KING, which, when combined, is another way to say *cogitating.* (Note that the constructor gives no indicator word.)

Another good example of a charade clue is "Seats made from 501 trucks (6)," in which you have the two halves of the clue: "seats" and "501 trucks." "Made from" is the indicator that what follows contains the charade. The phrase "501 trucks" implies two syllables in the six-letter entry. The first syllable is "501." Because you can't combine numbers and letters, replace the numbers with their equivalent in Roman numerals, and you get DI for the first syllable. The second syllable answers to "trucks" in four letters, which may be VANS. Combine the two syllables to yield DIVANS (seats).

Sometimes the indicator word subtly explains a sequence of words, as in "One hamburger roll before rumba is plenty (9)" to mean ABUNDANCE, or A BUN (one hamburger roll) *before* DANCE (rumba).

In his classic book on this subject, *Beyond Crosswords* (Prentice Hall), acrossionado Michael Miller refers to charade clues as *word chains.* That's a nice way to look at them because the letters are linked consecutively in a chain.

Deletions

A deletion is a fancy type of cryptic clue that works through the loss of one or more letters. Any part of the word may be removed to create the entry. To solve a deletion, begin by separating the dictionary definition part from the wordplay. You may be able to recognize where the wordplay falls if an indicator appears in the clue.

Sometimes the indicator for a deletion clue may be as obvious as *first off,* meaning that you ought to remove the first letter, or *omit.* Any instruction to remove or abbreviate indicates a deletion. Other times, you may find that one of the following indicator words in the clue tell you which letter to delete:

- *Headless* or *topless* indicates first letter (also *beheaded* or *without leader* or otherwise noting beheaded)
- *Tailless* or *bottomless* indicates last letter (also *endless, nearly,* and *almost)*
- *Heart* indicates center letter
- *Lost time* means take away T

Say, for example, that you're looking at a Will Shortz clue like "Sign of vindication after the guillotine (10)." Sounds grisly but not if you look at the parts. First, divide the clue into its straightforward and wordplay parts. "After the guillotine" seems to relate to a beheadment of sorts, which leaves "Sign." Taking "vindication" to the guillotine leaves you with INDICATION, which is the dictionary definition for sign.

In the clue "Insult Streisand? God, no (4)," the first half of this clue refers to the singer BARBRA. The second part of the clue tells you "God, no!" Don't mistake this phrase for a rebuke — it means *remove a god from BARBRA*. After you remove the god RA from BARBRA, you end up with BARB, which is a synonym for "insult."

Deletion clues are also known as *beheadments* and *curtailments,* depending upon where the letter removal occurs.

& Lit Clues

When you see a cryptic clue without an indicator word, the clue may be an & Lit clue, which stands for "and literally so." The straightforward and wordplay aspects of these clues merge in a perfect union, depending on the way you read the clue.

What is especially deceptive about this clue style is that deciphering it correctly depends on your reading skill, which is why some acrossionados refer to these clues as Read It Again clues. Yet another term for this clue style is Double Duty.

The indicator, if any, is the punctuation: an exclamation mark at the end of the clue. When you see that indicator, you know that you should read the clue once as a straight clue and again for wordplay.

For example, take the clue "Insane Roman at heart! (4)" by Will Shortz. You have to read the clue first, and then when you see the exclamation point, read the clue again looking for the entry indicated by the clue. In this case, the answer lies between ("at heart") the first two words, to yield NERO.

Sometimes cryptic clues combine types, such as an anagram plus a reversal. You see indicator words as you solve these *double whammies,* as I call them.

Cryptic clues must be specific

The world of cryptic crosswords has a rule known as *Afrit's Law* (*Afrit* is the pen name of one of the original compilers). It reads: "A clue may not mean what it seems to say, but it must say exactly what it does mean." As you gain experience in solving cryptics, you come to appreciate this maxim.

Other wrinkles in cryptic clues

The cryptic code is an organic one that expands with each constructor's amazing turn of mind. You may encounter clues that combine two types into one — for example, a cryptic clue may combine a charade and a deletion. To help you identify possible stray letters, add some standard indicator words to your solving lexicon:

- *Doctor* indicates DR and medic MD
- *Grand* indicates G (slang for *a thousand*)
- *Left* indicates the letter L *(to the left* indicates a reversal)
- *Little* or *short* may indicate an abbreviation
- *Love* indicates the letter O (as in the tennis term for *zero*)
- *Loud* indicates F (from the musical term *forte*)
- Numbers indicate Roman numerals (1 = I, 5 = V, 10 = X, 50 = L, 100 = C, 500 = D and M = 1,000)
- *Right* indicates the letter R
- *Point* may indicate one on the compass (E, W, N, S)
- *Soft* indicates P (from the musical term *piano*)
- *Time* indicates T (a scientific term)
- *Tom* indicates CAT

The World's Toughest Crossword: The Times of London

The course of crosswords changed forever in January 1930, thanks to an irate reader of *The Times* of London. A certain Lt. Commander A. C. Powell submitted a written complaint that the newspaper didn't offer a crossword for his money. Within the week, the mail poured in four to one in favor of a *Times* crossword. By February 1, the paper had recruited a constructor: Adrian Bell, a 28-year-old farmer with a published novel. Bell's dad, Robert, a crossword professional and constructor of the "Everyman Puzzle" for the *Observer,* recommended him.

For decades, the younger Bell was the main setter (as the British call constructors) of "the world's toughest crossword," as *The Times* of London calls its puzzle. He supplied *The Times* with two to four cryptics at the rate of three guineas each. Until 1970, Bell kept his identity under wraps — perhaps in an attempt to protect him from desperate solvers. In cahoots with his editor, Ronald Carton, Bell managed to wear out one dictionary per year. Bell's pithy opinion about his strange career: "I think you must be near dotty to spend your life setting crosswords." (Sounds like a cryptic clue to me.)

In 1947, when the editors moved the cryptic to the back page from the middle, a delighted acrossionado reportedly said: "It is no longer necessary to open the thing at all!"

Nowadays, *The Times* of London puzzle appears in English language newspapers that belong to the publishing empire of Rupert Murdoch. By way of explanation, a blurb tells readers that although the puzzle doesn't conform to the crossword in the "traditional sense" (or standard crosswordese), its clues are full of anagrams, double meanings, reversals, and buildups. And you're sure to encounter amusing clues such as "A hormone, possibly, used to build a heavenly body (8)." Could this clue be a charade-style clue that breaks down into A plus STEROID? Indeed.

According to the *Guinness Book of Records,* the record for persistence in tackling a *Times* of London puzzle goes to a woman in Fiji. This avid acrossionado completed the cryptic from *The Times* April 4, 1932 issue in May 1966. After reviewing the cryptic clue styles, I'm sure that you join me in applauding this tenacious solver on the magnitude of her achievement.

Keep in mind that the terminology used in the British cryptic differs significantly from the cryptic terminology of American compilers, which makes solving that much harder for American solvers. For example, in the British cryptic code, "sailor" in a clue represents the letters AB (as in able-bodied seaman), not a common usage in the USA. Of course, with enough solving practice and experience, you can come to know what these abbreviations are.

Where to Find Cryptic Crosswords

"Why do so many general interest magazines waste a whole page on crosswords?" a friend once asked me. "Even though I enjoy solving puzzles elsewhere, when I find one in a magazine, I can't seem to make heads or tails of it, so I flip right past." She meant that although she was an accomplished solver, she preferred her tried-and-true brand, which is typical of most solvers who get attached to a routine. Yes, I explained to her, you can derive a great deal of comfort from staying with what you know. But when you exercise your body, eventually you look for a change in routine — you jog in a different direction, you switch instructors, or make yourself a new tape. Sometimes freshening up your mental workout is good, too.

For the average acrossionado, solving cryptics may be an acquired taste. But dabbling in this crossword has special rewards. In the opinion of Mike Miller, author of *Beyond Crossword Puzzles* and a reporter for *The Wall Street Journal,* "Cryptic puzzles are to regular crosswords as four-star restaurants are to TV dinners." You don't want to limit yourself to microwaveable meals, nor do you want to limit yourself to "conventional" crosswords, as crypt people call the standard American variety.

After conducting a seminar in how to solve the cryptic, Mike Miller ordered a cake with the inscription "Farewell to muddle synthesis of ego and body (7)." His class understood the message as an anagram clue that "synthesizes" EGO + BODY to create GOODBYE ("Farewell").

To signal an anagram, cryptic clues use indicator words that introduce the notion of scrambled letters, as in *mixed up, wrecked, twisted,* or *muddled.* In Miller's clue, *muddle* serves as the indicator word of a synthesis (combination) of two words.

Magazine sources

Not surprisingly, magazines with a literary editorial tone tend to be the ones that include cryptic crosswords and other puzzles in the back of the book. In this section, I list the magazines by the number of issues per year.

Solving the cryptic in a monthly often involves a competitive edge. Some magazines offer free one-year subscriptions to those intrepid solvers who complete and mail in these diabolical diagrams in a timely fashion. Because the solutions aren't published until the following month, cheating is not even possible.

To say that the cryptic crosswords in magazines are wordplay gems is putting it mildly. Each month brings a unique challenge that may frustrate you at first. Familiarity with the clue styles is only the beginning of the decoding process. Sometimes reading the special instructions that accompany each puzzle may put you off. But if you stick with cryptics, you reap the rewards later.

Every publication offers to provide you with its copyrighted version of how to solve its cryptic free of charge if you mail in a self-addressed stamped envelope.

The Atlantic Monthly

Certainly, the most prolific team of puzzle pros in the specialized field of cryptic compilers these days is Emily Cox and Henry Rathvon. Their creative and whimsical puzzles appear on a full page in the back of *The Atlantic* (newsstand price, $3.95), as they have for years. Each advanced-level puzzle (a *variety* cryptic) comes complete with its own set of instructions peculiar to that particular theme.

Twelve times a year, this dynamic duo creates a unique seasonal challenge for its readers. Some examples of themes from 1997 include the following:

- "Celebrating the Fourth" (July issue) incorporates a theme particularly true to the month of fireworks. In the bar grid of 15 x 13 squares, the middle entry at 25 Across offers the key to them: GET A BANG OUT OF IT. Every time the letters IT appear in the answer, replace them with the word BANG in the grid.
- "Scoreboard" (August issue) uses a really funny-looking grid set up like a baseball scoreboard, 30 x 6, and divided into nine "innings." Instead of the standard numbers, the Across clues are labeled in six rows from A through D, while the Down clues are represented by numbers. The letters help you locate where the answers belong in the grid. Eighteen squares in the "scorecard" grid are shaded. By selecting out the letters from the shaded squares, the solver discovers the team scores. (Solvers who stick with the challenge find it to be a tie.)

A typical anagram clue from Cox and Rathvon is "Some politicians organized Persian club (11)." If you "organize" PERSIAN with CLUB, you meet "some politicians," or REPUBLICANS.

This productive team serves as the cryptic editors for Dell Champion magazines. They also produce two Sunday crosswords a month in the conventional American format for *The Boston Globe.* These puzzles can be purchased in book form (*Boston Globe Sunday Puzzles,* Times Books, $9). Their byline appears with some frequency in *Games* magazine, too. And they manage *The New York Times* Puzzle Forum on the Internet.

Harper's Magazine

For more than two decades, compiler Richard Maltby, Jr., has been an institution at *Harpers Magazine* (newsstand price, $3.95) producing variety cryptic crosswords. The Tony-winning director of *Ain't Misbehavin,* he joined forces with the late Ed Galli to create a monthly challenge for solvers in 1976. Galli created the diagrams; Maltby crafted the clues. The style of his advanced-level cryptics is awesome and serious. A lyricist by trade, he says he feels that he's using the same skill in setting words, whether to music by composer David Shire or to a grid created by Galli. A musical, in Maltby's view, is "a very large puzzle."

Maltby has been copying words out of the dictionary since he was in grade school. His formal introduction to cryptics came in the 1960s, thanks to his friend and colleague Stephen Sondheim (lyricist for the musical *A Funny Thing Happened on the Way to the Forum,* among other Broadway hits). He describes his puzzles as being on a wavelength that only dogs can hear. Although he aims to reach a wide audience through musicals, with puzzles he expects to play only to a select group. He compares his puzzle work to old-time jazzman Fats Waller: Despite the skill of the performer, that form of jazz attracted few fans. Ditto for the cryptic — yet the loyal few make the effort worthwhile.

In every issue, Maltby repeats one piece of advice: "Mental repunctuation of a clue is the key to its solution."

Here's a typical deletion-charade clue from a Maltby-variety cryptic for Valentine's Day: "Losing head, appeal to nurse to get some experience (5)." The indicator "losing head" tells us that the word to follow (appeal, or PLEA) is going to lose its first letter. The second portion of "appeal," combined with *nurse* (RN), yields the *experience,* or LEARN.

Types of tricks that Maltby incorporated into recent variety cryptics include the following:

- **RighTangles:** Maltby organizes clues by number and the direction in which you are to enter them — East, West, North, or South.
- **Head Hunting III:** The first letter for each entry appears out of sequence, which requires some "head" (initial letter) hunting.
- **Travel Document:** A search for hidden treasure within an oddly shaped grid.

The Nation

The Nation (newsstand price, $2.75) was the first American magazine to introduce the cryptic to the solving public. Frank Lewis has been compiling this puzzle since 1947. On October 9, 1997, *The Nation* honored Lewis with a Golden Anniversary party in New York City to toast this ongoing feature. At 85, Lewis doesn't show any sign of slowing down. In fact, he has stockpiled his square-dealing, advanced-level puzzles through the millennium, just in case.

A typical Lewis trick is using a number in a clue to refer to another clue in that puzzle. (Naturally, the number clue can only refer to a clue that keys in one direction so as to limit the choice to one entry.)

General-interest weeklies

When you're looking at tough puzzles, the Big Apple seems to have the corner on the weekly market at the moment. Because you receive these puzzles more often, they are less flamboyant than the ones you find in monthly magazines. They're more traditional in tone and appearance and are perhaps a bit more accessible if you want to try them out.

New York magazine

New York magazine (newsstand price $3.50) has had a cryptic in its pages since its first issue in 1967. Originally, award-winning composer-lyricist Stephen Sondheim did the honors. Eventually, Richard Maltby, Jr., succeeded him. Maltby moved his work to *Harpers* magazine in 1976. At that time, *New York* began to reprint puzzles from *The Times* of London. Nowadays the *New York* magazine crypt comes via England from the pages of *The Guardian,* so the crypt is traditional in style and medium in skill level, as cryptics go.

When *The Times* of London went on strike in 1978, British acrossionados became desperate. Only a copy of *New York* magazine with its reprint of the *Times* crossword satisfied their cravings.

A typical Guardian clue is "Mr Kelly has a twitch — it's hereditary (7)" The answer, for you curious folks, is GENETIC. The wordplay part of the clue comes first in the form of a charade, GENE + TIC. The dictionary definition for the entry is the final part of the clue, namely, "hereditary."

The New Yorker

In the summer of 1997, *The New Yorker* (newsstand price, $2.95) added a compact standard cryptic to its regular features. The bar grid measures 8 x 8 squares with about 20 clues per puzzle, a manageable number for the beginning crypt solver, although the skill level of the puzzle usually ranks in the medium range. Cryptics in this venerable weekly tend toward the whimsical. A different person compiles each puzzle, although some bylines do repeat.

Because the puzzle is smaller, the uninitiated acrossionado may find it an easier way to approach the cryptic.

A typical *New Yorker* cryptic clue is "Point of a changing seat (4)" Answer: EAST. The wordplay is introduced by the indicator word "changing," where "seat" is an anagram of EAST. The direct definition is "point" as in compass point.

Puzzle magazines

A variety of puzzle magazines include the cryptic in the mix of general puzzles. Because most puzzle editors enjoy this extra-challenging type of puzzle, I think they hope that if they expose enough readers to the cryptic, eventually it will catch on big-time. Happily, this tactic seems to be working.

Since its first issue in 1977, *Games* (newsstand price, $3.50) has always included a few cryptic crosswords in its pages. Its companion publication, *World of Puzzles* ($2.50), also features a couple of cryptics per issue. Each cryptic is ranked by number of stars from one to three for level of toughness where three stands for "proceed at your own risk." Most of the cryptic crosswords in *Games* fall into this three-star category.

A typical *Games* magazine cryptic clue: "Back at Bill's inaugural ball, nothing is forbidden (5)" Answer: TABOO. The wordplay appears in the first part of the clue, which combines a reversal ("Back at" = TA) and a charade linking the first letter of Bill (B) a ball or circle (o) and nothing (0). The dictionary definition appears at the end as "forbidden."

The *Games* clue reminds me that President Clinton is a well-known acrossionado who solves whenever he can. In fact, Will Shortz is considering an invitation to the President for a cameo on the Puzzler segment of NPR's Weekend Edition aired on Sunday mornings. Stay tuned.

Other sources

Once a month you find a cryptic in the Sunday puzzle page of *The New York Times* — and at no additional charge.

Book collections of cryptics

Some constructors whose bylines are familiar on the American-style puzzle are also master cryptic setters. I suppose that you can call these people bilingual.

Once you get the hang of how the cryptic operates, you may want to practice with some quality collections. Here are some tried-and-true series:

- *Henry Hook's Cryptic Crosswords,* by Henry Hook (Times Books)
- *Hooked on Cryptics,* by Henry Hook (Simon & Schuster)
- *Random House Cryptic Crosswords,* editor Stan Newman (Times Books)
- *Simon & Schuster Cryptic Crossword Series,* editor Eugene Maleska (Simon & Schuster)

Part IV
Other Pieces of the Puzzle

"Can't I just give you riches or something?"

In this part . . .

Unless you totally love puzzles, you may find this part of the book only mildly amusing. In it, I talk about the kind of subjects that make avid puzzle fans froth at the mouth. I'm talking truly juicy puzzle stuff like turning your love for crosswords into cold, hard cash, preparing for the puzzle by working other types of word games, and finding puzzles (sometimes for free!) on the Internet.

Chapter 14

Making Money with Crosswords

In This Chapter

- Turning into a puzzle pro
- Finding outlets that need puzzles
- Setting up your business
- Finding national tournament solving opportunities

Currently, you can earn money through puzzles in two ways: by creating and selling puzzles for publication or by entering the contest circuit. You may not be able to make a living by constructing or entering contests, but you can derive some degree of personal satisfaction from your efforts.

Sure, going public with your puzzle skills may seem like a stretch at first. But believe me, constructing puzzles and entering contests aren't about winning or losing; they're about broadening your enjoyment of the game. Either one just takes a little practice.

The New York Times puzzle editor Will Shortz says that he remembers one of the big thrills in his career as that first payment of $5 for a puzzle that he wrote while in his teens. Although I can't guarantee that your first efforts will have a similar impact, I'm glad to share the information with you about ways you may be able to earn a little extra money through this pastime. In this chapter, I do my best to explain how to tap into these special markets.

The Constructing Game

I got my start in constructing puzzles during my student days, shortly after my husband asked me why I didn't try to make up crosswords for sale instead of just compulsively solving them. After all, he reminded me, puzzles have a business side, too. Because my high school social studies teacher used to sell puzzles to *The New York Times,* I knew that I could send puzzles in over the transom, as the saying goes (meaning by mail). I took a stab at it, and my life has never been quite the same.

The only expense I incurred initially went toward a package of graph paper. I also used my desk dictionary for that first effort. In retrospect, I realize that using an abridged dictionary limited me in a good way from using the really obscure words that appear in the pages of the unabridged version. (Later, I visited the public library when I needed to verify entries.) After you get more involved in moonlighting this way, you may want to invest in a few references. I'll give you my advice on that subject in "Setting Yourself Up in Business," later in this chapter.

Getting your just rewards

If you want to try your hand at constructing puzzles, freelancers are welcome at a selection of newspapers and magazines (see the list of publications in "Finding Publications to Buy Your Puzzles" in this chapter). Be forewarned that even if a publication accepts your work, up to 12 months may pass before it gets into print, and you usually get paid only upon or after publication. You won't get rich quick constructing puzzles!

When you get paid, you have sold the *copyright* to that puzzle. Publishers buy all rights, which entitles them to reprint the puzzle at their discretion, whether through newspaper syndication or in a collection of crosswords. Constructors don't get paid for any reuse of their work.

Payment ranges from $35 to $75 for a daily-size puzzle and $100 to $350 for a Sunday-size puzzle, depending upon the publisher and the quality of the work.

Daily-size puzzles usually measure either 13 x 13 or 15 x 15; Sunday-size puzzles vary between 21 x 21 and 23 x 23, although 21 x 21 is the favored size.

According to Will Shortz, puzzle editor at the *New York Times,* some people just want that one published byline to their credit, and then they're satisfied. Others find themselves becoming serious constructors who develop a relationship with a particular publication or two and churn out material on a regular basis. But as retired constructor Michael Miller has observed, you're likely to make more money as a baby-sitter. The true reward, as he points out in his book *Beyond Crosswords,* is getting that puzzle byline.

Sizing up today's puzzle market

When I submitted a crossword to *The New York Times* in 1978, I received a personal note from then-editor Eugene Maleska inquiring about my age. He sensed that I was a student. Just as he'd been worrying about the future of crosswords, a crop of young constructors seemed to arrive on the scene. He was delighted to discover a new generation of acrossionados to carry puzzles into the future.

Times have changed again. With the introduction of the computer culture and video games, a new generation of puzzle experts has come on the scene. Youthful talent shows no shortage nowadays; in fact, competition is fairly fierce.

Supply is greater than demand in the market of puzzles these days. Although more puzzle publications fill bookstore shelves than ever before, opportunities to become a professional "cruciverbalist" (constructor) are limited. Constructing marketable puzzles isn't easy, as you may imagine; neither is conveying the art of puzzle making. As with any art, innate talent plays a part in the success of the artist.

To commemorate the Golden Anniversary of the Simon and Schuster Crossword series in 1974, constructor Father Ed O'Brien of Croton-on-Hudson, New York, decided to create a directory of fellow professional acrossionados. Officially called a *Compendium of Cruciverbalists,* Father Ed's research revealed that only a few hundred people make up the ranks of constructors. Because the market only supports a handful of full-time positions in this field, the number of people constructing on a regular basis hasn't changed significantly over time.

Finding Publications to Buy Your Puzzles

Your best bet is to start with the newspaper market, which has 365 "openings" per year. Magazines and books offer limited opportunities because publishers tend to rely on a stable of regular contributors. But once you break into the newspaper market, you can use your published puzzles as your "calling card" with the magazine folks. After all, they have plenty of pages to fill!

Newspapers

Always submit your puzzles with a self-addressed stamped envelope to facilitate communication. Puzzle editors need all the clerical support they can get! You won't necessarily receive a rejection, just a reply, possible recommendations, and, who knows, maybe an acceptance.

After you create your masterpiece, try sending it off to any of the following newspapers:

Los Angeles Times Syndicate
1165 Fifth Avenue
New York, NY 10028
Daily puzzles (15 x 15) — Attention: Trude Michel Jaffe, Editor
Sunday puzzles (21 x 21) — Attention: Joyce Lewis, Editor

The New York Times
229 West 43rd Street
New York, NY 10036
Daily and Sunday puzzles — Attention: Will Shortz, Editor

Newsday
P.O. Box 69
Massapequa Park, NY 11762
Daily and Sunday puzzles — Attention: Stan Newman, Editor

Tribune Media Services
6644 Hickorywood Lane
New Port Richey, FL 34653
Daily puzzles — Attention: Wayne Robert Williams, Editor

USA Today
P.O. Box 1040
Cambridge, MA 02140
Daily and Sunday puzzles — Attention: Charles Preston, Editor

The Washington Post Magazine
P.O. Box 32003
Washington, DC 20007
Sunday puzzles only — Attention: William R. MacKaye, Editor

Puzzle magazines

To prepare yourself for professional construction, you should closely review the magazine first for a few issues and request that publication's guidelines by sending a self-addressed, stamped envelope and a letter of request. You'll note that each editor has personal likes and dislikes and each magazine solicits different types of material.

Dell Champion Crossword Puzzles
1270 Avenue of the Americas
New York, NY 15020
Daily and Sunday puzzles — Attention: Joel Hess, Editor

Penny Press
6 Prowitt Street
Norwalk, CT 06855
Daily and Sunday puzzles — Attention: The Editor

Games* and *World of Puzzles
P.O. Box 184
Fort Washington, PA 19034
Daily and Sunday puzzles — Attention: Susan West, Editor

You can probably think of ten magazines off the top of your head that feature a new puzzle every month — *People,* for example. Unfortunately, most of those single puzzle features are by feature crossword constructors who have a contract.

Books

Although many books are collections of puzzles that have appeared elsewhere (newspapers or magazines), you still have opportunities to submit puzzles for review at any of the following:

Book of the Month Club
1271 Avenue of the Americas
New York, NY 10020
Daily and Sunday puzzles — Attention: Kathy Kiernan, Book Development

Running Press
125 South 22 Street
Philadelphia, PA 19103
Daily and Sunday puzzles — Attention: Dan and Roz Stark, Editors

Simon and Schuster Crosswords Series
1230 Avenue of the Americas
New York, NY 10020
Daily and Sunday puzzles — Attention: John Samson, Editor

Other publications

For the published constructor, the challenge is to compose a Sunday-size puzzle for publication. With so few Sundays in the year (and hence, correspondingly low chances of getting an acceptance letter), you may wish to try this smaller circulation outlet for the devoted acrossionado:

The Crosswords Club
c/o Wordsquare Publishing, Inc.
123 Elm Street
Old Saybrook, CT 06475
Attention: Mel Rosen, Editor

If you don't include a self-addressed stamped envelope with each submission, you cut your chances for acceptance to almost zero. Invest the cost of a stamp in your in attempts.

Getting Started in the Puzzle Business

The book that constructors swear by these days is Random House's *Puzzlemaker's Handbook* by Mel Rosen and Stan Kurzban (Times Books, $14). As you can guess by its subtitle, *How to Create and Market Your Own Crosswords and Other Word Puzzles,* this book leads you step by step through the fun (and sometimes frustrating) process of compiling a crossword worthy of publication. Meanwhile, I'm going to do my best to lead you through the fun (and frustrating) creative process and get your career started right here.

First things first: Before submitting a puzzle, get a copy of that publication's guidelines. Although I can give you some general tips, each editor must conform to the tone and style of his or her publication. You may need to take some personal preferences into account, as well. If you're familiar with the puzzles of a particular publication, you have a sense of the tone that it's going for.

General guidelines

I've adapted these guidelines from "The Basic Rules of Crossword Construction," issued by *The New York Times.* These rules apply to any publisher you may approach with your puzzle:

- **The pattern of black-and-white squares must be symmetrical.** If you turn the grid upside down, the pattern must look the same as when the grid is right side up.
- **No more than one-sixth of the squares in a diagram can be black.** Large areas of black squares anywhere in the grid are strongly discouraged.
- **Every letter must *interlock,* appearing in two words, one Across and one Down.** Therefore, your grid shouldn't contain any unkeyed letters (letters that appear in only one word, either Across or Down).
- **The grid must have overall interlock.** Black squares can't divide one part of the grid from another.
- **Theme entries must be symmetrically placed.** For example, if a theme entry is three rows down from the top, then a matching one must appear three rows up from the bottom.
- **No nontheme entry may have more letters than the longest theme entry.**
- **Entries may not repeat within the puzzle.**
- **Every entry must cite a reference book in which it is listed or be used in common speech or writing.** Artificially made-up phrases are unacceptable.

Note: Most publishers set the minimum word length at three letters per entry. Some puzzles do contain two-letter entries, but they are the exception nowadays.

Most publishers prefer a theme puzzle. The exception is the *wide open* crossword that features fewer-than-average black squares. In puzzles, a *theme* is a topic that ties together the longer entries. Anywhere from three to six or even eight entries may participate in a theme within a daily puzzle.

Constructing a puzzle

If you're motivated to create a puzzle and submit it for possible publication, here are my Ten Simple Steps to Making Up a Crossword. (Of course, these steps work just as well if you're creating a puzzle for fun — maybe to give to someone as a present on a special occasion.

I show you how to create a 15 x 15 square in this section. After you get comfortable with this grid size, you can graduate to the more complex patterns and longer clue lists necessary for a 21 x 21 puzzle.

Select a theme

The creative process usually begins with an idea about a central theme. Some constructors like to make up a good design first, but for beginners a theme often sparks the whole effort; a theme is a good idea, especially for your first few puzzles, because thinking about related words can help keep you focused.

Traditionally, a theme spans the width of the grid, consisting of three 15-letter parallel entries that cross at the third row, the eighth row and the twelfth row.

REMEMBER

Themes don't have to reach from one end of the grid to the other; you can select entries of 10 or 13 letters, if it works with your theme.

Any topic is fair game, although you may have a subject dear to your heart. Fun places to start your research are pairs of items, movie titles, job titles, favorite foods. (The puzzles in Chapter 19 may give you an idea of the scope of possibilities.)

PUZZLE PEOPLE

For my very first puzzle I selected a theme based on fruity entries: GRAPES OF WRATH, PEACHES AND CREAM, and APPLE POLISHER.

After you come up with your theme, jot down the three entries that build your theme and think up a title for the puzzle.

Locate a grid pattern that fits your theme entries

Eventually, you can create your own patterns, but for your first few efforts, you don't need this creative distraction. For beginners, I advocate the "instant cake mix" approach, which is based on using another diagram with a pattern that works for your purposes.

Scan your daily newspaper, a favorite magazine, or a puzzle book for a 15 x 15 diagram that offers the correct number of squares for your theme entries. After you find the grid, sketch out the pattern on a piece of graph paper, using a marker to blacken the appropriate squares. If you have access to a copier, I highly recommend making at least 10 copies of your grid so that you can start over if your grid becomes a mess during the construction process.

Insert your theme clues into the blank diagram

Returning to my first effort, I inserted GRAPES OF WRATH in the fourth line down, PEACHES AND CREAM at the "waist" (eight lines down), and APPLE POLISHER in the fourth row from the bottom.

Fill in words for the rest of the grid

After you position the theme, it's time to think about the stuff that fills in the rest of the diagram.

If you plan to submit your puzzle to a publication, you need to acquire a set of that publication's puzzle guidelines (each publication has its own distinctive style).

Write clues that match the words in your grid

This is where the fun really starts. Be as creative as you want. Check out Chapter 2 for a run-down on the basic clue types, and then have at it.

If you intend to submit your puzzle for publication, always keep the style of the puzzle editor at the publication in mind. For example, if you know that the editor at your target publication favors wordplay, remember to formulate your clues in this fashion (to a degree appropriate to the audience).

Insert numbers in the solving grid.

Double check to make sure that your clues correspond to the correctly-numbered entry in the grid, and then you're done.

Puzzle presentation

When submitting a puzzle to a publisher, you supply it in three parts:

- The empty grid diagram (on its own page) with numbers in place. The squares must be blackened.
- A double-spaced clue list, with answers listed at the far right, about 80 clues in all for the average 15 x 15 crossword.
- The solution grid on its own page with answers filled in. (Some editors prefer pencil so that changes may be made more easily.)

For identification, put your name, address, and Social Security number in the upper-right corner of each page. If appropriate, include the puzzle title at the top and a total word count.

If your crossword doesn't have a title, use the 1 Across entry when referring to your puzzle in correspondence.

Basic tools of the trade

Essential equipment for constructing puzzles includes graph paper and pencils with (clean) erasers. While more prolific constructors have access to computer and word processor programs, editors still accept hand-drawn grids as long as clues and entries are typed.

Some industrious people have developed software to help you create puzzles, and you can get that software through some Web sites. However, until you get rolling, some elbow grease is all you need to get started. Even in this computer age, you may prefer to resort to paper when constructing. Besides, a sense of humor, which has yet to be replicated in a computer, is a plus in the puzzle-making field.

Competing on the Contest Circuit

If you're like me, you'll be nervous the first time you enter a tournament. Don't let nervousness stop you! No one is going to watch you unless you're one of the top three players. (And if you do qualify in the top three, you have nothing to worry about in the embarrassment arena anyway.) Most of the other contestants remember what it's like not to know the ropes and are understanding of any faux pas you may commit. Just ask questions of the first quasi-official-looking person you see wearing a name tag, and chances are you'll make a friend in the bargain.

National tournament solving

Acrossionados have a limited window of opportunity to earn their 15 minutes of Andy Warhol fame by solving in public. The competitive market peaked in the 1920s when the solving fad was new.

After a 50-year hiatus, tournament fever came back into vogue in 1978 with the establishment of the Stamford Tournament. Will Shortz, current editor of *The New York Times* crossword, set up the tournament and has kept it going ever since.

Now renamed the American Crossword Tournament, Official Publications currently sponsors the event. The grand prize is $500 (which offsets the registration fee of $100). Over the course of the two-day event, you get the pleasure of solving six specially-crafted top-notch crosswords in the company of the country's fastest solvers. You can also attend a reception with the nation's top puzzle editors and constructors, who judge the competition (all of whom I mention in this book). And you get to make friends with others like you who understand your passion for puzzles.

The first grand prize winner of this tournament, Nancy Schuster, went on to an illustrious career as editor-in-chief of puzzle magazines (Official Publications and Dell Champion).

For information about the next tournament, visit the Web site at `http://www.crosswordtournament.com`. Or you may write to Will Shortz at *The New York Times* (find the address in the "Newspapers" section in this chapter).

The American Crossword Tournament officially kicks off with three rounds of puzzles on a Saturday, following a Friday evening of informal word games. As a contestant, you solve in a hotel dining room at a table divided by blinders. Not that anyone in this crowd wants to peek at his or her neighbor's sheet — this weekend is about fun, not rivalry.

Ivy League solving in the Roaring Twenties

On January 4, 1925, the first Intercollegiate Cross Word Puzzle Tournament was held in New York City. Yale prevailed over Harvard, Princeton, and The City College of New York in successfully completing a puzzle. Poet Stephen Benet and fellow Yale alumnus Jack Thomas made up the winning team. The entry that clinched the prize: ENTASIS. The clue: "Slight convex curve in the shaft of a column."

One square convention

Just 20 years ago, the American Crossword Tournament began as a way to fill the local Marriott during low season in early spring. Will Shortz (now the *New York Times* puzzle editor) organized the event, much to the delight of more than 100 avid acrossionados. As the ranks of contestants have swelled to over 200 and Shortz continues as emcee, the event has become firmly entrenched in the crossword calendar.

At the word "Go," all eyes are down, and the solving begins in earnest. When you complete a puzzle, you wave it in the air so that one of the judges can collect it and note your solving time on your paper. At the end of the day, contest officials post scores measured for accuracy and solving speed. On Sunday morning you participate in two more puzzles. The top three solvers complete the playoff crossword at the front of the room on giant screens as the other contestants watch in awe.

In an exciting recent development, you may participate in the tournament without leaving the comfort of your home through access at the tournament's Web site.

The American Crossword Tournament divides contestants by skill level, based on their past ranking. To encourage multiple winners, there are three to five levels of competition per year, depending upon who registers. In addition to the three overall fastest solvers, top solvers win special prizes based on age group, tournament history, and home state. The series of six puzzles that contestants solve in the course of the weekend event require more than 20 judges and referees. Naturally, computers tabulate all the data. But judges mark each puzzle for accuracy the old-fashioned way.

Mail-in contests

Solvers who prefer to compete through the mail have a wider selection of options. Some general-interest magazines offer one-year subscriptions as prizes for solving their crossword puzzles. Occasionally, puzzle publications offer cash prizes for timely submissions. Even the Book of the Month Club has taken to this type of promotional event in 1997. Greg Tobin, the editor-in-chief, happens to be an avid acrossionado. He collaborated with Stan Newman of Times Books to create a crossword that touched on an illustrious 20th-century American author, much to the delight of the members.

Perhaps the mail-in contest with the highest ticket prize occurred in 1988. Official Publications offered five couples a trip to Greece, including a cruise of some repeater isles (DELOS, IOS, and SAMOS) that most solvers only cruise on paper. Winners were selected at random and represented a fair cross section of solvers. I have it on good authority that these puzzle people kept their eyes glued to their puzzle magazines even when passing the glorious island of DELPHI.

Getting in on the big time in a small way

Although only one annual national crossword contest currently exists, smaller regional ones crop up from time to time. Most of these meets are scheduled in the North East or Middle Atlantic states. In 1997 the Barnes and Noble chain of bookstores in New York cosponsored a series of crossword events with Times Books at various locations in the metropolitan area. Bookstores have opened their shelves to solvers in the past, as well.

Back in 1978, a bookseller in Beachwood, Ohio, offered a $1,000 grand prize in a promotional crossword marathon. The hitch: The crossword by Jordan Lasher was nearly impenetrable. After 23 hours of straight solving using reference books in the bookstore shelf, Michael Donner, the first editor of *Games* magazine, took the top honor. Donner had completed most of the puzzle. (The following year, another *Games* magazine editor, Will Shortz, took the prize in a nine-hour session.)

Tips from the Winners Circle

Despite my long-term involvement in the field, the best rank I ever managed at the American Crossword Tournament was a middling 52nd. Solving against the clock is a completely different experience than working a puzzle at your leisure. The champions are folks who take their solving seriously and train between events. Many contestants simply aim for their personal best by improving on their prior year's time. As some judges observe, entering the American Crossword event takes a marathon mentality: the contestants are proud just to be able to finish.

In the realm of speed solving, puzzle pro Stan Newman holds the public record. In 1982, when he was a bond analyst at E.F. Hutton, Newman solved a *New York Times* daily crossword on live television in two minutes, 24 seconds. Now, as managing director of the puzzle division at Times Books, he shares these tips for solving success:

- **Look it up:** Whenever you come across a new word, consult the dictionary. A healthy curiosity about words and their origins and meanings helps to build your vocabulary as well as your solving prowess.
- **Write it down:** Try the index card system. Jotting down the newly discovered word on an index card is a handy memory device. (Newman accumulated over 8,000 cards in the course of his solving career.)
- **Solve regularly:** Practice makes perfect, as they say. And you acquire an eye for the various styles of constructors whose work dominates the contest circuit. Become cruci-compulsive!
- **Time yourself:** Speed and accuracy are crucial to tournament solving.
- **Practice with friends:** Mock contests can sharpen your reflexes.
- **Participate in contests:** Competing is fun, no matter how you rank. Sharing the experience is the added element.

Believe it or not, crossword contests used to be really popular

After the first wave of crossword fever in the 1920s, solving contests swept the nation. Cash prizes for solving in the Depression years titillated the readership of national newspapers, and they submitted bagloads of completed grids.

Eugene Sheffer ("Mr. King Features") crafted the Liberty contest for the *Chicago Herald and Examiner* in 1931. Each puzzle in the series of 30 crosswords contained the name of one signer of the Declaration of Independence, along with an excerpt from the document. A grand prize of $1,000 and cash prizes for 435 perfectly solved crosswords enhanced the incentive to participate. Responses flooded the Chicago post office with the appearance of the first puzzle shortly after Valentine's Day, 1932. Solvers decorated the grids in fanciful ways, trying anything to make their puzzle stand out from the crowd. Demand was so great that the paper recruited Sheffer to create a second contest series.

As political tensions began to mount in Europe, however, contest fever abated, and the fashion reverted back to solitary solving by 1940.

The key to sustained contest success? Broad but shallow knowledge, according to retired champion Rebecca Kornbluh of Illinois. A tapestry weaver by trade, Kornbluh kept in competitive shape by "training" for an hour a day between tournaments. Reportedly, Kornbluh has won the most prize money through speed solving, a total of more than $5,000. In addition, she has accumulated a sizable supply of unabridged dictionaries for her efforts.With accuracy and speed as the winning components, you need to focus on expanding your knowledge and developing some stenographic skills. Playing Scrabble and reading widely are good training grounds, according to top players of tournaments past.

Tournament winner David Rosen (a computer programmer) developed an interest in crosswords in fifth grade. In fact, he constructed them for the amusement of classmates. A spelling bee champion who read the dictionary for pleasure, Mr. Rosen still "collects" interesting words. Naturally, he's a member of the National Puzzlers League, an organization for serious solvers. His advice includes the following points:

- **Don't sweat it.**
- **Training for a crossword contest is like studying for an IQ test.** Read widely and be curious about words.
- **A good sense of humor and a flexible mind are assets for the acrossionado.**
- **Constructing your own puzzles helps you solve other puzzles, if you have the time to construct.**
- **The best asset for a solver is good eye/hand coordination for maximum writing speed.** Teaching yourself to write more quickly can help your score.

Tony Augarde's *The Oxford Guide to Word Games* (Oxford University Press, $18.95) may help sharpen your wits as you prepare to compete.

Maximizing your contest skills

Mensa, the high IQ society, has suggestions for maximizing your score during test-taking. Going into a "test situation" such as a crossword-solving contest with some preparation may help reduce the anxiety that slows down the thinking process. Herewith are tips from *The Mensa Genius Quiz Book* by Dr. Abbie Salny, Marvin Grosswirth, and others:

- **When being timed, skip any question you don't know.** Answer only those questions for which the answer comes to mind immediately.
- **Try guessing.** Your subconscious may have a hunch about the right answer.
- **Review your work.** Careless errors can be corrected instantly.
- **Get a good night's sleep.** Being fully rested can add 10 percent to your score.

Chapter 15
Flexing Your Mental Muscles

In This Chapter

- Training your brain for the puzzles
- Unraveling riddles
- Getting on the rebus trail
- Trying your hand at trivia
- Unscrambling anagrams
- Horsing around with Fictionary
- Scrabble and other spinoffs

When you're going to be in a marathon, you train your body prior to the race. When you're going to tackle a puzzle, you want to prime your mind. Granted, solving is not nearly as exerting or competitive a sport as running. But solving does require you to use certain brain "muscles" that you may not use in everyday life. Reviewing a variety of word games should help you get in tip-top puzzle shape.

Working Riddles

A riddle is a brain teaser. In other words, it's misleading.

You find riddles all over the crossword puzzle. This type of clue tests your puzzle wit and keeps you on your toes. On the other hand, it may also send your puzzle flying across the room. (See Chapter 2 for information about other clue types.)

The clue "Grand ending?" (3 letters) provides a great example of a riddle clue. You certainly need to go a long way to solve for this entry. Whatever *grand* means to you, the word *ending* in puzzles refers to a final syllable. In this case, the answer refers to the slang meaning of *grand,* as in a thousand dollars. You end up with the entry 000.

To keep puzzles fresh, constructors are on the lookout for new ways of disguising the same old repeaters. Much like cooks trying to use leftovers in new, appetizing ways, constructors rely on the riddle as an appealing new recipe for the same old dish. In fact, humorous riddles are often the central ingredient that provides the spice to the solving process. Especially in Sunday-size puzzles, which are by definition larger, constructors do their best to produce a fun-filled package.

In a riddle clue, every word is not always what it seems. Take a simple-seeming three-letter word like *saw.* As a clue, what does it mean to you? The grid has allocated five squares to this entry. Initially, you may interpret *saw* as the past tense of *see,* which is a natural first reaction and just exactly the trap your constructor had in mind. You may pencil in an entry like SPIED, a five-letter entry full of crossword compatible letters. Until you realize that the clue intends *saw* in the sense of "old saw" (proverb), ADAGE may elude you. To elicit the correct entry, a more obvious synonym clue would be "Saying" or "Proverb." But then you wouldn't have the thrill of seeing through the trick — or snapping your pencil in two.

The riddlin' tradition

Riddles go back as far as Samson, the fabled strong man from Biblical times. Before falling for Delilah, the longhaired hero married a Philistine girl. Instead of a toast, in those days, weddings included a riddling session. Samson composed this riddle for the occasion: "Out of the eater came forth meat, and out of the strong came forth sweetness." (Answer: What is sweeter than honey? And what is stronger than a lion?) Sad to say, Samson lost his sense of humor when presented with the correct answer, and the happy day turned into a massacre. Perhaps that explains why the tradition was discontinued?

In ancient Greece, cracking a riddle was considered a sign of advanced brain power and training. Sophism, a popular teaching philosophy of the time, is based on the sort of Q&A system inherent in puzzle solving. The highlight at many an ancient Greek banquet was the exchange of posers between wits. Rumor has it that Homer choked on a riddle, which led to his untimely demise. The killer was posed by the fishermen of IOS ("Greek isle"): "What we caught we threw away; what we could not catch we kept." (Answer: Fleas.)

The role of the ?

Luckily, constructors leave behind a few hints in the clues to tip you off that you have a riddle on your hands. A final question mark where there is no query tips you off to a brain teaser.

A brain teaser doesn't mean that you have to work extra hard to decipher the answer. It's all in the inflection: If you read the clue as a question, you understand that there is a subtext. If you see a clue like "Long-armed entity?" (3 letters), the question mark tells you that this is not a reference to a gorilla or an actual long-limbed creature, but to something conceptual. In three letters, you may recall the cliché "the long arm of the LAW." Instead of a straightforward missing-word clue like " — and order" or "Order's partner," this clue is designed to evoke a mental chuckle. After seeing the missing clue for LAW hundreds of times, this alternative may prove more engaging. When the crossing entries fit in with it, then you know you've got the right answer.

Getting some practice

Luckily, you can practice working with riddles so that they don't stump you when you come across one in a puzzle. Some riddle-type clues from "Courteous Lee," by Donna Stone (a Premier Crossword from King Features) can help you get the hang of how they work.

- **"Crop expert?" (6 letters):** The question mark implies that you're not in Kansas anymore, and the type of crop is not something for a FARMER despite the fact that FARMER is a six-letter entry that fits. Instead, the type of cropping has to do with haircuts, the sort performed by a BARBER.
- **"Beastly place?" (3 letters):** Again, remember the equation "? = riddle." The entry refers to a beast rather than the adjective *beastly,* meaning unappealing. The joke lands you in a place where beasts live — for example, ZOO or DEN, depending upon the intersecting words.

- **"I specialist?" (7 letters):** Here you have a double entendre: It sounds like "eye specialist," which is the type most people know about. Someone who's hung up on the self ("I") takes the solver into Freudian territory. You don't have to dig back to the myth of Narcissus to know that an egomaniac can be called an EGOTIST.
- **"Type of ship?" (6 letters):** Instead of taking *ship* in its literal meaning, think of the word as a suffix for puzzle purposes. One use of this suffix is with the six-letter word FRIEND.

In his book *The Fun of Answering,* prolific author and confirmed puzzler Isaac Asimov claimed that the sweetest victory is to make up a poser that elicits the response, "I give up." Better than a set of tennis or handball, he was proud to note that this victory doesn't even raise a sweat.

For the A to Z in riddles, check out *Riddles: Ancient and Modern* by Mark Bryant, published by Peter Bedrick Books. You get two for one in this book: an overview of the evolution in riddles and nearly 1,000 quips compiled in a Worldwide Riddle Anthology.

Looking at Pretty Pictures: Rebuses

Meet the rebus, first cousin to the riddle. A *rebus* is a picture puzzle that depicts words visually — like hieroglyphics. You may already be acquainted with the rebus if you've ever drawn a heart to symbolize the word *love* — as in "I (♥) U." Another popular rebus you may have encountered in grade school is "ICURYY4 me." (Translation: "I see you are too wise for me.")

You also see rebuses used in advertising on a daily basis. When you see a certain symbol, you understand that it represents a specific manufacturer. Like a ransom note, a rebus puzzle looks like a motley combination of recognizable words and pictograms that together convey a message.

Rebuses rarely appear in crossword grids. After all, creating one of these amazingly clever diagrams requires extra work without the promise of extra compensation. And the demand isn't that great in the current market. However, sometimes you still find this elaborately tricky type of theme in a larger Sunday puzzle format.

A rebus theme crossword offers a lively alternative to the solver, and it's an incredibly clever way to incorporate multiword entries in condensed form. But until you figure out that you're dealing with a rebus, you may wonder how so many letters can fit into so few squares.

Rebuses weren't always just for fun

The rebus craze was introduced in 16th-century France through the Catholic Church. In order to reach out to illiterate parishioners, the priests of Picardy, a northwest province of France, designed pamphlets combining words with pictures. Due to the puzzle element of these brochures, entitled "De Rebus Quae Geruntur" (Concerning Things Which Are Accomplished), they were instant best sellers. Much like crosswords grabbed the global fancy in the 1920s, the rebus became the rage of its era.

I have found the ingenious use of rebuses in the following crossword entries:

- **Card suits:** You may find an entry that includes the symbol for diamond, spade, club, or heart in one square rather than the spelled-out word. For example, "♥"ENED (to mean HEARTENED).
- **Math symbols:** The plus (+) and minus (–) symbols in one square represent the words MORE and LESS. These words are then combined with others, sometimes with themselves, as in CARE – (meaning CARELESS).
- **Weight abbreviations:** The letter combinations LB, GM, OZ, DM, or TN may appear in the entry as part of a longer word, as in LBS THE PAVEMENT (where LBS reads as POUNDS).
- **Triangle with a circle at the top:** This rebus indicates LOCK and is used in one square to represent that syllable in a longer entry. One example of this rebus is (🔒) HART (to mean LOCKHART).
- **Triangle representing itself:** As in BERMUDA (▲).
- A blank square may be a rebus for the word BLANK, as in (❑) ET in three squares to read BLANKET.

Taking the Trivia Quiz

Trivia plays a big role in the crossword puzzle via clues of relation. For variety in dictionary-definition-type clues, an entry may be described in relation to a similar object. I call this type of clue the *cousin clue.* An obvious example of this relation is the clue "Osprey's cousin" (3 letters). The word "cousin" implies that the object named — osprey — is closely related to the bird in the entry. It's another way to clue that ever-popular "Sea eagle" in crosswords, namely the ERN or ERNE.

Everyone has expertise in some area of study, whether it's names of movie stars, artists, birds, sports, or rock stars. On the other hand, everyone has an Achilles' heel, a weakness. Mine is rock music. I am woefully stuck in a rock-n-roll time warp that hasn't progressed since 1975. Luckily, many repeaters hark back to that era, such as Mrs. Lennon, also known as YOKO ONO, (two crossword-compatible names) and Fleetwood MAC.

Making note of "trivial" facts, figures, and names is bound to pay off in your solving by allowing you to make connections referred to in cleverly-constructed clues. Whenever you hear a puzzle-friendly placename or person name, make a mental note to yourself. (A word is *puzzle-friendly* if it is five letters or less and contains a balance of vowels and consonants.)

A twist on the cousin clue is the implied example clue. Instead of using the word "cousin," you have to decode what the example in the clue is trying to convey. The example may be expressed in a variety of ways. The repeater DEE can help me illustrate my point:

- **"Ruby, for example":** Due to where it's placed in the clue (first), you can't see that Ruby is meant to be capitalized. Okay, the tricky aspect of this clue is in the interpretation of that first word. Although Ruby is July's gemstone, it's also the given name of the actress whose surname is the entry.
- **"Ruby, e.g.":** This is the Latin version of "for example," so it is also a clear-cut definition by example, only in a more compact format.
- **"Ruby or Sandra":** The either/or example is usually most transparent because it gives you two examples. In this case, it clearly identifies *Ruby* as the name.

Aside from memorizing the solutions of every grid you work, how can you acquire a working vocabulary of these slippery little entries? Subliminally, you're already absorbing good information through watching TV and reading the newspaper. You're gathering names of crossword celebrities, common abbreviations, and geographical locations that all appear in the diagram.

Measure your crossword trivia fluency against the questions below by matching items in Column A to items in Column B. You find the answer in Appendix A.

Column A	*Column B*
"Hilo volcano"	AMAH
"Opposite of spring tide"	IMAM
"October gemstone"	ODE
"Kimono belt"	ESNE
"Asian governess"	MAUNA LOA
"Lily's cousin?"	NEAP
"Nabokov heroine"	ALIT
"Snick's partner"	ADA
"Leftover, puzzle style"	OBI
"Oolong, e.g."	ASTER
"Mosque prayer leader"	YSER
"Keats' preferred format"	ATES
"Filipino sweetsop"	OPAL
"Starchy rootstock"	DDE
"Rhone feeder"	SNEE
"Serf"	TEA
"Heraldic wreath"	ORLE
"Fall bloomer"	ALOE
"Dismounted"	ORT
"After HST"	TARO

You can score your success according to the following scale:

- **Above 15:** You're a full-fledged acrossionado if you score above 15
- **Above 10:** You're an ICP (inveterate crossword puzzler)
- **Less than 10:** You're an OCP (occasional crossword puzzler)

Pulling words out of thin air

Some spelling games can help raise your consciousness about letter combinations that you encounter in the grid. Norman Cousins, renowned author of *The Healing Heart* and longtime editor of the *Saturday Review,* devoted many spare moments to spelling games. A favorite, "Ghost Front to Back," can easily be played by two. The point of this exercise is to create a word of any length by working from the inside out. You begin with two letters that appear in the middle of a word, say P-C. The next player then adds a letter to the beginning of the letter combination, say O. Now you have O-P-C. If the first player adds an L to the end you get O-P-C-L. At this point, the second player may wish to make a word from these letters such as STOPCLOCK. If one player can't add a letter, that player challenges the opponent to finish the word. As long as the word is valid, that person wins.

Playing with Anagrams

An *anagram* is a rearrangement of the letters of a word (or words) into a new order that reads sensibly. Besides being of critical importance to solving Puns and Anagrams-type puzzles, anagrams are a great tool for improving your mental sharpness in general. Anagrams force you to look at words and letters from many different angles, which is a skill that takes you a long way in the crossword grid. (I discuss anagrams in depth in Chapter 12.)

Please take a look at a few of my favorite anagrams to flex your mental muscle:

- MIGUEL DE CERVANTES SAAVEDRA = GAVE US A DAMNED CLEVER SATIRE (to describe the man who wrote *Don Quixote*)
- DANTE GABRIEL ROSSETTI = GREATEST BORN IDEALIST (to describe the romantic 19th century British artist)

In his work *The Philanthropist,* British playwright Christopher Hampton works these thought-provoking anagrams through the character Philip the philologist:

- LA COMEDIE FRANCAISE = A DEFENSE O'RACIALISM
- SHAKESPEARE'S HAMLET = MAKES THE REAL SHAPES

For more background on the subject, *The Oxford Guide to Word Games* by Tony Augarde charts the evolution of word games and puts them in social context.

Talk show host nonpareil Dick Cavett is known to have a flair for anagrams. Lyricist Richard Maltby was bowled over when Cavett scrambled the letters in ALEC GUINNESS to read GENUINE CLASS after looking up at a movie marquee for *Lawrence of Arabia.* This skill at anagrams was sharpened in the 1970s through the avid pursuit of Perquacky, a type of spill-and-spell board game. (Cavett is among the few to play Perquacky at Hugh Hefner's mansion.) What does this knack reveal about his brain power? Cavett is humble, in fact self-deprecating, by classifying this skill in the idiot-savant department. The anagram he gives himself is CATCH IT A RARE VD, using his full name, Richard A. Cavett.

Another kind of trivia game

Botticelli is a great trivia game that sharpens your puzzle wit (and travels well from point A to point B). Celebrity names provide the fodder for the game.

You need at least two people to play, one to think of the name of a well-known person while the other(s) identifies that person through a series of questions with yes or no answers. If playing with more than two people, then each player gets a turn to ask a question. The winner correctly identifies the secret person. If one player makes an incorrect guess, he drops out.

Acting Up with Fictionary

Besides providing hours of amusement, this fanciful word game can help sharpen your synonym-clue solving skills (see Chapter 2 for more information on the different types of clues, including the synonym clue). All you need is a dictionary, paper and pencils, and three or more participants.

In Fictionary, you give a viable definition to an obscure word. One player selects the word to be defined and spells it aloud. That player then writes the true definition on a piece of paper. Meanwhile, the other players make up their own definitions and write them down. The first player then collects the papers and reads each one aloud, preferably with a straight face. The other players then vote on which is the correct choice. It's surprising how many votes the fake definitions can get.

After you enter the universe of the acrossionado, you acquire a new attitude toward words. Part of the flight of fancy that you embark on after you embrace the puzzle habit includes a certain whimsy about the definitions of odd-looking words. You acquire a confidence about the language, and that confidence gives you the air of possessing great knowledge. Funny thing is, you often have gained information through osmosis. You may find yourself able to get the gist of a word or term even without any conscious effort. Recently, someone asked me the meaning of the term "paper tiger." With complete self-assurance, I offered the definition by looking at the components: If a tiger (or any ferocious beast) is made of paper, then it has no real power. This sounded reasonable, and when I later checked in my dictionary, my definition did match. What luck!

What's in a name?

In the 17th century, anagrams of names were thought to contain insights into your character. An antiquary of the time, William Camden, defined the game as the "dissolution of a name truly written into his letters, as his elements, and a new connection of it, by artificial transposition without addition, subtraction or change of any letter, into different modes, making some perfect sense to the person named." If this is true, then I may as well hang it up — my name, MICHELLE ARNOT, works out to be an anagram of AM HITLER CLONE!

Can puzzle solving build your IQ?

Although it's debatable whether solving crossword puzzles actually boosts your intelligence, some academic evidence suggests that puzzles may keep your brains agile at an advanced age. Sherry Willis, associate professor of human development at Penn State, found that older people's mental skills may grow rusty through disuse, and that the mental exercise involved in puzzles can help avert that process. She followed 29 people from age 65 to 95 for 14 years. Her conclusion: Solve crosswords on a regular basis (or enroll in continuing education courses) to help keep your mind sharp.

Scrabble®

Scrabble, manufactured by Milton Bradley, sharpens your crossword skills by allowing you to practice combining letters to make words. Scrabble and crosswords overlap in the way words intersect with each other and the strange lexicon of short words intrinsic to each. A passing knowledge of crosswordese provides you with a lexicon that may help your Scrabble game.

Scrabble is a spelling game that consists of a board and 100 letter tiles. The board looks like a 15 x 15 daily-size crossword grid consisting of 225 squares with a colorful pattern design involving about one-quarter of the squares. The game may be played with two to four people.

Each player selects seven tiles without looking at them. You use your seven tiles to create a word. You may use any or all of the tiles in a single move. (An average move uses four letters.) After each move, you replace the number of tiles you used to make the word, always restoring the number of tiles to seven (of course, you can only replace tiles as long as there are extra tiles left). The challenge is to earn maximum points by attaching your word to one letter on the board so that your letters fall on special squares that double or triple the point value of a letter or word.

When all the tiles are in the hands of the players, the first player to use all of his or her tiles ends the game. That player is entitled to add double the value of the opponent's leftover tiles to his or her total score, according to U.S. rules. If neither player can use every tile, then each must deduct the value of the leftover tiles from their final scores.

GRIDLOCK BUSTER

Forget about standard crossword construction rules in this arena. When you finish a game of Scrabble, the board looks like an openweave "Kriss Kross" pattern with words interlocking at one point or two at most. (In fact, before Scrabble, the spelling game was known as Criss Cross.)

REMEMBER

Rearranging your seven letters to form a word is akin to making an anagram. The difference is that you're not required to use all seven letters in Scrabble. Also, the letters are selected at random and may not work together to form any word.

TECHNICAL STUFF

If you use all seven letters in one move, consider yourself an ace. Using all seven letters in a single move (called a "scrabble," "slam," or "bingo") earns you a bonus of 50 points.

The tiles

The distribution of popular letters from crosswords in English applies in Scrabble, too. Tiles are divided so that E rules. Distribution of letters in order from most to least is as follows:

- **E** = 12
- **A and I** = 9
- **O** = 8
- **N, R, and T** = 6
- **D, L, S, and U** = 4
- **G** = 3
- **B, C, F, H, M, P, V, W, and Y** = 2
- **J, K, Q, X, and Z** = 1

You also find two blank tiles, which can be used to represent any letter. A total of 100 points are available in the tiles.

Each letter has a point value on a scale from one to ten, with E at the low end with a value of one and Z worth ten points at the high end. The challenge is to earn the higher score by using a less popular letter in your move. In addition, you may assign any letter value to the two blank tiles when you use them, although they have no point value.

The value of your leftover tiles is deducted from your total score. It behooves you to use the higher-value tiles right off the bat.

The board grid

A black star against a pink background lies at the center of the diagram on the board. That star indicates where the opening move is placed. From that star, four diagonal lines reach to the corners of the grid. The diagonal lines include colorful squares that change the value of your entry word:

- **Light blue:** Double Letter Score
- **Dark blue:** Triple Letter Score
- **Pink:** Double Word Score
- **Deep pink:** Triple Word Score

When a player sets a word across one of these colorful squares, the score reflects the additional amount indicated in the highlighted square.

What's the Swedish word for Scrabble?

The magazine *Financial World* estimated 1995 sales under the Scrabble brand name at $39 million, which tells you something about the Scrabble game's timeless and universal appeal. You can buy Scrabble in 31 languages in over 100 countries.

Strategy and tips

Experts recommend that your rack of letters is balanced, with a mix of vowels and consonants. If you find your rack heavy in either direction, you may elect to skip a turn, throw your tiles back, and select a new rack of letters.

Scrabble champions Nick Ballard and Joseph Cortese of Chicago have identified various racks that combine well on the board. One winning sequence is SATIRE. The letters in this word can be rearranged into anagrams when combined with another letter, such as:

- Retails
- Baiters

A champion player aims to make a scrabble in the first four moves and again in the final four, where the average game lasts 15 rounds.

Words beginning with capital letters are not allowed in Scrabble. These include geographical references and proper names. Although some Scrabble champions train by solving crosswords, this is not universally acceptable because crosswords contain many proper names and abbreviations, neither of which are permitted in the Scrabble arena.

In general, if you keep the following in mind, you'll do well at the board:

- Save potential suffixes ING, TION, and EST for possible bingos.
- Go for bonus boxes whenever possible.
- Use more than one letter per move.
- Make "hook" words that enable you to add on a letter in your next move. For example, GAM becomes GAM+E when you add a crossing word later.

Playing serious Scrabble: Scrabble tournaments

In order to get into the tournament circuit, you have to belong to a club and earn a rating by playing a round. The National Scrabble Association (NSA), a subsidiary of Milton Bradley, licenses these events. Membership ($18 a year) is encouraged in order to participate officially. You can obtain information by writing to the NSA at 120 Front Street Garden, P.O. Box 700, Greenport, NY 11944.

Under tournament conditions, you can expect two aspects of the game to gain new meaning: namely, time allocation per move and validity of words:

- **Time per move:** According to tournament rules, 25 minutes is the maximum amount of time allotted per move. In a game where each player may make ten moves or so, this limit is a blessing. For those players who go over the limit, the penalty is ten points per minute.
- **Word validity:** The bible of Scrabble is the *Official Scrabble Players Dictionary* (OSPD, to those Scrabblers in the know). If a player challenges the opponent's move, the clock stops while a neutral party checks the source. If the word proves unacceptable for any reason, the player who made that word loses that turn. If the word is approved, the challenger may lose a turn under North American rules.

Another club for puzzle people

If you're looking for like-minded puzzle lovers but don't necessarily want to compete, The National Puzzlers League may fit the bill. Members communicate through a newsletter, *The Enigma*, which is chockablock with brainteasers and other such posers. Every member goes by a special handle or nickname. (*New York Times* puzzle editor Will Shortz, for example, is *Willz.*) Nearly every tournament winner is a member, which tells you something about the caliber of those who belong. For more information on the NPL, visit the club's Web site at www.puzzlers.org/.

Scrabble dictionaries

The last word for Scrabble players in North America is the *Official Scrabble Players Dictionary* (OSPD), published by Merriam Webster in hard or soft cover. It contains words limited to eight letters or less.

For words over eight letters (if your game includes entries of that length), players refer to *Merriam Webster's Collegiate Dictionary,* 10th edition.

Overseas, the Scrabble player's source is *Chambers Dictionary,* which lists Official Scrabble Words (OSW) in a separate form. Because the OSW include many foreign words excluded from the OSPD, its lexicon is richer.

Scrabble clubs

Milton Bradley supervises the National Scrabble Association (NSA), which licenses tournaments and club directors. With more than 100 clubs in the North American division, chances are you live near one. If not, the NSA can help you start one. A newsletter circulates the latest information in the field, including tips on improving your game. Annual dues of $18 entitle you to play in tournaments nationwide.

You can contact the NSA at the following address:

National Scrabble Association
c/o Williams & Company
120 Front Street Garden
P.O. Box 700
Greenport, NY 11944
info@scrabble-assoc.com

For instant information on a club near you, check the Milton Bradley Web site at www.scrabble.com/home/htm.

Scrabble clubs are recruiting everywhere, and English-language players may pick up a game as they travel. Here are some far-flung places of interest to the player on the road. You can contact these clubs on the Internet at the following addresses:

- **The Australian Scrabble Players Association:** rjackman@ozemail.com.au
- **Jerusalem Scrabble Club:** orbaum@netvision.net.il
- **Thailand Crossword Club:** crosword@ksc.th.com
- **United Kingdom:** J.W. Spear and Sons PLC; 101354.3235@compuserve.com

The ABC's of Scrabble

Poor Alfred Butts, the architect who invented the Criss Cross board game. Although the game he invented in the 1930s has sold consistently over the years under the brand name Scrabble, Butts sold off his rights to his word game in 1948. After unsuccessfully trying to market the game for over ten years, Butts sold his invention to civil servant James Brunot, who went on to the big time with the game when he renamed it Scrabble.

Although Butts couldn't interest manufacturers in his homemade cardboard spelling game, he did attract a small group of enthusiasts among his neighbors. In fact, over time he produced 500 sets for personal friends. The Brunots were among those who had enjoyed playing Criss Cross. After the war, Butts turned his attention back to architecture. Meanwhile, Brunot's position as executive director to the President's War Relief Control Board was winding down. The men struck a deal, and Brunot took out a trademark under the new name of Scrabble.

Until 1952, the Scrabble game posted an annual loss in a limited edition. It was advertised in select places like *The Saturday Review* and *The Smith College Alumnae Quarterly*. Things turned around quickly in the summer of 1952 due to the interest of an influential player, Jack Straus, the owner of Macy's department store. No sooner did he stock up his store than sales shot through the roof. From 18 sets a day, the Brunots suddenly were hit with orders for more than 300 a day. After a week's holiday, the Brunots found back orders for 2,500 sets. They recruited everyone they knew to help fulfill demand. Even with a staff of 35 working double shifts, orders kept stacking up. When they saw no end in sight, Brunot cut a deal with Selchow & Righter, manufacturers of Parcheesi, and, after February 1953, of Scrabble. These days, Milton Bradley (a division of Hasbro, Inc.) owns the Scrabble trademark in the U.S. and Canada, while J.W. Spear and Sons PLC (a subsidiary of Mattel) controls the trademark outside these countries.

Scrabble spin-offs followed in 1957: Travel and Revolving first, then Scrabble for Juniors. When he was approached by a little girl who spoke of her desire to grow up to be able to play Scrabble, Brunot jumped on the idea. The Juniors board has words spelled out so that players must match their tiles to those in the grid. On the reverse side, the board is a version of the adult game for older children.

Other Games with Words

Although Scrabble reigns supreme, some relative newcomers have become modern standards for acrossionados like me who enjoy parlor games. Two standbys are Boggle and Pictionary:

- **Boggle:** A Parker Brothers Hidden Word Game, Boggle is a personal favorite of mine. Like a hidden word puzzle, your challenge is to pick out words from a grid of letters. The letters may connect in any direction, including diagonally, as in a word twist. Any number of players can participate, armed with a pad of paper and pencil. Sixteen lettered cubes are embedded into a 4 x 4 grid with a plastic cover. You shake it roundly and allow the letters to settle into the slots. When the cover is removed, a three-minute timer is set while each player races to list the most words from that grid that consist of three or more letters.
- **Pictionary:** This game is a combination of Hangman, that schoolchild's word game, and Charades. In Hangman one player has a word in mind, represented by a series of dashes. Beside the dashes is a platform with a noose. The guesser starts naming off letters. For each letter that does not appear in the word, the other player draws in a part of the body at the noose. Each letter that does appear in the word gets filled in. The guesser wins if he or she gets all the letters of the word before the entire body is filled in. In Pictionary, one player has a word in mind, which the other players must guess through a series of drawings. Although your artistic skills come in to play, good guesswork on the part of the players is crucial.

Etiquette expert Letitia Baldrige recommends formal solving gatherings to be held after dinner, provided that all are forewarned and that nonplayers may retreat to another room. As a big fan of "Facts in Five," I am all for the return to parlor games.

The ABC *Scrabble* show was the first TV program based on a board game. These days, you may find Pictionary on your local station in the afternoon.

Chapter 16

Finding Puzzle Stuff Online

In This Chapter

- Surfing the World Wide Web in search of puzzles
- Finding free puzzles online
- Bookmarking other types of puzzle sites
- Reading about puzzle contests

If you can't tell the Internet from a castanet, then please feel free to skip this chapter — you can find hundreds of magazines and puzzle books at your local bookstore to keep you busy. (Turn to Chapter 3 for more information on finding a puzzle if you couldn't care less about computers.)

Even if you're new to the Internet, you may have heard about the wide variety of stuff you can find online. The subject of puzzles, naturally, proves no exception. Solvers can have a field day on any one of the scores of puzzle-oriented Web sites — and new puzzle Web sites seem to pop up every day, some offering their goods for free.

The Internet opens up some new angles on solving. When you're not actually solving a puzzle, you may wonder what's going on in the greater world of puzzles — such as who won the last big tournament. You can find out on the Internet. Or you may even want to meet other people who like puzzles. You can find them, too, on the Internet. Solving, which used to be strictly a solitary pastime, has become interactive, thanks to the Internet.

Of course, the Internet changes all the time as Web sites come and go and electronic mail *(e-mail)* addresses change. You may find that some of the sites and addresses listed in this section no longer work — hey, that's just the way it goes in the fast-changing online world. Just keep in mind that search engines (such as Yahoo!, which you can find at `http://www.yahoo.com`) can help you find new sites, and most sites link you to other sites, and so on, and so on.

For the full scoop on the Internet, e-mail, and the World Wide Web, you need to pick up *The Internet For Dummies,* 4th Edition (by John R. Levine, Carol Baroudi, and Margaret Levine Young), or *Netscape and the World Wide Web For Dummies,* 2nd Edition (by Paul Hoffman), both published by IDG Books Worldwide, Inc.

Although you locate the puzzles on your computer, most sites intend for you to print them out and work them the old-fashioned way: on paper with a pencil. Most of the time you need special graphics software (Lyriq, for example) in order to read and print out the grids. Some sites offer the necessary software; just follow the instructions offered at the site for downloading the correct version of the program for your machine.

Finding Free Puzzles Online

What's better than a free puzzle, I ask you? Good quality puzzles, you say? By "name constructors"? You can find a veritable treasure trove of good quality, free crossword puzzles by popular constructors on the World Wide Web. Additionally, you can explore some new horizons, puzzle-wise. I want to clue you in on a few of my favorite sites.

Index of Crossword Puzzles

`http://www.primate.wisc.edu/people/hamel/cp.html`

Ray Hamel, whose work appears in publications like *Games*, maintains this obviously-labeled site. He offers links to hundreds of other crossword-related sites, from original puzzles to newspaper archives, which guarantee hours of amusement. Links also lead to reference information on tournaments and clubs, as well. Puzzlers of every solving level can find something to link to at this page.

MacNamara's Band Crossword Puzzles

`http://www.macnamarasband.com`

The prolific constructor Fred Piscop, whose work appears in *101 Crossword Puzzles For Dummies* (published by IDG Books Worldwide, Inc.) as well as in the Simon & Schuster *Crosswords* series, The Crossword Club, and elsewhere, features about two dozen medium-level 15 x 15 crosswords at this Web site.

In order to print the puzzles on hard copy, you need to download a program called Acrosslite. This program is available for a variety of platforms, including Windows 3.1, Windows 95, Mac, and UNIX. After you download the software, you can either work the puzzles online or print them and work them with your trusty pencil. I highly recommend working at least one puzzle online — the site offers three different layout options for each puzzle, and it's just so cool watching that little hand fill in the letters as you type them in. You just have to try it.

For a fee (visit the site for more information) MacNamara's Band also offers custom puzzle design for corporate purposes (some companies use crossword puzzles in their newsletters and on their Web sites) or for your favorite acrossionado. Just e-mail a topic to MacNamara's Band and receive a uniquely designed crossword for that special occasion or publication.

You may be "puzzled" as to why a crossword Web site is named after a band. This riddle is easy to solve: By day Fred Piscop crafts crosswords, and by night he's a keyboard musician (alias Fred MacNamara) with a special interest in Irish tunes. These days Piscop/MacNamara plays in a band called Wes Houston, which you can find out more about at this site.

Newspaper archives

If you have a hankering for a crossword from a specific publication, or you missed out on your favorite puzzles while on vacation, you may want to research the publication's online archives. In fact, you can get the same-day crossword from these sites everyday if you happen to be away from your newspaper source for any reason. Here are some addresses to get you started:

The Los Angeles Times

`http://www.student.net/xwords`

I can't figure out why this student-oriented Web site archives the *Los Angeles Times* puzzle every day, but it does. Hey, why question good fortune, especially when you can access the past six months of daily puzzles? You can work the puzzles online, or print them and take them to the park.

It took me a while to figure out how to work the puzzle online, so let me tell you how to do it, just to save you the trouble. First of all, the page is packed with advertisements, and so I didn't even see the clues on the left-hand side of the page until I really concentrated! To answer a clue, click either the Across or Down box (whatever is appropriate for the clue), type in your entry, and then click the first box in the grid for the entry. Your answer should appear! You can save a puzzle and come back to it later if you want — now that's what I call service.

Multimedia (TV Guide)

`http://www.tvguide.com/tv/xwords/archives.htm`

Sorry Mac users — only Windows 95, Windows NT, and Windows 3.1 users can download the MultiMedia Crossword Software needed to read the puzzles available from this Web site. After downloading the software, treat yourself to a puzzle from the archive, which lists puzzles from almost two years ago. All the puzzles come directly from the weekly publication *TV Guide.*

NY Newsday

`http://www2.uclick.com/client/new/cx/`

Don't be intimidated by the solving clock that starts ticking as soon as you click the first square of the puzzle on this page. Go ahead and take all the time you want to enjoy this very handy page. You get a daily crossword, plus tons of help, if you want it.

The site offers a Solve Letter button if you want a leg-up on a particular square; click the Solve Word button if you can't get past a troublesome clue; or click the Solve Puzzle button if you give up on the whole darned puzzle. And if you don't like one puzzle, just click the Archive button, and you see a list of puzzles (from up to a month ago) to choose from.

The New York Times Archives

`http://www.nytimes.com/diversions/welcome.html`

This service is free if you have a seven-day subscription to *The New York Times.* If you don't, you need to subscribe to the service (which currently costs about $10.00). Instructions at the site walk you through the process of signing up.

In addition to the daily and Sunday crossword puzzles, you also get the puzzle that appears at the bottom of the Sunday page and access to a puzzle archive and online chat forum. If you aren't sure you want to sign up, click the Samples button to see a sampling of the goods.

The Washington Post

`http://www.washingtonpost.com/wp-srv/style/longterm/cross/crossw.htm`

If you're a Sunday puzzle lover, you should bookmark this Web site. Every week *The Washington Post* puts its famed Sunday puzzle up at this site for you to work online. You can choose from puzzles from the last two months.

Puzzability

`http://www.puzzability.com`

You get crosswords plus riddle-based and visual puzzles from Puzzability. Daily or weekly puzzles are available at this site from three top-flight constructors (and former *Games* magazine editors) Mike Shenk, Robert Leighton, and Amy Goldstein.

Special puzzle features at this site include a hangman-type word game entitled *Common Knowledge* for which you need a Java-enabled browser; wordplay in the form of a Daily Poser competition, for which subscribers may earn a slot in the Web site's Hall of Fame; a Teaser of the Week, which is a challenge using words that is guaranteed to get you thinking; and a visual puzzle (called *Two Timers*). Some interactive puzzles are available from time to time. These folks also offer custom puzzle design for a fee to corporate or private clients.

Puzzle Depot

`http://www.puzzledepot.com/index.shtml`

Puzzle Depot operates both as a library and as a clearing house for updates in the world of puzzles. In addition to a variety of sample puzzles, this site supplies information about the latest board games, software, educational materials, and book collections. You can get news on upcoming puzzle contests, as well, in the weekly newsletter. This site also offers links to non-crossword puzzle sites that may be of interest, such as the Enchanted Mind, and a chat room.

Web Word Search

`http://www.geocities.com/WestHollywood/2555/puzzle.html`

Plain and simple, Web Word Search provides a wide selection of word searches on topics such as television, movies, and sports, as well as mazes, which are visual puzzles that lead you through winding pathways to a goal (see Chapter 4 for more information on word searches). Each puzzle is rated with stars according to the following scale so that you can find a puzzle that's right for you:

- **One Star:** Piece of Cake!
- **Two Stars:** Getting Harder
- **Three Stars:** Medium to Hard
- **Four Stars:** Pretty Darn Difficult!
- **Five Stars:** Are you Nuts?!

Word Puzzle of the Week

`http://www.smartcode.com/isshtml/weekwsk.htm`

This site offers a variety of puzzles, and a new challenge is posted every Tuesday. For example, this week the site offers an enormous word search called "X" Words. The people behind this Web site must really put time into designing these puzzles — "X" Words is a beautiful red puzzle with an "X" design cut out of the middle. Much better than any dull black-and-white word search.

To work the puzzles, just print them from within your browser and go for it with a pen or pencil.

Wordsearch Center

`http://www.geocities.com/Enchanted Forest/1786/alpha.htm`

A selection of more than 200 puzzles of all types are available at this site for the puzzle glutton. You can choose from puzzles of every shape, size, and difficulty range. Just visit the site and follow the instructions that you find there — this well constructed site will lead you directly to exactly the puzzle you crave.

Educators may want to visit sites that link to Wordsearch Center, which feature material geared to grammar school students. Christmas Word Search Puzzles, for example, leads to seasonal puzzles, while Early American Crossword Puzzles are designed to instruct as well as entertain.

Paying the Price for Online Puzzles

Some sites charge a small fee for the privilege of belonging to a club of solvers who specialize in a certain type of word game. You gain entry to these sites by using a password that the site sends you after you submit a credit card number for billing purposes. The password entitles you to access a download area where you can make your puzzle selection.

American Cryptogram Association (ACA)

`http://www.und.nodak.edu/org/crypto/crypto`

Sorry, Charlie, you gotta pay to get in here, but you do get what you pay for, which is top-notch cryptograms (see Chapter 4 for more information on cryptograms). The ACA has published a bimonthly journal of coded messages composed by its members since 1932. At last count, 700 people are actively enrolled in this intellectually challenging and entertaining pursuit. Visit the site for instructions on getting started with cryptograms and the ACA.

ClueMaster

`http://www.cluemaster.com`

The solver with an appetite for cryptics may click in as a guest and access archived material at no charge (check out Chapter 13 to find out everything you need to know about the cryptic puzzle). Members receive new puzzles for a nominal fee. Special features at this site include the following:

- A jumbo-sized 25 x 25 cryptic crossword known as the *2-Way Giant,* which comes with two sets of clues. One set of clues is in standard cryptic format, such as "One of a pair upset for example by sudden pain (6)"; the other is a straightforward dictionary definition, such as "Sudden pain (6)". (See Chapter 13 for more information on the cryptic puzzle and its clue structure.)
- 50 daily-size crosswords that you can sit down and work quickly.

- Logic puzzles, which require you to make connections between variables in an everyday situation.
- A set of FAQs (frequently asked questions) about puzzles of every kind.

Because British *setters* (constructors) create these puzzles, clues may not follow the standards developed among American cryptic folks. Just think of the British lingo as an extra hurdle in the solving process — or a bonus, depending upon your point of view.

Crossword America

`http://www.crosswordamerica.com`

You get a daily-size American-style puzzle every weekday during the week and a Sunday puzzle on the weekend at Crossword America. Constructors like Frances Hansen and Alfio Micci, whose work you may be familiar with through other publications, contribute material to this site.

If you have the program Lyriq on your computer, you may choose to download and work the puzzles offline. You can download Lyriq at the site if you don't have it already.

Squizz's Cryptic Crosswords

`http://cuiwww.unige.ch/-squire/cryptics/`

Over two dozen cryptic crosswords by Australian constructor David Squire, offered in various formats, highlight this site. If you enjoy a cryptic crossword challenge, this is the place to be. While the puzzles may seem hard to crack at first, with a little practice you may impress yourself. (Check Chapter 13 for more information on the subject of cryptic crosswords.)

Winning Big at Puzzle Contest Sites

Just to show you the diversity of sites out on the Web for puzzlers, I put together the following collection of sites related to puzzle contests. Surf away and enjoy.

Puzzle Contest Sites

`http://www.yahoo.com/Recreation/Games/Puzzles/Puzzle__Contests`

Maybe you're looking for a little something extra with your solving. You may find that something in a puzzle competition. Most competitions involve word games rather than crosswords. Some online contests actually offer cash prizes without any obligation. Check out the three sites listed at this address for the details.

Puzzles @ Random

`http://www.randomhouse.com25/puzzles/challenge/register.cgi`

Stan Newman, managing director of the puzzle division of Times Books (part of Random House and perhaps the world's largest book publisher of puzzles), maintains this site. To keep surfers up-to-date on the latest puzzle materials produced by Times Books, Stan offers a weekly challenge at this Web site. If you methodically solve the one-a-day crossword clues, by week's end you can identify a secret celebrity through the profile depicted in the answers. (The celebrity may be a real person or a fictional character.) A chat forum allows you to respond and comment on the latest entry. Stan also throws in some solving hints and tips, just to make sure that you walk away satisfied. Three cheers for Stan!

To access sample crosswords at this site, look for the New Releases button, which looks like a book, and click the book's jacket. In any given month, you find about six different books with one puzzle per title featured for your solving pleasure.

Riddler

`http://www.riddler.com`

Riddler offers a choice of daily riddles from a contest puzzle site. From trivia to crossword competitions, you may select from a range of puzzle categories. To qualify for prizes, you need to register. (If you don't care about the prizes, you may play without registering.) As you play, you accumulate tokens that you can later redeem for prizes.

Yoyodyne

`http://www.yoyo.com`

Here's your chance to win a free vacation. By participating in trivia contests via e-mail, you may be eligible for some big-ticket items. Contest subjects vary widely, but an interest in sweepstakes helps.

Miscellaneous Puzzle Sites

When you just can't get enough of puzzles, you may want to try any of the following sites, which are definitely for the confirmed puzzle addict.

The Cruciverbalist

`http://www.cruciverb.com`

This site is the place to eavesdrop on conversations among noted American constructors as they trade quips, help, and advice on an electronic message board. The thrust is on American-style puzzles. If you have any serious desire to construct, this is the place to see and be seen.

National Puzzlers' League

`http://www.puzzlers.org`

For $13 a year you can enjoy the company of the country's top puzzlesmiths through a monthly publication, *The Enigma,* produced by the National Puzzlers League. While many eminent crossword constructors are members, the material in *The Enigma* focuses exclusively on word games. (A sample from the publication is available on the site.)

Currently over 300 members participate in the fun and games. Each member assumes a *nom de plume* upon joining and uses that sobriquet in all correspondence. The league historian Willz (better known as Will Shortz, puzzle editor of *The New York Times*), chairs the League's annual convention, which takes place in Connecticut.

Words and Stuff

`http://kith.org/logos/words/words.htm/`

If you're interested in words, you may find this weekly column by Jed Hartman of interest.

Sometimes older is better

One expert constructor observed that because portability is key to solving pleasure, the Internet can never fully replace paper and pencil in this hobby. Unless you have a laptop with you at all times, when the urge to solve hits, you may need to grab a newspaper, book, or magazine for instant puzzle gratification.

Part V
The Part of Tens

In this part . . .

In this part of the book, I give you a quick rundown on important puzzle people, solver types, frequently asked questions, and solving tips. Hey, and if that wasn't enough for one part, I also give you ten practice puzzles that you can really cut your teeth on.

Chapter 17

Ten Puzzle VIPs

In This Chapter

- Arthur Wynne
- Margaret Farrar
- Will Weng
- Eugene Maleska
- Will Shortz
- Stan Newman
- Elizabeth Kingsley
- Doris Wortman
- Thomas H. Middleton
- Edward Powys Mather
- Derrick Mcnutt

Crosswords are the million-dollar industry they are today thanks to the efforts of a handful of talented and motivated editors and a select group of prolific constructors. The rare soul sets out to be a puzzle professional, although the field is a dynamic one that seems to be growing constantly. At the risk of starting an argument, in this chapter I focus on ten key people who have guided the puzzle industry (meaning American and cryptic crosswords and the acrostic) to its current level of popularity. (The names I mention in this chapter may already be familiar to you if you've been reading other chapters of this book.)

As one generation of puzzle pros passes the baton to the next one, the crossword continues on its fluid evolutionary course. Here are the folks who led the way, presented by puzzle type, in the order in which they appeared on the scene.

Crosswords

Without the hard work and inspiration of the creative word-loving people listed here, I wouldn't be writing this book today. Since 1913 the work of a handful of people who take fun very seriously has impacted the 20th century in a profound way. What could possibly take the place of the ubiquitous crossword puzzle? Neither television nor the Internet has yet toppled its hold on people's scraps of free time or captured their collective imaginations.

Arthur Wynne

Why do inventors never seem to collect the financial rewards on their great ideas? Crosswords are no exception. The brilliant mastermind behind crossword puzzles belonged to Arthur Wynne, an editor at *The New York Sunday World.* A native of Liverpool, England, Wynne was weaned on the clever puzzles in the Riddle Box section of the popular British children's magazine, *St. Nicholas.*

The source of inspiration for the first crossword may have been a puzzle that Wynne spotted in *The London Graphic,* a colleague later speculated. That puzzle was a geometric shape built from words. Faced with a deadline to come up with a puzzle for the eight-page Fun supplement of *The World* just before the holidays in 1913, Wynne recalled this diverting puzzle. Rather than come up with one more enigma or riddle (typical Fun fare), he decided to devise something new. A little sketching produced a diamond-shaped grid of 31 odd and pedantic words that read differently across and down. He numbered the entries and spent a few more hours hammering out a list of clues. Despite protests from the layout department, which viewed the puzzle as a graphic headache, the *Word Cross* made its debut that December. When readers sent in requests for more, the Word Cross became a regular Sunday feature.

When did the Word Cross become *Cross-Word?* During the month following its debut. Perhaps the instructions ("Find the missing cross words") influenced the title change.

Almost immediately, Wynne began to solicit freelance crossword puzzles from readers, who were happy to oblige. Until 1924, the Cross-Word continued in this way as a local feature, moving from the Fun section to the Sunday magazine as space permitted.

Wynne retired from puzzles in 1920, after years of fielding complaints about missing numbers and clues. With *New York Tribune* columnist Franklin P. Adams on his case to improve the crossword's quality, Wynne decided to appoint a full-time person to the department. Little did he know that this new person, Margaret Farror, was to set the crossword on a meteoric rise in its fortunes in the next four years.

Margaret Farrar

Imagine that your first job out of college had such worldwide impact that it changed the course of the publishing industry and created a universal sensation. That's the story of Margaret Farrar, NEE ("Wedding announcement word") Petherbridge, whose career began after World War I. Margaret Farrar started it all — the ongoing crossword series for Simon & Schuster, *The New York Times* crossword, and the *Los Angeles Times* syndicated puzzle.

Fresh out of Smith College, Margaret joined the staff of *The New York World* in an entry-level job. By 1921, her editorial duties included a pesky little feature peculiar to that newspaper — the crossword. Arthur Wynne, her boss, had designed the pencil game some eight years earlier and was losing interest in it, so Margaret inherited a drawerful of clues and diagrams.

At first, Margaret was cavalier about her position as keeper of the puzzles. But after receiving complaints from readers who were upset about absent clues or misnumbered grids, she changed her tune and her system. The editor herself subjected each puzzle to a rigorous test-solving prior to publication. At that point, Petherbridge took a vow on a stack of dictionaries to improve the quality of the crossword. Ultimately, her oath produced a healthy global industry that shows no signs of old age.

The watershed year for puzzles (and Margaret) was 1924. Two young Columbia graduates, a Mr. Richard Simon and a Mr. Max Schuster, approached the puzzle editor with an idea for a crossword collection. On a hunch that the puzzle could attract a wider audience, the enterprising publishers went to the one and only source of the game: Margaret. With the assistance of two newspaper colleagues, Prosper Buranelli and Gregory Hartswick, each editor pocketed a $25 advance and set to work. Publication date was April 1924; by year's end, the volume had set a record in sales — over 150,000 copies. Not only did the book launch the Simon & Schuster company, but proceeds went toward establishing a second publishing house — known as Farrar, Straus, Giroux.

Naturally, the mother of crosswords conducted all her correspondence on graph paper. In 1979, I received a graph-paper note from Margaret about a letter she had received from an unhappy solver in Denver. After a 15-year hiatus, this solver had returned to puzzles and found them lacking in "the educational premise." Margaret begged to differ with this view. She acknowledged that over time, crosswords had expanded to include phrases and slang entries so that constructors gained additional options in the making of puzzles. And these new entries were meant to inject fun — "wholesome fun, a good time," as Margaret said in her missive to me. She based her philosophy on good taste and the motto "Good news preferred." According to Margaret, finding out something new along the way serves as a bonus rather than the goal.

Margaret's final pronouncement to me on the game was that *a solver should emerge feeling refreshed and accomplished.* As for herself, the reward that she claimed was a ragbag vocabulary. Her legacy, in addition to the worldwide pastime at large, is the Margaret Award, which the Simon & Schuster folks bestow upon one especially clever puzzle in each of their puzzle collections.

Will Weng

Most observers agree that *The New York Times* has wielded tremendous influence in the field of the American crossword, and that Will Weng played a major role during his tenure as Margaret's successor.

When Margaret reached mandatory retirement age at *The New York Times,* management had no idea where to turn for a replacement. The only in-house candidate appeared to be the head of the Metropolitan copy desk, namely Will Weng, an occasional constructor. Circumstances threw him into the post, without any proper training, while Margaret was in bed with the flu. He spent his first year keeping his head down as acrossionados threw tomatoes his way. Any successor was bound to suffer from fallout after the long reign of "Mrs. Crossword." (Even puzzles that had been edited by Margaret but printed under Weng's byline were criticized publicly by noted solvers such as authors Jean Stafford and E.J. Kahn.)

Eventually, Weng asserted his editorial style, characterized by a tongue-in-cheek tone. Light-hearted experimentation and an extensive and graceful command of idiom were his stock in trade: He believed that the crossword was a game without any educational merit. Soon he jettisoned three themes perpetually submitted by new constructors, his personal peeves:

- **The Bermuda onion school of crosswords:** No more countries and foods combined (for example, BRUSSELS SPROUTS or FRENCH TOAST)
- **The Blue Danube school of crosswords:** No more colorful geographical locations
- **Farewell to Hemingway:** No more ERNEST HEMINGWAY, A FAREWELL TO ARMS, and THE SUN ALSO RISES, despite their 15-letter configurations

Instead, Weng looked for innovations such as theme entries that read backwards or omit vowels. He also introduced the pun clue, which I discuss in Chapter 12.

Despite his penchant for fun and different approaches, he never cottoned to the cryptic (see Chapter 13), which he called a "pointless exercise with a perverted sense of humor." Weng claimed that his greatest achievement during his tenure on the *Times* puzzle page was keeping the page cryptic free.

Eugene Maleska

As a lovestruck college student, Eugene Maleska created his first crossword in 1934 as a valentine in tribute to his future wife, Jean. Little did he know to what proportions this labor of love would grow.

Upon retiring as Bronx Assistant Superintendent of Schools in 1977, Dr. Maleska embarked on a second career as puzzle editor for *The New York Times* crossword and co-editor of the Simon & Schuster puzzle series with John Samson.

Maleska's puzzle career was not without its bumps. He weathered an estimated 40 rejections by the puzzle editor at the *New York Herald Tribune* before his first acceptance in 1943. Based on that success, he began to contribute puzzles to Margaret Farrar at *The New York Times.* Together they collaborated on the following innovations that have become industry standards:

- The use of phrases as single entries
- The introduction of the *Stepquote,* which spells out an excerpt from a literary source in zigzag course from the upper left to the lower right of the completed grid

Because of his background as a professional educator, Maleska approached puzzles as learning tools. He reduced the number of words in the grid from 80 to 76 in order to open the crossword to longer entries. As for clues, he favored rhyming pairs, as in "Tot's cot" for CRIB. A published poet, he did his best to marry his two passions where possible.

Will Shortz

Whether you realize it or not, you're familiar with the work of prolific puzzle master Will Shortz. He's the mastermind behind the quips used by *Batman*'s Riddler, as portrayed by Jim Carrey. His voice enters the homes of National Public Radio listeners each Sunday as the Puzzle Master on Weekend Edition with Liane Hansen. (Overseas, he broadcasts puzzle news on Radio Free Europe.) One of the original masterminds behind *Games* magazine, his byline has appeared both as constructor and editor. He is the author of a series of books called *Brain Games* and serves as coordinator and host of the American Crossword Tournament, which he founded (see Chapter 14 for more information on the tournament).

What kind of credentials do you need to be a puzzle wunderkind? A degree in the study of puzzles (enigmatology) from a curriculum that Shortz developed at Indiana University, for starters. A law degree from the University from Virginia doesn't hurt. (Shortz has yet to put that degree into practice.)

Although he began his career as a constructor in the fourth grade, he entered the field professionally in high school. Shortz' extensive personal collection of all things related to puzzles reflects his unabated passion for the subject.

As the fourth (and youngest ever) editor of *The New York Times* crossword, Shortz is leading that puzzle institution into the next millennium. One of his first innovations as *Times* editor was to credit the constructors of the daily crossword by inserting a byline below the left corner of the grid. A second innovation is allowing the use of brand names, in a campaign to keep crosswordese to a minimum. Wordplay is the rule rather than the exception on his clock. But Shortz hasn't changed the way the *Times* crossword challenge escalates during the week: The ones in the Monday edition are the easiest, with the level of difficulty building up to Sunday. (Some folks would argue that Saturday is the toughest of all.)

Stan Newman

Stan Newman won three crossword tournaments in 1982, worth $2,000 in prize money. After setting the world record in speed solving (under three minutes for a *New York Times* daily), he retired from competition undefeated. At the same time, he switched career paths from bond analyst to self-described "crossword crusader."

The closest thing to a crossword activist, Newman is a visible and vocal force on the solving scene. Currently the managing director for the puzzles and games division of Times Books, Newman began his puzzle career with a newsletter on the subject sponsored by his organization, the American Crossword Federation. Originally, his gripe with puzzles was that they included too many obscure terms. He "cured" this problem by launching his own brand of syndicated crossword with *Newsday.* Now he's on a campaign to bring in new solvers through contests in bookstores as well as on the Times Book Web site (`www.puzzles atrandom.com`). The way he sees solving, the key to sharpening your skills is to evaluate where you are and then devise a program to grow stronger.

A believer in populist puzzles, he encourages slang and pop entries. According to Newman, good puzzles shouldn't require a trip to the library. His philosophy: After you get the answer, you should say "Ah!" not "Huh?"

Acrostics

In the 1930s, a decade after the crossword craze swept the world, a new style of puzzle that became known as the *acrostic* came on the scene. Chess is to checkers as acrostics are to crosswords: in other words, acrostics are more challenging than the average crossword puzzle. Turn to Chapter 11 for more information on the acrostic.

Elizabeth Kingsley

Some solvers wonder about the educational value of the crossword; others do something about it. Mrs. Kingsley leads as a do-something type-solver. A reunion at her alma mater, Wellesley College, spurred her into action some 65 years ago. Concern about how the galloping popularity of James Joyce was overtaking the classics on campus gave her pause. Determined to promote her personal favorites (Shakespeare, Defoe, and Keats), she went home, grabbed her anagram tiles (the predecessor of Scrabble tiles), and set to work. She named her invention the *Double Crostic* and bought the copyright.

A literary influence is the heart of the double crostic: The diagram contains a quote or book excerpt spelled out in a rectangular grid. The clues are straightforward dictionary definitions. The "double" aspect of the puzzle is in the bonus you find in the answers to the clues: The initial letters, when connected vertically, spell out the author and title of the work from which the excerpt comes.

For her first subject, Mrs. Kingsley selected Alfred Lord Tennyson's "Ulysses" — possibly a dig at Joyce's version. The *Saturday Review* published her first double crostic effort on March 31, 1934, bought the copyright, and kept Mrs. Kingsley in business submitting a double crostic weekly through the end of 1952. In fact, the magazine kept the puzzle on as a regular feature until the *Review* folded and passed the trademark along to *The Nation,* where it now resides.

"Our Queen Elizabeth," as fans called her, held court while she worked. Seated with anagram tiles strewn on a black velvet cloth in front of her, she welcomed interruptions. Admirers included Cole Porter and Ogden Nash, who claimed that "Double Crostics have saved my sanity in the grim loneliness of hotel rooms when I lecture my way around the country." In the days before e-mail, this industrious lady kept up a hectic correspondence with many of an estimated 10,000 fans. The *Crostics Club* column that accompanied the puzzle provided a forum to the regular readership. Her work was so all-consuming that she never had time to check out the "competition" — crossword puzzles.

According to a reliable source (Margaret Farrar), Mrs. Kingsley spoke of little else but the Double Crostic in her later years. During her lifetime, she produced more than 2,500 of these clever puzzles. With such an invention to her credit, I suppose she was entitled to brag.

Doris Wortman

In 1952, Kingsley handed over her prize jewel, the Double Crostic, to her editor, Doris Wortman. Mrs. Wortman's credentials were excellent: She'd been proofreading Double Crostics for the Simon and Schuster series and had taken over Double Crostic editorial responsibility at the *Saturday Review* in 1944. But her presence was very much behind-the-scenes. When the first Wortman constructed D-C appeared in the pages of the *Saturday Review,* she was unknown by the solvers. To ease the transition, the puzzle retained its original name as the Kingsley Double Crostic.

According to Wortman, her relationship with Kingsley, "was a pleasant union of Smith and Wellesley," referring to their alma maters. Less academically narrow than her predecessor, Wortman expanded into contemporary authors and relied on her memory rather than reference books. Occasionally, she indulged her own fanciful phrases. For example, she clued GIRAFFE'S EYE as the entry for "The corn is evidently higher than Hammerstein thought." (It's ELEPHANT'S EYE in the "Oklahoma" song.)

Despite the license she took with her clues, Wortman dedicated herself to her puzzle work. Her daughter reported that she worked without a break from 5:00 am until nearly midnight every day. Part of her dedication, it was later revealed, was due to the fact that she was the family breadwinner. While Mr. Wortman tried to find work, the family lived on the $15,000 salary that the Double Crostic afforded her.

Eventually, the liberties Wortman took with her word lists brought her down. When author Laura Z. Hobson was named puzzle editor, it was the beginning of the end for the Wortman era. Hobson killed two puzzles that she considered unsuitable (one quotation was anti-labor, the other a downbeat poem on the assassination of John F. Kennedy).

Thomas H. Middleton

If ever a byline and a puzzle have become one and the same, it's the acrostic and Thomas H. Middleton. Middleton is a one-man industry, having picked up where Elizabeth Kingsley left off (with Doris Wortman in between). For over 30 continuous years, this prolific constructor and former professional actor has produced quality acrostics.

As with most puzzle VIPs, Middleton stumbled into his position. In 1967, The *Saturday Review* was desperate for a Double Crostic constructor when Mrs. Wortman, Mrs. Kingsley's successor, passed away. Only a handful of people were eligible to handle the post. The decision was left to Laura Z. Hobson, the author, double crostic enthusiast, and friend of the magazine's editor, Norman Cousins. As it happened, she selected Thomas Middleton as the most qualified candidate. (By the way, Mrs. Middleton, nee Cousins, is the sister of Norman.)

Over the years, this master constructor has provided *The New York Times* with two acrostics per month and produced books of the puzzles for Simon & Schuster, as well as the weekly acrostic that now appears in *The Nation.* He designs his clues to be fair and accessible to all. A gentleman compiler, he includes chapter and verse in missing-word clues from sources such as Shakespeare or the Bible. Although reference books are more widely condoned with the acrostic, expert solvers resent Middleton's hints, but he points out that the more experienced solvers are free to ignore such references.

One of the strangest queries Middleton says he's encountered over the years came from a fan who was unclear about the format: She worked the acrostic by placing the answers directly into the grid rather than filling in the word list first (you can read more about the acrostic in Chapter 11). She wondered what those horizontal spaces were meant for. (She'd completely missed the double message of the author and title spelled out in the initial letters of the answer list.) Putting a positive spin on his answer, Middleton replied that "One of the things that sets puzzle-heads off from the saner members of society is that we do enjoy making things tougher for ourselves."

Cryptics

Diabolical, that's what cryptic puzzle constructors are. When the crossword hit the shores of England in the 1920s, it acquired a new format that took hold of the English populous. Eventually, Americans grew curious about the cryptic, which only began to develop a following in America after the 1980s.

Turn to Chapter 13 for more information about the cryptic.

Edward Powys Mather

Shortly after the crossword reached England's shores in 1925, the British press debated how long it would take for the fad to fizzle out. What they hadn't bargained on was the magic of cryptic constructor Edward Powys Mather. A literary critic and translator, Mather insidiously transformed the American crossword into the witty cryptic. Mather took it upon himself to experiment with the clue structure and came up with some diabolical results.

At first, Mather circulated his puzzles privately among his friends. One of these recipients was a literary agent, who recognized an opportunity to promote this new type of puzzle. Although concerned about his academic reputation, Mather relented — by publishing these crosswords under a pseudonym. Under the heading "Crosswords for Riper Years," *The Saturday Westminster* published Mather's puzzles with the byline "Torquemada" (the Spanish Grand Inquisitor). By 1926, he was ensconced as the puzzle compiler for the *Observer,* a post that he held until he died.

Mather was convinced that the puzzle audience was divided into low- and highbrow categories. For his highbrow following, he abandoned the black-and-white diagram for the bar grid, which became his trademark. At the same time, he discarded the notion of symmetry. In this way, "Torquemada" developed the ground rules for the cryptic crossword and its distinctive types of clues (see Chapter 13 for more on the cryptic crossword).

During his lifetime, Mather revealed little about the creative process. After his death, however, Mrs. Mather told all. Each puzzle took two hours of effort, and Mr. Mather preferred to work in the bedroom or the garden. After he selected a topic and listed related words, Mrs. Mather constructed the diagram.

With the cryptic, each clue is a unique invention. Mrs. Mather discovered that over the course of time, her husband had come up with 50 different clues for the same entry.

Derrick Macnutt

Senior Classics Master at Christ's Hospital School in England, Derrick Macnutt took over from "Torquemada" in 1939. In keeping with his position, he assumed the name of the original Torquemada's successor as his pseudonym: Ximenes. (Originally, he'd used the pseudonym Tesremos, which is Somerset backwards.) For decades to follow, Macnutt contributed two cryptics per month to the *Sunday Observer,* each of which he knocked out in about 90 minutes. During his lifetime, he created about 1,200 puzzles in total. Ximenes favored unkeyed letters (those surrounded by black squares) and symmetrical diagrams.

Recognizing that puzzles lovers come in two varieties (the passionate solver and the occasional one), Macnutt catered to both. For the former, he produced the *Observer* puzzles, complete with a contest. For the latter, he created the solver-friendly Everyman series.

A sociable man, "Mr. X" encouraged competition among *Observer* fans. He regularly offered an award to the solver who could create a clever cryptic clue. Periodically, his readers honored him with a special dinner to mark certain milestones, a tradition that outlasted his work. The event even caught the attention of *Time Magazine,* which covered the celebration of Ximenes' 200th crossword in 1952.

Macnutt wrote the first book on cryptic construction, *Ximenes on the Art of the Crossword Puzzle.* A devout disciple of "Torquemada," he also adhered to the "square dealing" philosophy of the father of the modern cryptic, Afrit (also known as Alistair Ferguson Ritchie, 1887 to 1954). A phrase adapted from Lewis Carroll's Mad Hatter forms the basis of this philosophy: "You need not mean what you say, but you must say what you mean." (If you've ever attempted to decipher a cryptic clue, you can appreciate this bit of advice.) Ximenes maintained that the solver prefers entries based on a vocabulary familiar to the man on the street. In other words, the entries must be everyday idioms, no matter how wacky the clue sounds.

Personally, Macnutt confessed once that "only a lunatic with a distorted mind could devote his life to constructing these fiendish puzzles."

Afrit a cryptic man, just like his puzzles

The cryptics of Alistair Ritchie (Afrit), which appeared in the BBC publication, the *Listener,* are the forerunners of the modern cryptic. Unfortunately, not much is known about this great constructor. The headmaster of Wells Cathedral by day, Afrit left his puzzles to posterity in a volume called *Armchair Crosswords* (which is now out of print).

Chapter 18
Ten Solver Types

In This Chapter

- Revealing your inner puzzler
- Gaining insight on the scope of the solver's universe

In the other chapters of this book, you explore the universe of puzzles and get a basic grasp of the elements involved. However, in this chapter, I invite you to turn your focus to the most important element of the puzzle universe: You.

Who Is the Typical Solver?

In my 20 years of professional puzzling, I've met the gamut of solvers. The thing I have noticed most is the diversity of folks who seem to flock to solving puzzles. Why others tend to clump the puzzle dabbler together with the confirmed acrossionado under one umbrella is beyond me. That whole way of thinking totally ignores one of the great things about puzzle solving — puzzles are a great pastime because they offer something to interest everyone. From "can't concentrate" to "speed solver," you can find something for every level and personality in the world of puzzledom.

Of course, you must dispel any preconceived notion of John or Jane Q. Solver as an opinionated, hypereducated, nerdy know-it-all. Okay, a small band of puzzle solvers *do* come across as unbearably patronizing — every hobby has its spoilsports. If you happen to meet someone who speaks in anagrams, my advice is to run in the opposite direction. But why let a stereotype ruin your fun?

The Rooster: Rise and Solve

The everyday type of crossword solver is the Rooster. Much like a vitamin, one-a-day is the rule for this confirmed puzzler. The wake-up call includes a hot cup of coffee and a crossword — one to wake the body, the other to wake the brain, and each equally indispensable. (That's how I got started.)

Usually, the Rooster was raised on puzzles, as "Oscar contender Celeste" (HOLM) has told me she was. Like brushing your teeth, the habit sticks with you for life.

The Commuter: Next Stop — Puzzles!

The Commuter has a mandate to complete the puzzle within a prescribed amount of time, whether it's the time it takes the bus to cross town or the brief interlude while waiting for the train. The Commuter gets a special thrill from the challenge of finishing the puzzle before her or she reaches the appointed destination. (The Rooster and most other puzzlers don't have a vested interest in this bit of bravado.)

Author E.J. Kahn, a Commuter who turned into an Acrossionado, shared with me vivid memories of racing others in the Conrail car en route to New York City from Connecticut. Of course, you need at least one other player to turn solving into a competition. But with puzzles, you don't have far to look to find a sympathetic soul.

The Doodler: Color Me Puzzles

The use of creative solving utensils characterizes the Doodler, who often uses highlighters, markers, rulers, and other tools to add an aesthetic side to the solving experience. After all, the typical black-and-white puzzle grid could use some sprucing up!

Actually, the Doodler's approach is not entirely creative in nature. Many solvers use different colors of ink to help them gauge the progress that they make on a puzzle during any given sitting.

Pulitzer Prize winner Russell Baker sometimes uses the Doodler's technique when he works an acrostic in more than one sitting. (You can read about acrostics in Chapter 11.)

The Bull: The Solver Sees Red

For some solvers, completing the grid is a matter of pride.The Bull feels compelled to complete every puzzle undertaken — without another solver's help. That personal commitment includes searching for answers, whether by using reference books or by dialing the 900 numbers provided by some newspaper puzzles. For the Bull, the goal is to get those squares filled in any which way and by any means necessary.

Cartoonist Roz Chast captures the frustration of the Bull perfectly in her work entitled "A Toughie." Sometimes Chast struggles between two possible entries, squeezing two letters into a square until she decides on the correct one. Her pet peeve is when the Across entries look correct, but the Down ones make no sense at all. (Roz also fits the Night Owl profile, which you can read about in "The Night Owl: Undercover Work" in this chapter.)

The Jekyll: Two-Dimensional

The Jekyll solver approaches a puzzle expecting to crack another Rosetta Stone. Nothing thrills them more than the challenge of breaking the code, learning the lingo, and deciphering the mindset behind the puzzle.

Author Laura Z. Hobson, who made her name as the author of *Gentleman's Agreement,* was a classic Jekyll. In addition to writing books, she worked as a freelance cryptogram constructor and as puzzle editor for the Double Crostic at *The Saturday Review* for more than two decades (for more information on the cryptogram, see Chapter 4). After she wrote a profile of *Saturday Review* editor Norman Cousins, she eventually took control of the puzzle page at that publication.

The Scoper: The Riddle Unraveler

Know any whiz kids? The type of brain who can eyeball a phrase and then scramble it up to create a suitable anagram from the same letters? These folks are the acrossionados who like to read clues as though they're reading a book and to solve puzzles in their heads without bothering to put pen to paper.

Clues with pizzazz — that's what a Scoper wants. Grids are completely secondary in the solving game. That's why the British-style cryptic crossword puzzle, with its clue structure based on complex wordplay, draws Scopers. Each clue acts as a small riddle unto itself within the greater framework of the crossword. (Find out more about the cryptic crossword in Chapter 13.)

Scratch a librettist and you find a Scoper. Musical folks have a natural affinity to the art of cryptics, ever since Oscar Hammerstein began dabbling with them. Many of the greatest names of contemporary American musical theater are also avid cryptic constructors, such as Stephen Sondheim and Richard Maltby, Jr.

The consummate Scoper is Mike Miller, perhaps the only constructor to be published by *The New York Times* at the age of 13. When I had the pleasure of making his acquaintance in the early 1980s, he observed that baby-sitting pays better than writing puzzles for money. (It still does, which explains why Miller became a reporter for *The Wall Street Journal.*)

The Actor: The Public Puzzler

Solving by committee is the Actor's modus operandi. The Actor fills in a few entries and then begins to shout out clues. "Does anyone know the name of an antique car in three letters, beginning with R?" (Yes, the answer is that old crossword chassis with well over 150,000 miles on it by now, the REO.)

For the Actor, the goal is to gather the answers from the resources at hand, which can turn the game into a sporting event. After the momentum picks up, you can gear up for an impromptu form of *Jeopardy!,* with the players pitting themselves against each other in a race against the clock to complete the grid.

Because opportunities to solve as an ensemble present themselves at specific times, a routine emerges. Shouted out replies aren't always correct, so the Actor solves in pencil.

Ruth Warrick (Phoebe Tyler on *All My Children*) is a confirmed Actor through and through, from her career to her approach to crosswords. In her case, the inclination to solve by committee was an outgrowth of the teamwork required by a role that spans nearly three decades on television. Ms. Warrick prefers solving with a pencil in honor of one of her early collaborators, Walt Disney, a careful solver who shunned ink solving.

The Daredevil: Solving with a Grid

Playfulness describes the Daredevil, who is usually a longtime solver. After years (perhaps decades) of working crosswords, the Daredevil tries to enhance the challenge by customizing the solving process in some way. Often a Daredevil attempts to work a conventional puzzle as a diagramless puzzle — without looking at the grid (you can read more about the diagramless in Chapter 11). Daredevils usually work the puzzle using only the list of clues and a piece of graph paper where they sketch in the entries.

In his long tenure as editor of *The Washington Post,* Ben Bradlee became notorious around the office for the amount of time he spent with puzzles. (Screenwriter Nora Ephron says that he spent more time with puzzles than anyone else she's ever known with a full-time job.) Bradlee was famous for the stash of graph paper in his desk, which confirmed him as a dyed-in-the-wool Daredevil.

The Acrossionado: The Inksters

Rumor has it that Grumpy Old Walter Matthau can complete a Sunday crossword in *The New York Times* in 20 minutes — in ballpoint pen, naturally. These feats are the giveaway traits of the Acrossionado.

The Acrossionado has solved for a lifetime and is conversant in crosswordese. Some of those experts solve using only the Down clues: They completely ignore the Across clues. Most professional puzzle folks are former Acrossionados. Yes, Acrossionados know the answer to "Heraldic wreath" (ORLE) and "Fragrant resin" (ELEMI) because they've seen those clues a million times before.

Puzzle pro and Acrossionado Stanley Newman wowed TV viewers in 1982 when he solved a *New York Times* daily puzzle in under three minutes. Just filling gibberish in all the boxes can take that long!

The Saver: Stack 'Em Up!

All solvers take pride in their work. The Saver, however, loves a finished crossword puzzle so much that he or she can't throw it away, even when it's months old.

You know you're in a Saver's home when you see that telltale pile of magazines. If they're not puzzle magazines, then they're open to the puzzle page. (And the puzzle may or may not be completed.)

Okay, I confess: I'm a Saver! It's simply that when I'm interrupted while solving, I put that puzzle aside for another day. But before I know it, there's another issue to work on and I'm on a new puzzle. That doesn't mean I'm ready to throw out the old one!

The ties that bind

Puzzles often bring families closer. Liza Minelli and her mom Judy Garland shared a passion for puzzles that helped them through some rough patches. Actress Michael Learned once told me that she enjoyed solving with her children as a way to make reading and homework less of a chore and to spend some fun time together as a family.

Night Owl: Undercover Work

Some solvers unwind from the events of their day with crosswords. The Night Owl seeks a mental midnight snack — the mental equivalent of taking a bag of Chips Ahoy into the bedroom. By definition, when you're doing something sneaky like that, you can only do it alone. You can't ask others for help, and you certainly can't turn to reference books.

Cartoonist Roz Chast (a regular in the pages of *The New Yorker*) epitomizes the Night Owl profile. She once confided to me that she considers crosswords to be a luxury comparable to treating yourself to a pair of $300 gloves. Instead of reading the front page and studying about world affairs, how can you justify time spent staring at a grid? That's why she relegates solving to bedtime.

Opera impresario Beverly Sills is also a Night Owl. Because she suffers from insomnia, she once told me, she likes to solve herself to sleep. Because she's on the road quite a bit, she makes sure to rip out a few puzzles from the papers and magazines now and then in order to have an emergency supply in her purse.

Chapter 19

Ten Practice Puzzles

In This Chapter

- Working out your puzzle prowess on five daily-size puzzles
- Testing your solving mettle with five Sunday-size puzzles

When it comes to crossword puzzles, practice really does make perfect. The more puzzles you work, the more comfortable you become with the special language of crosswords. You may also find that as you gain experience as a solver, you get more fun and pleasure out of the grid as you work harder puzzles, faster.

In this chapter, I give you ten puzzles to help you on your way to solving stardom. Included are five daily-size puzzles for you to think over, plus five Sunday-size puzzles to round things out.

And don't forget to pick up a copy of *101 Crossword Puzzles For Dummies,* Volume 1, which gives you 101 of the best crosswords, cryptograms, acrostics, and diagramless you ever saw.

Puzzle 19-1: Woodsy Cities

An abbreviation in a clue tells you the entry is shortened, too.

Across

1 Actor Fiennes
6 DEA buster
10 Johnny's successor
13 Krazy —
16 After the last act
18 Length times width
19 Kind of trip
20 U.N. labor arm
21 Iowa town
23 Roger Moore role
25 Trifling amount
26 Citrus drink
27 Wanes
29 Military measure
30 Outlawed insecticides: abbr.
32 Bosc, e.g.
33 Cleo's nemesis
35 Look up to
38 City near Chicago
40 Clerical garb
43 *Giant* ranch
44 Chopper
45 Wedding cake feature
46 German pronoun
47 Rock band's need
48 Bach work
52 Like Marietta
54 Dance, in Paris
55 Adjective for shoppe
56 TV alien
58 Sports events
59 Peachy person
61 City on the Arkansas
65 First lady
66 Downgrade
68 — Aviv
69 Spree
71 Gershwin brother
73 Suffer over
76 Act like a wave

78 Wgt. units
79 Pair
80 Attack with snowballs
82 Provide weaponry
83 Pips
85 But, to Brutus
86 Former atomic research center
89 Err at cards
90 Blow up, for short
91 Singles
92 Skirt length
93 Cartoon Betty
96 Pierce
97 Goal
98 Enemy
101 Craftsman
104 California resort
108 Here, to Pierre
109 Ostrich's kin
110 Feminine suffix
111 Sculptured slabs
112 Tic-toe center
113 Rug, slangily
114 Dick Tracy's love
115 Pastoral poem

Down

1 Kind of room, for short
2 Tarzan's friends
3 Resort near Venice
4 Huzzah
5 Not vert.
6 Place for a bun
7 Jackie's second
8 Save
9 Algiers native quarter
10 Airport users
11 Go gray
12 — Kippur
13 Oast
14 Jai follower
15 Civil wrong
17 Rasp
22 Commercials
24 One of a litter
28 Dry, as wine
31 Constellation
32 Court action
33 Confused
34 Play the guitar
35 Bedouin
36 Unprincipled politician
37 Suburb of St. Paul
38 Range
39 First third of a movie dog
40 Southern tourist resort
41 Untidy discarder
42 Turkish rulers
44 "The King —"
49 Pcak
50 Set aside
51 The works
53 Word with whiz
57 Kind of tense
60 Crew
62 Racket or rocket ender
63 Mold
64 Airport closer, at times
66 Boys
67 Inclemency
70 Wire, briefly
72 African fox
74 Ardor
75 Lodge member
77 Droops
81 Meadowlands gait
84 Joined forces
87 Irate
88 Argue
89 Highway exits
90 Prefix with "gram"
92 Re followers
93 Lure
94 Killer whale
95 Of the ear
96 Like a bug in a rug
97 Iowa town
99 Golden's "— in America"
100 Equal, in Paris
102 Emulate Betsy Ross
103 Brigitte's friend
105 Mil. officers
106 Important U.S. highway
107 Poivre's partner

Puzzle 19-2: Open Wide

Across

1 U.C. Berkeley
4 Frozen dessert
9 Famous fibber
14 Today, in Tuscany
18 Latin I word
19 Sun on the Seine
20 Like a rowboat
21 Split hairs?
22 Director Howard
23 Extract quickly?
25 Top exec.
26 Sties
28 H.S. exams
29 Go on and on
30 "— You Again" (Coward tune)
31 Put a lid on
32 Flemish art family
34 Sweetened ground corn
36 Home orthodonture?
38 Singers James and Jones
39 Get along!
41 — Ababa
42 Evening hour, in Essen
43 That's what it's all about
44 Ambles, with "along"
46 Sandburg poem
49 Haggard novel
50 Dental equipment?
52 Come full circle
54 Stun guns
56 Something to go on
58 "The Sun — Rises"
59 Bladed runner
61 Enlisted man: abbr.
62 Mass arrival
64 Where homeboys hang
65 Go quietly
69 Tropical rodent
71 Impede, legally
73 Very expensive dental work?

76 Lincoln center?
79 Volcanic ejecta
80 "Give — figgy pudding"
82 Region of Ephesus
83 "The — Duckling"
84 "There — atheists in foxholes"
85 Lace piece
86 Photographer Adams
87 Painful dental work?
92 Singers Baker and Bryant
93 Most abundant
94 Precisely
95 Jai alai ball
97 Incited, with "on"
98 German import
99 ICBM component
102 Jordan's queen
103 Dentist's motto?
106 Cornered, with "bind"
107 Kind of buggy
108 McCarthy co-worker
109 Metropolis daily
110 Signs off on
111 Jeanne d'Arc, et al.
112 Basket for 95 Across
113 Tears
114 "The Science Guy"

Down

1 Find fault
2 Pierre's possessive
3 Like an aging dentist?
4 Foreign exchange
5 Fran's friend
6 Row
7 Slant
8 Polar toiler
9 Window picture
10 Range rovers
11 Big, in Bordeaux
12 Dusk, to Donne
13 Dutch commune
14 Weigh on
15 Sale spot
16 Humperdinck miss
17 What history repeats
19 Relieves
24 "Take —" (waiting-room directive)
27 Be smug
29 Nitpicker
31 Early bloomers
32 Northern California bay
33 Mayor Giuliani of NYC
34 Sidedish
35 Seventh year sympton
36 Cookbook instruction
37 Co-Nobel winner Shimon
39 Evening, in Paris
40 Noncoms
43 16th century Church council site
44 Exec.'s job
45 Morsel
46 Dentist's chair?
47 Approximately
48 Incandescence
50 RAF honor
51 Something to contemplate
53 It's in the air
55 Environmentalist Leopold
57 Plains people
59 Queens venue
60 Part of a service
61 Vatican resident
63 Faulkner's "Requiem for a —"
66 "— what you think"
67 Geometry assignment
68 Tiny one
69 "Rule, Britannia" composer
70 — alone (solo)
72 Gave the axe
74 Number of bits in a byte
75 Speadsheet segs.
77 "The Alexandria Quartet" finals
78 Olive and family
81 Dates
83 Squad cars
84 Sticks to it
85 Word with born
86 Consecrate ceremonially
87 Mingles
88 Pull the — from under
89 "The thrill —"
90 Tudor successor
91 Salt additive
92 Axis opposite
95 Sun worshipper
96 African grazer
98 Gorillas
99 Tree trunk
100 Black
101 Social work
103 CIA's big brother
104 Quarter of four
105 PBS counterpart

Puzzle 19-3: Paving the Way

Across

1 Stage prompts
5 Seaside cities
10 Catnap
14 Help in crime
15 To no — (fruitlessly)
16 Butter stand-in
17 Loughlin of "Full House"
18 — cotta
19 Chowder morsel
20 Sinclair Lewis novel
22 Crinkly cabbage
23 TV's "Remington —"
24 Like a wallflower
26 Select from a menu
30 Enticing smell
34 Rush-job letters
38 Cathedral part
39 Symbol of affection
40 Eliot's — *Marner*
42 Cambridge univ.
43 See-through food wrap
44 Opening bars
45 Pal, out West
47 Go out with
48 Crannies' partners
49 Nose (slang)
51 "+" on a double-A
53 William Jennings Bryan, for one
58 October birthstone
61 Place for a nostalgic "trip"
65 Prefix with legal
66 Clock-radio buzzer
67 "It's a sin to tell —"
68 Rocker Clapton
69 Tenant's contract
70 — turtle soup
71 Give over, as property
72 Dud
73 Rightmost column, in math

Down

1 Pacifies
2 WW II predator
3 Inspiring dread
4 *Goosebumps* author R.L. —
5 Dressmaker's diagram
6 Walkie-talkie message ending
7 One-in-a-million
8 Poop out
9 Venetian blind components
10 Ice cream flavor
11 Cinders of old comics
12 Circus animal
13 Huge volume
21 Construction-site sign
25 Haberdasher's wares
27 Deadens, as piano strings
28 Bottled water brand
29 Prefix with active
31 Gumbo essential
32 Potatoes partner
33 Charles' sister
34 M, — Mary
35 Chinese: prefix
36 Kind of sax
37 Boardwalk's Monopoly partner
41 Not too bad
46 Hotel attendants
50 Take a stab at
52 Lowercase
54 Crockett's last stand
55 Eagle's grabber
56 In the cooler
57 Stinks
58 Oil cartel
59 Reduce, as expenses
60 Like a desert
62 "Waiting for the Robert —"
63 Courteous address
64 Words of approximation

Puzzle 19-4: Dance Party

Names in the grid often begin with the letter E.

Across

1 Rain-delay cover
5 Capone facial feature
9 Word with hanger
14 "— close to schedule"
15 Director Kazan
16 Michelangelo sculpture
17 Russo of *In the Line of Fire*
18 Uncool fellow
19 Hesitant
20 Unexpected change
23 Farrah's ex, for example
24 Corn unit
25 Policeman, in action
27 More expensive
31 Division word
32 Volcanic residue
33 Playful mammal
35 Jason's vessel
38 "Caught you!"
39 — "King" Cole
40 "— Were a Carpenter"
43 Lilly of pharmaceuticals
44 Scolds
46 Ruhr industrial center
48 Moray
49 Irene of *Fame*
52 Mythical strongman
54 College life
57 Hip-hop music
58 Mal de — (seasick)
59 Playful prank
64 Anti-pet-abuse org.
66 Lions or Tigers or Bears
67 Bad day for Caesar
68 Dutch master Jan
69 Deceptive move
70 In case
71 Filled to the gills
72 Hold at least a pair of jacks
73 Past due

Down

1 Civil offense
2 One more time
3 Rice-a-—
4 Oven button
5 Mexicali miss
6 Musical sign
7 Flight expense
8 Air-traffic detector
9 Abdominal organ
10 Draw
11 Kind of tape recorder
12 "— Grows in Brooklyn"
13 One who treats
21 Owl's claw
22 Prefix with angle
26 R.R. stop
27 James of *Brian's Song*
28 Workplace watchdog org.
29 Floor covering
30 Suffix with kitchen
34 "All —!" (court phrase)
36 Jubilation
37 Gets the squeaks out
41 Commuter-boat operators
42 Ancient Peruvians
45 Bummed out
47 Management realignment
50 Return, as to custody
51 "—, amas, . . . "
53 Sisyphus direction
54 Build up, as a fortune
55 Jai alai basket
56 Opening remarks
60 Effortlessness
61 "What's the big —?"
62 Robin's home
63 Italian noble family
65 So-so mark

Puzzle 19-5: Rare Birds

Across

1 "Georgia Peach"
5 Jokers
9 Pack
13 As far as
17 Combat cover
18 Lab heater
19 No way!
20 Son of Abraham
21 Globetrotter
23 *Network* star
25 Kind of home
26 Goddess of strife
28 Small birds
29 They're all charged up
30 Bingo call, perhaps
31 Synthesizer name
32 Nutlet
35 Sappho, for one
37 Supercharger
41 Churl
42 — *and Sensibility*
43 Newsroom newcomer
46 Sigh of relief
47 Intimidate
48 Pre-Hellenic deities
50 Relaxed
52 *Die Zeit* article
53 Typewriter key
55 Stumble
56 Erudite herb?
57 *Key Largo* Oscar winner
58 See?
59 Cleaned the floor
61 Prohibitionist
62 Noted archer
66 70 Across sign
67 Giggles
70 Nobel prize category
71 Frightened, in Dogpatch
74 Word of woe
75 Fuel rating

■	1	2	3	4	■	5	6	7	8	■	9	10	11	12	■	■	13	14	15	16
17					■	18				■	19				■	20				
21					22					■	23				24					
25								■	26	27			■	28						
■	■	■	29				■	30					■	31				■	■	■
32	33	34				■	35						36	■	■	37		38	39	40
41				■	■	42					■	■	43	44	45	■	46			
47			■	48	49					■	50	51				■	■	52		
53			54					■	■	55						■	56			
■	57						■	■	58					■	59	60				
■	■	61			■	62	63	64						65	■	66			■	■
67	68				69	■	70					■	■	71	72				73	■
74				■	75	76					■	■	77							78
79			■	■	80					■	81	82					■	83		
84			85	■	86			■	■	87					■	■	88			
89				90	■	■	91	92	93					■	94	95				
■	■	■	96		97	98	■	99					■	100				■	■	■
101	102	103					■	104				■	105					106	107	108
109							110			■	111	112								
113					■	114				■	115				■	116				
117				■	■	118				■	119				■	120				■

77 Mussed
79 Jag rival
80 Bowe bluff
81 Midshipmen
83 Bighorn bleat
84 Mischievous god
86 Bill of Rights number
87 Temperamental
88 Modern agora
89 Orgs.
91 Origin
94 Score
96 Grand finale?
99 Unpleasant encounter
100 Newcastle nuggets
101 Caliber
104 Sail support
105 Ring sites
109 *Peter Pan* portrayer
111 "Right or Wrong" country singer
113 Ph.D. preliminaries
114 Mil. honcho
115 A TV Taylor tot
116 Tendon
117 High wind
118 Patella position
119 Nothing, in Nogales
120 First-rate

Down

1 Brag
2 Melville novel
3 More dictatorial
4 Surrealism founder André
5 Sports
6 LLD recipient
7 Serengeti sight
8 Uniformity
9 Flat on one's back
10 Graduate school output
11 Linesman's call
12 Swamp
13 Exhausting
14 Window part
15 Diplomacy
16 Phil of folk
17 FBI guy
20 Otherwise
22 Attitude
24 Sugarloaf sight
27 Ceremony
30 Beethoven's birthplace
32 Rudiments
33 Appropriate
34 *Rio Bravo* director
35 Bosc, for one
36 Soprano Renata
38 *Cheers* regular
39 Light brown, as hose
40 Held title to
42 Bart, Belle, or Brenda
44 Wear
45 Protective mound
48 *Fiddler on the Roof* role
49 Eastern Nigerian
50 Wood-working machine
51 Mishmash
54 Harvest goddess
55 Hedge
56 Address an audience
58 Jumbo
60 Hot spots?
63 Making a choice
64 Long legume
65 Kim of *True Grit*
67 Hindu drum set
68 *Saint — Fire*
69 Yielding
72 For shame!
73 Handled with "with"
76 Mark of mediocrity
77 Says "I do"
78 "Lacey" portrayer
81 Antimatter particle
82 Meat cut
85 Elegantly
87 Clothing store section
88 Ariose
90 Inner-city areas
92 Winter weasel
93 Subtle expression
94 Spelling
95 Polish Nobelist
97 Coach Parseghian
98 Pharmaceutical giant
100 Cretan capital
101 Pollution
102 Mitchell mansion
103 Uzbekistan's sea
105 Sooner city
106 Talus or tibia
107 Pre-holiday periods
108 Darn
110 Calamine component
112 Gretel's grandfather

Puzzle 19-6: Necessary Items

The Bible supplies great entries — see 66 Down.

Across

1 Q-tip, e.g.
5 Model material
10 Attention-getter
14 Radar response
18 Olympian
19 Morning sound
20 Marching band members
22 Take on cargo
23 Make an impression
24 Gig for Mr. Ed?
26 Viking Ship Museum site
27 French cleric
29 Idle and Ambler
30 Charlemagne's capital
32 Period a machine is operational
35 Sandwich sheath
37 Certain NCO's
38 See 13 Down
39 Material for Santa?
43 Campground co.
46 Scholarly volumes
48 Fewest
49 "Three Times —"
50 Treasury agcy.
51 Lamb, to some
52 Reduce, briefly
53 Name for a Colleen
54 Boss of 37 Across
55 Coleman and son, for short
56 Hotel room furniture
60 China setting?
61 Spin
63 Enthusiastic about

64 More meddlesome
66 Abaci, e.g.
67 *Compulsion* author
68 Unstable nuclear particles
69 "All bets —!" (forget it)
70 Femme fatale
71 Floor material
72 Transept transector
73 Torero on strike?
76 "— your pardon"
79 Rainbow goddess
80 — Hari (German spy)
81 Word of woe
82 Firm up
83 PC alternative
84 Yahoo
86 — the face (embarrassed)
88 Long time
89 Partook
90 Eavesdropper's station?
93 Short-lived Egyptian king
94 Col.'s command
95 "— moi, le deluge"
96 Short O'Neill play
98 Hard-shell clam
101 Jason's first wife
103 "By hook — crook"
104 Impulse
105 Skater's need?
109 Murmurs of mutton
113 Inkling
114 — living (support oneself)
115 Brought to a conclusion
116 Prepare for publication
117 Mug
118 Social gatherings
119 Desert fruit
120 Flat-bottomed boat

Down

1 Haggard heroine
2 Dampen
3 Football's flight
4 19th century Muslim movement
5 Tonsorial specialist
6 "I cannot tell —"
7 Stripling
8 — Lanka
9 Aida rival
10 "— of beauty . . .": Keats
11 Former anti-communist comm.
12 Wanes
13 Rum drink with 38 Across
14 Coalitions
15 Bind
16 Pass the time
17 Menial worker
21 In segments
25 Johnson successor
28 Beemers
31 Give it — (attempt)
32 State
33 Sao —
34 Comic's need?
35 Coin of the realm
36 Separate
37 Bridge segments
40 Forewarns
41 Reprieve
42 Visitor from Venus
43 Place to pucker?
44 Bacchanals
45 — *Is Born*
47 Be careful, with "it"
52 Small stars
53 — on (inciting)
54 Fiberboard ingredient
57 Portugal's peninsula
58 Bond portrayer
59 Rings solemnly
62 Sports auth.
65 Bionic Woman's org.
66 Where Noah landed
67 Rich, e.g.
68 La Scala city, to Sophia
69 Persona
70 Play first-string
71 Popular garden bulbs
74 "— be off" (so long)
75 Western star?
77 Tedium
78 *Beau* — (Wren novel)
84 Role for Liz
85 Bargain
86 Mature
87 Furious
88 "Three men in —"
91 Comaneci, et al.
92 Tatters
94 Big birds
97 Shifted a sail
98 Clever comment
99 Pakistani language
100 See 88 Across
101 Former filly
102 Ms. Millay
103 Pointed arch
106 Chow down
107 Bambi's aunt
108 Banned chem.
110 Fuss
111 Broadcast
112 Hog haven

Puzzle 19-7: Heavenly Bodies

Across

1 Not of the clergy
5 Hemingway nickname
9 — Martin (classy car)
14 "Ignorance — excuse!"
15 Puts to work
16 Hotelier Helmsley
17 Countenance in the nighttime sky
20 "— Johnny!"
21 Mets' stadium
22 Creole vegetable
23 Pull a scam
25 Small brook
27 Salesman's pitch
30 — pig (domesticated rodent)
34 Airport letters
37 Right-angle joints
39 Granny and Square
40 Science fiction classic (1954)
44 What the Queen of Hearts baked
45 Arab chieftain
46 Dogpatch's Daisy
47 Substitute
49 In pieces, with "fall"
52 Caroler's song
54 Verdict
58 Patriot missile's target
61 — avis (unique person)
64 Part of a drum kit
65 George Harrison tune
68 Farewell, to Pierre
69 Olympic dueler's weapon
70 Aide: abbr.
71 *Steppenwolf* writer
72 Colorful horse
73 Civil rights figure Parks

1	2	3	4	■	5	6	7	8	■	9	10	11	12	13
14				■	15				■	16				
17				18					19					
20					■	21			■	22				
23					24	■	■	25		26		■	■	■
■	■	■	27			28	29	■	30			31	32	33
34	35	36	■	■	37			38	■	39				
40			41	42					43					
44					■	45				■	■	46		
47					48	■	49			50	51	■	■	■
■	■	■	52			53	■	■	54			55	56	57
58	59	60		■	61		62	63	■	64				
65				66					67					
68					■	69				■	70			
71					■	72				■	73			

Down

1 Loose-limbed
2 Pallid
3 Chemically nonreactive
4 Fresh arrivals, with "new"
5 Wordplay
6 Sale caveat
7 Phnom —, Cambodia
8 Fall bloom
9 Drink with shepherd's pie
10 Wheat used in pasta-making
11 Captured, as in checkers
12 — about (circa)
13 Grandmother, affectionately
18 "Pronto!" to a CEO
19 Reagan Secretary of State Alexander
24 Pizzeria units
26 *Cool Hand —*
28 Model Macpherson
29 Camel's cousin
31 Standard
32 Kett of old funnies
33 Tennis legend Arthur
34 Suffix with major
35 "— she blows"
36 Puts on the radio
38 Do some pruning
41 Rush-hour riders, perhaps
42 Proportion words
43 Main — (principal street)
48 Worst possible score
50 Mr. Limbaugh
51 Unmusical quality
53 Poorer, as excuses go
55 Cowpoke's rope
56 Builder's framework
57 Gossipmonger
58 Iranian leader until 1979
59 Sign away
60 *Exodus* novelist Leon
62 Nonpayment takeback, for short
63 On the briny
66 Fast Eddie's stick
67 Noted Downing Street address

Puzzle 19-8: In the Cards

Across

1 King with a golden touch
6 Hinged fastener
10 Wall Street pessimist
14 Prizefight venue
15 Raines of old films
16 Ticklish Muppet
17 *Grumpy Old Men* star
19 Moises of baseball
20 Book of maps
21 Where to find a stalactite
23 Grads, last year
26 Wrestling victory
27 Diminished gradually
28 Regional dialect
30 Bread supplier
31 Proficient
32 "Certainly!"
33 Geometry-proof letters
36 Ready for picking
37 — rata
38 Fisherman's decoy
39 The — -i-noor diamond
40 Count calories
41 Davis of *Thelma & Louise*
42 Indoor mile record-holder Coghlan
45 Milk protein
46 Kentucky Fried Chicken Colonel
48 Train unit
49 Jacqueline Kennedy, — Bouvier
50 Skinflints
51 Auks and hawks
53 Colored portion of the eye
54 Fictional pet detective
59 Broadway hit show
60 Suffix with folk
61 Fudd of cartoondom
62 Outer perimeter
63 Transmitted
64 Cook, as a turkey

Down

1 Capt.'s superior
2 Tax-deferred acct.
3 Yule mo.
4 "Diana" singer Paul
5 Where NaCl is collected
6 Macho male
7 Charitable donations
8 — -mo (replay technique)
9 Breakfast stack unit
10 Cleaver, e.g.
11 Fictional sleuth created by Dannay and Lee
12 Martin's "That's —"
13 Three minutes in the ring
18 Yalies
22 King Kong, e.g.
23 Type of plug
24 Sound system component
25 *Nightmares and Dreamscapes* author
27 Fortuneteller's card
29 Unlock, in verse
30 Martin Van —
32 Takes a turn on *Wheel of Fortune*
34 Comic Kovacs
35 Revolutionary diplomat Silas
38 — *Misérables*
40 Upper-side fins
41 Perry Mason creator Erle Stanley
43 "— Fideles"
44 Debussy's "La —"
45 Give a hoot
46 Cathedral topper
47 Televised
48 Catlike animal
51 Swiss capital
52 Normandy city
55 Cedar Rapids college
56 Thurman of *Pulp Fiction*
57 Legal matter
58 Louvre display

Puzzle 19-9: Crosswordese

Across

1 Felon's out
6 Type of powers
12 June honoree
15 Greek coin
19 Was concerned
20 Melodic
21 Yalie
22 Island on the Adriatic
23 Unau
25 Vied
27 Hostelry
28 Ade flavor
29 Usher's beat
31 Kurt's wife
32 Stow cargo
33 Hudson or Essex
35 Trattoria order
37 Count chaser
38 On the losing side
40 Perfumes
42 M.I.T. grad
44 Court figure
45 Anoa
47 *The Art of Love* poet
50 — the other
51 City near Decatur
52 Paging sound
53 Nixon's attorney general
54 Esne
55 Spoil
56 Turndown vote
58 Letter
60 Seedsmen
63 "— moi, le deluge"
65 Rotating piece
66 Seadog
69 Abas
71 "— Pinafore"
72 "— Ape" (Sedaka song)

73 Blue Ribbon beer
74 Of a Swiss theologian's doctrine
76 Italian infant
78 Hit letters
79 Part of a yen
80 Greek peak
84 Actor Maurice
85 Like some excuses
88 Dull sound
90 Ceremonies
91 Rockfish
92 Oda
94 "— Fables"
95 Anger
97 Some Black Sea natives
98 Depose
99 — Borch, Dutch artist
101 Precise
103 Monogram for 100 Down
104 — in the bud
105 Crazy as —
107 Map
109 "Tell — the marines"
110 Salamander
113 Eggnog garnish
115 Attu
119 Seep
120 "Exodus" hero
121 Took it easy
122 Eden visitor
123 Young or old ender
124 Finale
125 Vein
126 Correct

Down

1 Play start
2 Sod
3 Press
4 Put money on
5 Worshipper
6 Maniacs
7 Gaelic
8 Zilch
9 In addition
10 Phoenician goddess of love
11 City on Utah Lake
12 Lowered in rank
13 Succulent plants
14 Low wattage
15 Butterine
16 Ers
17 Dramatist Clifford
18 Mine veins
24 Down duck
26 Outline
30 Binge
32 Pink slip
33 City on the Orne
34 Home of the Braves
36 Ritter
38 Curse
39 Wide-mouthed jug
41 "Dear —"
43 Departs
44 Angeles lead-in
45 Central American tribe
46 Ran
48 Muslim religion
49 Considers
51 Curve
53 Beethoven's "— Solemnis"
55 Actress Erin
57 Lou Grant portrayer
59 Striped silk fabric
61 — lazuli
62 Make a lap
63 In the manner of
64 Play — (fool)
66 Rome's river
67 Century plant
68 Aes
70 Tropical shrubs
75 Dins
77 — B'rith
78 Big rig
81 Portico
82 Aug. follower
83 Fool
86 Mite
87 Hostess Perle
89 Stockings
90 Reply
92 Curse
93 Deadly snake
94 Ms. Loos
96 Ms. Horne
98 Messy
99 Mexican noshes
100 *The Waste Land* poet
102 Future oak
106 Unique person
108 — avis
109 Roman road
110 Villa d' —
111 Custard
112 See to
114 West of Hollywood
116 Superlative suffix
117 Salt Lake City player
118 "Today — a man"

Puzzle 19-10: Chuckles

In a missing-word clue, you see only one dash — even when two words are missing.

Across

1 "— Well That Ends Well"
5 Cook book
9 Medical insurance term
14 Borscht base
15 Tennis edge
16 Give a keynote address
17 Poet Lazarus
18 — slip (termination notice)
19 "Olympia" painter Édouard
20 Serengeti scavenger
23 October 31 goodie
24 Ready-go connector
25 Seance sound
28 Scott Joplin tunes
31 Long-faced ones
33 Surgery memento
36 *Bus Stop* playwright William
38 Pub pints
39 Vegetable-huckstering character
42 "— , poor Yorick!"
43 Verve
44 — Major (Big Dipper container)
45 Marx Brothers foil Margaret
47 Sandwich shop
49 Curvaceous letter
50 Diving bird
52 Put on cloud nine
56 Turtles hit of 1967
61 Compete in a bee
63 Kemo — (the Lone Ranger)
64 Trevi fountain coins
65 Stan's comedy partner
66 "— go bragh!"
67 Has — (is connected)
68 Nuts and — (basics)
69 Sax or clarinet
70 Garden intruder

Down

1 Eve's second-born
2 *Melvin and Howard* actor Paul
3 Tree-dwelling primate
4 Put on, as a play
5 Per — income
6 Thor's father
7 Famous vase
8 Looped crosses
9 Regain consciousness
10 Port of Algeria
11 Slender cigars
12 Munched
13 "Are we having fun —?"
21 Escape artist Houdini
22 Land on the Red Sea
26 Sports facility
27 "Hey, you!"
29 Lass
30 "Slammin' Sammy" of golf
32 Two aces, for example
33 Script notation
34 Shucker's throwaway
35 In addition
37 Actor Hackman
39 Mick's daughter
40 Hop out of bed
41 Skillful deceit
46 City near Mount Vesuvius
48 List of symbols on a map
51 "Three Little Fishies" bandleader Kay
53 Attorney- —
54 Belonging to thee
55 Really strange
57 Came to earth
58 Gross-weight deduction
59 N.Y. theater award
60 Tear to pieces
61 Weep loudly
62 Arafat's org.

1	2	3	4	■	5	6	7	8	■	9	10	11	12	13
14				■	15				■	16				
17				■	18				■	19				
20				21					22				■	■
■	23					■	■	24			■	25	26	27
■	■	■	■	28		29	30	■	31		32			
■	33	34	35		■	36		37		■	38			
39					40					41				
42				■	43				■	44				■
45				46		■	47		48		■	■	■	■
49			■	50		51	■	■	52		53	54	55	■
■	■	56	57				58	59						60
61	62				■	63				■	64			
65					■	66				■	67			
68					■	69				■	70			

Chapter 20

Ten Frequently Asked Questions about Crossword Puzzles

In This Chapter

- Deciding whether to work the puzzle in pen or pencil
- Making money with nothing more than a pencil, a puzzle, and your brain
- Steering clear of the most common crossword pitfall
- Finding a puzzle that's right up your solving alley
- Understanding why solving is a great hobby
- Answering other commonly-asked puzzle questions

Whenever someone finds out I'm involved with puzzles on a professional level, I get barraged with a series of the same questions about the way things work in puzzledom.

Unlike professions that grant degrees, such as medicine, law, or journalism, working and constructing puzzles is one of those quirky fields that you wonder about yet take for granted. Until this very minute, you probably wondered who could possibly answer your questions about the puzzle world. In this chapter, I address some of the main queries I've heard over the years.

Pen or Pencil?

In the foreword of the very first collection of crosswords issued by Simon & Schuster in 1924, the editors advised readers to approach the solving process gingerly and with a pencil. The editors wisely advise, "This saves erosion of paper and temper. But never hesitate to try a word that may be right. The trial and error method holds in puzzling as it does in life."

Certainly, on occasion you will make mistakes or get caught with a wrong answer that fits — but it's just a phase. Making errors is how you gain experience in the game of solving. No one attains master status in solving without a little trial and error. You make more progress in crosswords by figuring out why you fell into a hole rather than in spending hours reading a crossword dictionary in hopes of avoiding that pitfall.

Especially when you first get interested in puzzles, allow yourself the opportunity to take a few wrong turns — use a pencil and sketch in your answers lightly. That way, you can always "take it back" if you discover, ahem, a *better* answer to an entry. In addition, sketching your entries in lightly allows you the unparalleled thrill of going back over your answers in pen after you have solved the entire grid (which you will, with this book's help).

How Can You Make Money with Crosswords?

Crosswords offer three potential paychecks: through construction, through contests, or (less often) employment, listed in order of opportunity.

Constructing puzzles

You can count on one paycheck if you write a puzzle that is accepted for publication. That paycheck may range anywhere from $25 to $75 for a 15 x 15 crossword (depending upon where the puzzle appears and the quality of the puzzle). Will Shortz, puzzle editor at *The New York Times,* reports that in 1996 he alone used 122 different constructors to obtain the 365 puzzles for the newspaper. About half of the 122 constructors are satisfied with a single byline, while some of the others get hooked. Those who get the solving "bug" develop a little sideline business with regular magazine or book clients.

By the way, Will fondly recalls his first $5 paycheck for a puzzle that was published when he was in high school. My first puzzle sale earned me a cool $20.

If you get the urge to try crossword construction, it's a good idea to begin by requesting a set of guidelines from the publisher you plan to approach. Guidelines help you to format the puzzle according to the specifications of that puzzle editor for optimal results. There are some computer programs that can help you get started with this enterprise, if you choose to go that route. Of course, a sheet of graph paper, a pencil with an eraser, and a good idea are all you really need to get started.

Solving

Solving offers another option to earn some extra bucks. Some magazines feature contests with prize money if you complete and mail a puzzle within a brief time frame. Although there's only one national event (the American Crossword Tournament), smaller regional competitions do crop up, especially in the Northeast. You can find out about these by inquiring at the Web site for either the American Crossword Tournament or Puzzles at Random (turn to Chapter 16 for more information about crosswords in Cyberspace).

Puzzle piecework

Currently, magazines and books support about two dozen puzzle editors in total, and good editors are always welcome. Tournament champs also find steady work as proofreaders for puzzle publishers.

Tournament winners may find new career opportunities suddenly opening to them. For example, in 1978 the very first Tournament winner, Nancy Schuster, a homemaker, went on to an illustrious career as editor-in-chief at Official Publications and retired as editor-in-chief at Dell Champion in 1997.

For more information on making money through the grid, turn to Chapter 14.

What's the #1 Grid Pitfall for Beginners?

Novice solvers are always tempted to insert an "S" in the final box of a clue that appears to be plural when they can't guess the complete entry. I don't advocate this strategy for two reasons:

- **Filling in the "S" doesn't lead to real progress.** I find it discouraging to have a lonely "S" all by itself in an otherwise lightly filled grid. As S-fillers already know, that single letter rarely, if ever, unlocks any intersecting words to help you along.
- **Constructors often plant tricky clues to convey the impression of a final "S" where none exists.** Many constructors are very devious. They know how attractive it is for beginning solvers to fill in that "S" whenever they get the slightest suggestions that a plural entry may be in the works. For that reason, these sly constructors go out of their way to suggest an "S" when one is really not called for in the entry.

  For example, Norman Hill, noted crossword expert, notes that he has been caught time after time with a speculative "S" in the answer for the clue "Letters" only to be reminded that the answer is MAIL. Other booby traps he cites are DICE for "Cubes" and ARISTAE (a Latin plural) for "Grain bristles."

  On the other hand, a clue that appears singular may result in a plural response as in RUINS for "Tourist attraction."

Part of being a proficient solver is acquiring the sense to recognize a potential booby trap. It's part of the "Aha!" sense of satisfaction and accomplishment that you get as you jot in the correct entry. Just like Sherlock Holmes or Angela Lansbury, you get better at interpreting clues over time, so that you can crack the case.

Archaeologist Iris Love has compared her work in the field to solving a crossword puzzle. She's absolutely right: Working crosswords is all about digging — digging into the recesses of your mind, digging into your knowledge bank, or digging into the dictionary and the other reference books you may suddenly find in your personal library.

Instead of filling in that easy "S," switch your focus away from word parts by compiling a personal list of repeaters (some avid crossword junkies have been known to keep such a list in their wallet). This list can act as a handy reference tool and as a vocabulary builder.

Where Can You Find Easy Crosswords to Get You Started?

Until you get into the solving habit, the best places to turn to for beginner crosswords are newspapers and magazines. (Books tend to be slightly more advanced and more expensive — they are usually for acrossionados with established tastes and preferences.)

When you look at your newspaper crossword, note the source in small type near the grid, which is often listed as a "Syndicate." Generally, syndicates provide crosswords and other featured columns (horoscope, advice, and cartoons, for example) to your daily newspaper.

King Features Syndicate is a great source for simpler puzzles. Its crossword by Eugene Sheffer and crossword by Thomas Joseph are small (13 x 13 and 11 x 13) but fun to solve.

Smaller grids translate into a simpler challenge. When you're ready for a step up, try the *Los Angeles Times* Syndicate for a medium-level challenge.

Another handy place to find an easy puzzle is somewhere inside the pages of a consumer magazine like *TV Guide* or *People.* If you have an interest in the subject of the puzzle, even better — you find yourself whizzing through the clues on a solving tear. Chances are, you can find answers to the crossword in the pages of the magazine, which is also a solving boost. In fact, should you really develop an appetite for puzzles about television, you may want to look for two newsstand puzzle magazines on the subject: *TV Crosswords* and *TV Guide Crosswords.*

As for puzzle magazines in general, don't get overwhelmed by the choice of 200 magazines crowded at the store. Begin your search by looking for key words like "Easy," "Fun," or "Simple" in the title of these magazines to tip you off to the level of puzzles and request the magazine by name. Consult Chapter 3 for the details on finding a puzzle that's right for you.

Can Puzzles Help Build Your Vocabulary?

Puzzle editors don't intend for puzzles to be educational — puzzles should be fun. The intention of crosswords is to divert and amuse. If you learn something along the way, that's like finding a penny on the street — your personal good fortune.

However, in the early days of crosswords, they were considered both educational exercises and vocabulary builders. When crosswords hit the national scene in 1924, the University of Kentucky included "solving" in its curriculum for a brief period of time. The director of the New York Zoological Society was pleased to report that from AI ("Two toed sloth") to YAK ("Tibetan ox"), more solvers were familiar with zoo animals than ever before. (Unfortunately, your opportunities to study puzzles at college are considerably slimmer these days; except for master puzzler Will Shortz, who earned a B.A. in Enigmatology from Indiana University, I don't know of any accredited courses or degree programs on the subject.)

If you are bent on getting an "education" through puzzles, check out the acrostic, which you can read about in Chapter 11. This puzzle was designed in the 1930s by Elizabeth Kingsley, a librarian who deliberately set out to create a puzzle that would promote literature. In a time when James Joyce and Gertrude Stein gained an audience, Kingsley dedicated her efforts to bringing Shakespeare back to the solving masses. (Naturally, Joyce or Stein may appear in the acrostic nowadays without causing a stir.)

Although crosswords are really more entertaining than educational, getting good at solving does say something positive about your gray matter. Although "Crossword U." doesn't issue diplomas, plenty of Sunday solvers have earned their stripes as top-notch acrossionados with formidable verbal powers. Studies have shown that puzzles are good exercise for your memory, which may have a spill-over effect on enhancing your vocabulary.

Do Puzzles Go through Fads?

Absolutely! As in any artistic undertaking, crossword "styles" go in and out of vogue and actually have created factions. Crosswords evolved from a straightforward synonym matching game to game that stresses wordplay and clever twists both in entries and clues.

Two criteria determine the style of a crossword:

- The type of entries that are allowed
- The clue structure

Today's trend is anti-obscurity: no more genuses or remote Slavic towns are condoned in the grid. And where possible, a clever clue replaces a synonym. The trend is to exercise your wits rather than strain your brain.

In fact, an educational tone in crosswords is most definitely "out" right now. By solving a *New York Times* crossword, which is the measure of quality, you can get an idea of what the trend is.

When Eugene Maleska served as the editor of the *New York Times* puzzle page, he brought his background as an educator to the post. As a result, Maleska allowed entries to lean toward the obscure in the name of learning. Until his death in 1993, he advocated this editorial tone in his work. Perhaps in reaction to his policy, a backlash movement developed that came to be known as the New Wave revolution.

Opposed to obscure terms (or anything smacking of academia), the New Wave of constructors and editors emphasizes the clever aspect of crosswords that challenges the wits. Current *Times* editor Will Shortz was a staunch member of the rebels, most of whom are now in top editor positions in the field.

What's the next trend in crosswords? My crystal ball tells me that puns & anagrams (which you can read more about in Chapter 12) will fade away as the millennium approaches. I predict the cryptic crossword will become more commonplace in the United States, although it won't topple the American crossword in the foreseeable future. (See Chapter 13 for more information on the cryptic puzzle.)

Is Aptitude for Puzzles Hereditary?

No studies have been conducted (to my knowledge) to prove that good solving skills can be passed from fathers and mothers to their children.

A more likely connection exists between seeing people solve and acquiring the interest and skill yourself. After all, until this book came out, unless an acrossionado showed you the ropes, nothing in writing walked you through the process. (It may appear that the interest is hereditary if someone in your house showed you how it worked, and you caught on.)

My guess would be that if anyone in your family showed you the ropes, it was most likely a grandparent. At least in my own family, I've observed that the interest skips a generation. My grandfather, one of the original solvers, compulsively solved puzzles and often wondered aloud whether someone could make a career from puzzles. Although my father, an artist, never touched a puzzle, I came along to prove my grandfather right about working in the puzzle field.

How Do You Know If You Have the Dreaded Puzzle Fever?

Just like any other pastime, you must approach the crossword with some modicum of moderation. If you aren't careful, you may contract Puzzle Fever.

Puzzle Fever is a bug associated with the crossword since its early days. Overt symptoms of puzzle mania really hit a peak in the 1920s when crosswords were still considered a passing fad. At that time, crosswords' black-and-white grids appeared on a line of dresses, each sold with a book of puzzles to go with the dress. The wise shopper was eligible for a discount on a future purchase if she returned the puzzle book correctly completed within a few days. Just the right accent for this nifty outfit was crossword puzzle jewelry. Collar pins, gold link bracelets, and a French enamel ring were available, each based on the familiar checkered grid. They were advertised as "the talk of Fifth Avenue and the most intriguing jewelry at the smartest shops." Even Broadway was struck with the mania. The revue "Puzzles of 1925" featured a skit set in a sort of Betty Ford clinic for acrossionados seeking to "kick the habit."

Take this test to determine whether you have caught the bug. A score of over 40 points means you may need to march down to your local newsstand for a quick dose of jumbles to help you out of your Puzzle Fever:

- Sometimes you solve the puzzle in a magazine without even looking at the front cover of the magazine. (10 points)
- You experience an almost unearthly thrill when you fill in that last missing entry. When you complete the daily puzzle grid, you leave it on the refrigerator or open on the corner of your desk so that passers-by can make note of your accomplishment. (10 points)
- When you pick up a newspaper or magazine, you turn instinctually to the puzzle (yes, you already know where the puzzle is located in every nationally syndicated publication available at your newsstand). (10 points)
- You know more than three four-letter entries that correspond to the vague clue "Farm building." (20 points)
- You try to use the word ESNE in a sentence. (20 points)
- You write words down in a special clue journal you keep for when you see a new crossword-friendly word. (20 points)
- You catch yourself wondering what Will Shortz is doing tonight. (20 points)
- You have vanity license plates that read XW LOVER. (You're a goner — 30 points.)

Is Puzzle Solving Good for Your Health?

As long as you enjoy solving, and solving doesn't cause you stress, I would hazard to say yes. I also like to remind everyone that solving is a low calorie pastime (unless your habit is to work your puzzle over a danish).

According to the first lady of crosswords, Margaret Farrar, crosswords are intended to distract you from worries of every sort. "Who can worry about paying the rent when you're working on a clue?" she posed rhetorically.

Of course, if you find puzzles frustrating or annoying, the distraction may turn into a blood pressure issue. That's why it's important to find the right puzzle for you.

How Did You Get Involved in Puzzles?

Inevitably, whenever I meet someone, he or she ends up asking me how I entered the domain of puzzle publishing. While my solving interest may be inherited from my grandfather, the motivation to turn my hobby into a job came from my husband. During my grad school days he observed me solving puzzles daily, and he challenged me to solve for money. That gave me the idea to compose a puzzle for publication.

In high school I had a social studies teacher who was a freelance puzzle constructor, and so I knew it was possible to send in unsolicited submissions to certain publications. I put together a puzzle in a few days and mailed it to Eugene Maleska at *The New York Times*. It appeared in the *Times* in June 1978 (I tell you all about submitting your own puzzles to publication in Chapter 14).

By strange coincidence, Eugene Sheffer, the King Features Syndicate constructor, was also a professor emeritus in my department at Columbia. He recruited my help, and I've been involved with puzzles in some professional capacity ever since. My story is living proof that you can do what you like for a living.

Are All Crosswords in English?

I'm happy to report that the world of crosswords is almost as diverse as the non-grid world. You can find crossword puzzles in almost every language, frequently in the newspapers and magazines that publish in those languages.

Here's a quick sampling of non-English-language crossword puzzles:

- **Arabic:** The language reads from right to left, and so does the puzzle. Typically these puzzles feature a smaller-than-usual grid of 9 x 9 squares, and you find the first Across entry in the upper-right corner.
- **French:** Called *mot croises* (pronounced *moe krwazay*), French-language puzzles are divided into columns. Across the top the columns are numbered from 1 through 11. Down the side, each row is assigned a Roman numeral. By finding the intersections, you solve the clues.
- **German:** The German-style puzzle, called a *Kreuzwortratsel* (pronounced *kroytz-vort-rates-l*), combines the clues and the grid into one compact challenge. For example, in the left-hand corner of the first Across square, you see a two- or three-word clue that ends in an arrow showing you the direction (and length) of the entry.
- **Hebrew:** Sometimes these puzzles are not the typical square grid that you find in English-language puzzles — often Hebrew-language puzzles are non-traditional sizes, such as 15 x 13 squares. In addition, Hebrew reads from right to left, so you find the first Across clue in the upper-right corner of the grid.
- **Italian:** In Italy, solvers look forward to asymmetrical patterns in a rectangle or bar-shaped grid. In some puzzles, many of the letters do not interlock with other letters.

- **Japanese:** Solving in Japanese involves symbols, rather than letters, using the *hiragana* writing system. The *hiragana* system consists of 51 symbols, each of which represents a syllable.
- **Spanish:** Called *crucigramas* (prnounced *kruseegrammas*), these south-of-the-border puzzles often sport asymmetrical grids.

How Do You Construct a Crossword?

When you first start out with puzzle constructing, you can follow some simple steps to compose a crossword puzzle. Basically, you can discover good constructing techniques by looking at the puzzles you see in newspapers and magazines. For more detailed information on constructing puzzles, turn to Chapter 14.

Where Can I Meet Other Puzzle People?

Face to face, the best place to meet the biggest group of crossword puzzle people is the annual American Crossword Tournament. In early spring, this event takes place in Stamford, Connecticut. About 20 judges, mostly editors with names you see in your solving travels, attend the event. During the informal games, you can meet 200 solvers from everywhere and compare notes on this passionate pastime.

Thanks to the Web, though, it's never been easier to communicate with other puzzle lovers. If you visit some of the sites described in Chapter 16, you can find like-minded people the world over. You are not alone!

Chapter 21
Ten Solving Tips

In This Chapter

- Knowing the shortcuts to solving success
- Looking out for the chuckholes on the grid
- Scrolling for missing-word clues
- Judging a crossword by its clues
- Admitting when you've made a mistake
- Reviewing different crossword repeaters

Unlike most games, crosswords don't come with instructions or a book of rules. Part of the beauty of the solving process is the fact that it's free-form: You can approach the clues in any order you choose. For example, experienced solvers sometimes give themselves an extra hurdle by looking only at Down clues and completely ignoring the Across column. Beginners may look for "easy" clues first, focusing on the harder clues later in the solving process.

Because there is no established way to approach a puzzle, one solving system may work perfectly for you, but be totally useless to someone else. I take this into account as I present the following solving tips, which represent the ten hints I've found help beginners the most.

In this chapter you find some basic steps for optimal solving success.

Avoiding Common Traps

Many solvers want to fill something in — anything — just to get rid of those blank squares. You must resist this temptation, along with the following mishaps that oft befall the over-enthusiastic solver:

- Sticking in an "S" when you suspect an entry may be plural
- Assuming that an entry is a past participle (ends in ED) before you know the rest of the entry
- Mistaking a noun for a verb, and vice versa
- Mistaking a proper name for a noun or adjective
- Using a writing utensil that can't be erased

Cheating! (Call It Research)

When you pick up your first few crosswords, you may get stuck behind a clue — one you can't get no matter how many intersecting letters you fill in or how many times you've combed this book for an answer. In cases such as these, I want you to forget everything your first-grade teacher, mother, and preacher taught you — I want you to brazenly, unabashedly cheat.

Cheating is the best tool I can think of when it comes to solving the grid. I guarantee that if you take the time to look up the answer to a stubborn clue, you will remember the answer the next time it comes up in the clue list.

Consult Chapter 9 for my short list of the best cheating tools, I mean *reference books,* for your crossword library.

Checking for a Theme

Most crosswords include some entries that are related through a common topic, called a *theme.* In a 15 x 15 puzzle, you may be looking at anywhere from three to eight theme clues in the puzzle. You can spot theme entries because they are typically among the largest entries in the grid. Theme clues may relate to each other in subject matter, or not at all.

Theme entries appear in parallel places in the grid for easy identification.

Some puzzles offer a title, which tells you something about the theme. For example, if the title of a puzzle is "Getting the Last Word" then you could hypothesize that the theme entries may have to do with words you use to end a phrase.

Themes cover a vast range of material, from common elements in the entries to common elements in the clues. Constructors like to incorporate wordplay in the theme, which makes decoding that much trickier. But after you get the idea behind the theme clues, you're golden.

Concentrating on the theme clues allows you the following advantages:

- The information provided by each of the theme clues creates a synergy that allows you to "get" all the theme clues a little more easily.
- Solving the longer theme entries allows you to make more headway into the grid, and faster.

E-Gads! Looking for Words Beginning with E

Wherever you find your crossword, you encounter a plethora of three-letter entries beginning with E. Constructors like words that start with E because they key well in both directions.

My favorite E-word (and one guaranteed never to be used in everyday conversation) is ERG. To a scientist it is a unit of work representing the efforts of one dyne. To you and me, it answers the clue "Unit of work or energy." (For some reason, ERG seems to gravitate to a grid corner.)

Another personal favorite is EKE, as in " — out a living" or "Squeeze by." As loathe as you may be to utter this verb, you find yourself spelling it on a regular basis in the grid.

Not all common E entries are proper dictionary words. As an example, take EEE for "Shoe width." (Narrow shoes are rare in puzzledom, which may indicate that constructors prefer Birkenstocks.)

Another common non-word three-letter "E" entry refers to which way the wind is blowing. Most often the crossword weather vane points ENE (east northeast) with SSW a close second (south southwest). Sometimes the direction may refer to placement of one city in reference to another to heighten the challenge. Or, in more challenging puzzles, the same letters may be clued as "Chemical suffix," as in propylene.

Also included in the three-letter "E" entries are shapes of letters, as in ELL ("Building addition") or ESS ("Curve").

Poetic touches come through in the world of E entries. If you can hold onto E'ER, E'EN, and ERE, you'll be covered. Bird watchers will be happy to spot ERN ("Aquatic bird") and EMU ("Flightless bird") in the grid.

However, the most important three-letter E entry is ETC ("Common catchall").

The following four-letter A words also appear in the grid with amazing frequency:

- **ACTA** = "Deeds"
- **ACTE** = "French play segment"
- **ADIT** = "Mine Entrance"
- **AGAR** = "Seaweed"
- **ALOE** = "Tonic plant"
- **ALII** = "Et — " (and others)
- **APAR** = "On — with" (equal)
- **APER** = "Copycat"
- **AREA** = "Word with code"
- **ARIA** = "Operatic solo"
- **ARTE** = "Commedia dell' —"
- **ASEA** = "Confused"
- **ASTA** = "Nora's dog"

Erasing Bad Combinations

If you fill in two parallel words and notice kooky letter combinations forming, such as JT or ZB, you should throw a flag up to yourself and question one of the entries that contributes to the combination.

Keep your puzzle antennae raised for consonant combinations that are acceptable in the puzzle lexicon, even if they aren't allowed in the English vernacular. Two types of entries fall into this category:

- **Abbreviations:** For example, NDAK (for North Dakota) or SDAK (for South Dakota).
- **Roman numerals:** For example, the answer to a clue may involve a combination of Roman numerals, such as LXV or MDC.

Go ahead and use your eraser — that's why they put it on the end of the pencil at the factory. Even if you make the wrong choice and find that you've erased a correct word, it's better to start again than try to make a wrong letter work. You should feel that the crossing words confirm a correct choice by making reasonable letter combinations.

The crossword's most popular letters are E, S, R, T, D, and A. The odds of seeing J or Z in a puzzle are lower.

Filling In the Gaps by Reciting Your ABCs

After you have filled in a majority of the clues, you may have a few incomplete entries left over that are missing just one or two letters. Test the options for those missing letters by running the alphabet through that spot for each word until you find the letter that works.

If you enjoy working your crossword on the bus or train home from work, I advise that you sing or recite the alphabet mentally — unless people can see your crossword puzzle, you may get some strange looks from fellow passengers.

Finding the Missing-Word Clues

A good way to get a toehold into the grid is to begin by answering a clue that contains a blank in it. (The puzzle world calls this type of clue a *missing-word* clue.) You can easily identify these clues because they contain a dash or line which indicates that a word (or sometimes words) are missing from the clue. (The entry is the missing word.)

You should start with these clues because constructors usually make them pretty easy. Typically a constructor won't ask you to supply the article that goes in front of an obscure type of Bavarian goat cheese, available only in the mountain markets of the Alps.

Usually, the answer is obvious to you — perhaps along the lines of supplying the missing words from the following phrases:

- *"It's a Wonderful —"*
- "It had to be —"
- " I — New York"

(In the case of the first clue, if you're not familiar with this Jimmy Stewart film, *It's a Wonderful LIFE,* which is traditionally aired around the holidays, then I highly recommend the movie for after your crossword break. As for the second clue, music fans and romantics all around the world will recognize that "It had to be YOU." Finally, you don't have to be a fan of the Big Apple to recognize the phrase "I LOVE New York.")

Constructors usually incorporate at least one missing-word clue in the puzzle just for beginners — these clues are often the break that a beginner needs to get going in the grid. If you don't see a missing-word clue in the Across or Down clues, it's a signal that you're in deep waters.

Focusing on a Corner

Zero in on a corner, preferably the corner with the most entries, and try to work on the intersecting entries. Work on as many intersecting entries as you can get that extend into the body of the puzzle.

In fact, I usually take a swipe at all the corners before heading into the rest of the grid. I find that if I can get the answers to one of the corners, I have corresponding luck in the matching corners.

Knowing When to Give Up — for Now

When it comes to crosswords, it just doesn't pay to be stubborn. If you don't know the answer to a clue, leave the clue and come back to it after you've supplied a few of the missing letters via other clues.

In crosswords, quicker is often better. If you can't make headway within a reasonable amount of time (say about 10 minutes), chances are you'll throw in the towel. Or worse — you'll try to make incorrect entries work and end up spinning your wheels. If, instead, you use your opening moves to identify some easy entries, your ultimate goal of solving the entire crossword eventually comes within your grasp.

Obscure entries are on the wane in crosswords. Modern puzzlesmiths are dedicated to removing weird nonvernacular terms from the grids. Instead, the trend is to include more brand names and acronyms that are common in your everyday life. This is not to say that heraldic terms have been eliminated entirely, or that obsolete words are banished, but today's repeaters *are* less esoteric than they were in the past. Besides, they're just that — repeaters. Eventually, you come to know them and anticipate them as the crossword clichés that they are.

Looking for Foreign-Language Clues

In the interest of expanding the lexicon of short words that fit into puzzles, a limited number of foreign words appear regularly. These foreign words fall into the everyday variety, and should be simple to remember.

Sometimes clues for foreign words are obvious through the use of a tag at the end of the clue as in "Three: Fr." (TROIS). Or, the clue may imply the country of origin through a reference to a local name or town as in "Three, to Pierre" or "Three in Lyons."

Making Note of "Trivial" Information

Knowledge of a wide variety of subject matters proves invaluable when you sit down with the crossword. In real life, it may not help you too much to know that Switzerland is divided into CANTONS, but when the clue reads "Swiss regions," that same little bit of "trivia" suddenly becomes quite useful.

The following true-and-false test should help you gauge the depth of your knowledge of trivia about crossword puzzles:

- **Princess Margaret is the only known member of the English royal family to have won a crossword puzzle competition.**

  True: She won the 1954 crossword contest held by *Country Life* magazine.

- **Crossword puzzles were first introduced in New York City.**

  True: *The New York World* introduced a feature entitled the Word Cross during the holidays in 1913.

- **The first collection of crossword puzzles launched the publishing house of Simon & Schuster.**

  True: In 1924 the first crossword collection set the world on its ear, launched a fad and began a series that continues through today.

- **Crossword puzzles date back to Cleopatra.**

  False: Its ancestors predate 1913, but the crossword evolved around the time of WWI.

- **A lawsuit by a "crossword widow" has been filed in an American court.**

  True: This lawsuit occurred during the crossword fever that swept the United States in 1924. The woman filed suit against her husband, who she said had abandoned her for the crossword puzzle.

- **One third of the American population indulges in crossword solving.**

  True: According to the Gallop Poll, over 33 percent of all Americans solve on a regular basis.

- **The term "crossword puzzle" entered the pages of the standard dictionary in 1934.**

  True: Although as "cross-word" it had been added to the "New Words" section of many dictionaries in 1927.

Scanning for Geographical Repeaters

Puzzles have favorite hotspots that seem to make the cut regularly. Often a geographical clue is straightforward such as "Lake port" for ERIE or "River into the Caspian Sea" for URAL. If URAL escapes you, an atlas may help. (Chapter 8 can help you gain your bearings in the crossword map as well.)

Scrolling for Implied Missing-Word Clues

Sometimes you may scan a list of clues and not come across any of the dashes or blanks that normally alert you of a missing-word clue. Despair not — at least not until you have a closer look at the clues.

Instead of a blank line or dash where the entry should be, a missing-word clue may often describe an entry through its connection to another word. For example, instead of " — branch (peace symbol)" you see "Word with branch" for OLIVE. Constructors call this type of clue an *implied missing-word* clue (obviously belying its close relation to the missing-word clue I describe in "Finding Missing-Word Clues" in this chapter).

A few key terms signal an implied missing-word clue: The entry may be a "partner" or "word with" the clue word. Or the entry may be described in the clue as "like" something else. The following clues show you a few variations of the implied missing-word clue:

- "Word with code" = AREA
- "Partner of bill" = COO
- "Like old news" = STALE

To be tricky, the word "partner" may follow the other member of the pair. For example, you may see COO with a clue that reads "Bill's partner." In three letters, you know that HILLARY is not the answer (as in the Clintons).

Skipping Right Past 1 Across

The crossword puzzle is not a book. Without a plot line to follow, you have no reason to start at the beginning when solving a crossword.

Well, having said that, I now have to eat my words. Actually, the crossword puzzle is very much like *this* book. Throughout this book, I present information in such a way that you can pick up the book, open it up, and start reading on any page. Likewise, the crossword constructor builds a puzzle such that you can start answering clues at any point in the clue list. You may read the clues in order as you browse the crossword, or you may jump in at an intriguing spot.

Of course, if the answer to 1 Across speaks to you, then by all means put it in the grid! I'm simply granting you the freedom to begin anywhere.

Spotting Proper Name Clues

Every crossword has some entries that qualify as *repeaters,* meaning those words that tend to appear in puzzles due to their crossword-compatible letters. I'm talking about strange little words like the birds that frequent the grid, such as EMU, RHEA, or MOA.

Among these repeaters you find certain celebrities who tend to pop up in the entries. You may be surprised how well you do in the category of Crossword Hall of Fame. With a smattering of names, you can gain ground in the grid.

Specifically, keep the following half dozen names handy as you scan the clues:

- **ALOU** = "Baseball family"
- **ARI** = "Onassis nickname"
- **ERLE** = "Author Stanley Gardner"
- **INA** = "Actress Balin"
- **INGE** = "*Bus Stop* playwright"
- **UTA** = "Actress Hagen"

Consult Chapter 6 for more information on crossword celebrities.

Thinking Like a Constructor

The art of puzzles lies in the presentation, making the constructor and the editor the driving forces behind any puzzle. No easy rules can explain how the minds of the constructor and editor conspire to put together this deceptively easy-looking little brain game.

As a strategy for approaching a puzzle, try to think like the constructor and editor who bring you the puzzle. In order to do this, you must become familiar with their work, which you can easily do by reading and working your daily newspaper puzzle every day.

After a week or so, you will begin to discern subtle flavors in the clues. Some constructors and editors favor wordplay; others enjoy peppering the clues with references to silver screen actresses.

With time, you will become familiar with the tastes of your favorite constructors — and consequently, their favorite tricks will become your best tools for entering the grid.

Part VI
Appendixes

In this part . . .

After you finish a puzzle (or after you find it impossible to resist the temptation to cheat), turn to Appendix A in this part to find out the answers that inquiring minds want to know. In Appendix B, I provide a very handy list of common three- and four-letter repeaters. If you get stumped on a clue, you can consult this list and see if you find an entry that fits your bill (or squares, as the case may be).

Appendix A

Answers

Chapter 1

Puzzle 1-1

Page 9

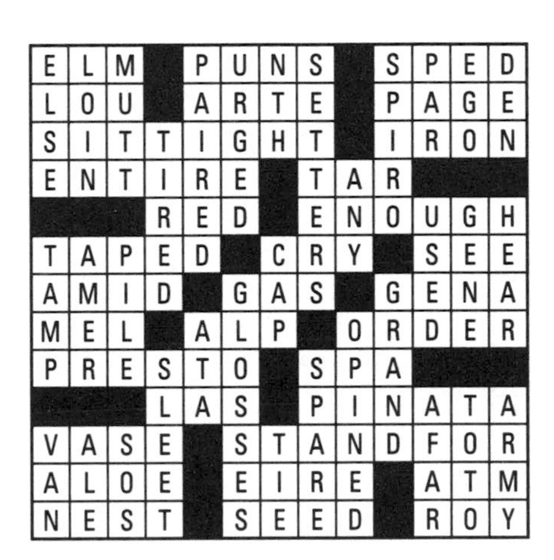

Chapter 2

Puzzle Prep

Page 21

Rolltop desk, Jai alai, Alley Oop, Hale and hcarty, Cain and Abel, Salt and pepper, Shish kabob, Cease and desist, Peyton Place, Angela's Ashes.

Puzzle Prep

Page 22

Coco Chanel, Ira Gershwin, Arlo Guthrie, Greer Garson, Enid Bagnold, Ina Balin, Mia Farrow, Ken Kesey, Frma Bombeck, Estee Lauder, Regls Philbin, Ruby Dee

Puzzle Prep

Page 24

AGAR = "Seaweed;" ASEA = "Without a clue;" AWAY = "Not in;" ASTA = "Nora Charles' pet;" AERO = "Prefix with dynamics;" AGRA = "Taj Mahal city;" ALOE = "Skin creme additive;" AMAH = "Asian governess;" AFAR = "At a distance;" ARIA = "Operatic solo;" AREA = "Word with code;" ADIT = "Mine entrance;" APER = "Copycat"

Puzzle Prep

Page 25

"Me, in Metz" = MOI; "Love, in Roma" = AMORE; "Place: Fr." = LIEU; "Dernier —" = CRI; "Nino's unclc" - TIO; Life: Fr." = VIE; "Home to Jose" = CASA; "German article" = DER; "Saint: Sp." = SAN; "Quid — quo" = PRO

Puzzle Prep

Page 26

"A frame up?" = ART; "Turn red?" = RIPEN; "Complains in a fishy way?" = CARPS; "Flat piece of paper?" = LEASE; "Respectable people?" = ELDERS; "Green land?" = EIRE; "Ram's dams?" = EWES; "Pest's rest?" = NAP; "Tot's cot?" = CRIB

Puzzle Prep

Page 28

"I cannot tell —" = A LIE; "— bad example" = SET A; "Stuck in —" = A RUT; "Put — on it!" = A LID; "What's — for me?" = IN IT; "— first you don't succeed . . ." = IF AT; "— was saying . . ." = AS I; "Thanks —!" = A LOT; "Hole —" = IN ONE; "Snug as —" = A BUG; "Blind as —" = A BAT

Chapter 3

Puzzle 3-1

Page 32

Puzzle 3-2: For Chocoholics

Page 34

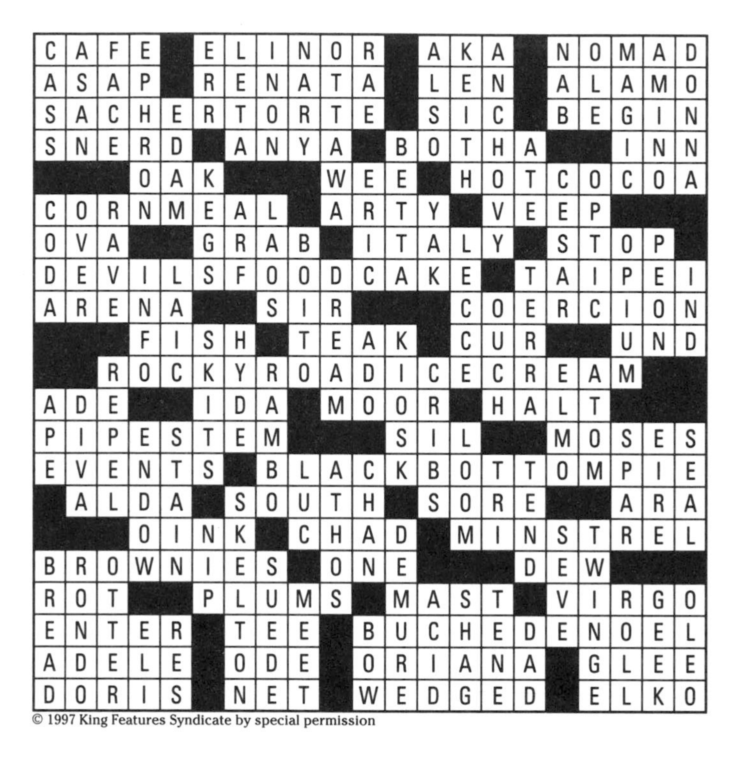

Puzzle 3-3: Dog Day

Page 36

Puzzle 3-4

Page 38

Puzzle 3-6: Shivery

Page 43

Puzzle 3-5: Hi Again

Page 40

H	I	H	I	■	R	E	R	U	N	■	G	O	E	S
I	T	A	L	■	O	M	E	G	A	■	L	I	L	T
P	H	I	L	O	S	O	P	H	I	C	A	L	L	Y
S	E	R	■	N	I	T	S	■	S	U	S	S	E	X
■	■	■	A	D	E	E	■	A	M	E	S	■	■	■
B	A	S	K	E	R	■	A	M	I	S	■	H	A	L
O	P	T	I	C	■	S	M	I	T	■	S	O	M	E
T	H	I	N	K	S	N	O	T	H	I	N	G	O	F
H	I	E	S	■	W	A	R	Y	■	L	E	A	N	T
A	D	S	■	G	E	R	E	■	S	L	A	N	G	Y
■	■	■	F	L	A	K	■	R	E	I	D	■	■	■
A	R	M	O	U	R	■	C	A	A	N	■	A	L	A
C	H	I	N	E	S	E	H	I	B	I	S	C	U	S
T	E	N	D	■	I	N	U	S	E	■	K	I	R	K
S	E	G	A	■	N	A	M	E	D	■	I	D	E	S

Puzzle 3-7

Page 45

M	A	R	Y	■	S	P	A	T	E	■	D	D	A	Y
E	Z	I	O	■	C	O	M	E	S	■	R	U	L	E
L	U	N	G	■	A	T	O	N	E	■	F	E	T	A
D	R	K	I	L	D	A	R	E	■	P	E	T	E	R
■	■	■	■	E	S	T	■	M	E	T	E	O	R	S
P	A	N	D	A	■	O	N	E	I	L	L	■	■	■
L	E	A	R	N	S	■	E	N	D	■	G	A	S	H
A	R	I	D	■	H	A	R	T	E	■	O	L	E	O
R	O	L	O	■	R	I	V	■	R	H	O	D	E	S
■	■	■	L	A	U	R	E	L	■	A	D	A	P	T
S	Y	R	I	N	G	E	■	I	S	R	■	■	■	■
M	E	A	T	Y	■	D	R	Z	H	I	V	A	G	O
I	S	I	T	■	M	A	I	Z	E	■	O	U	R	S
T	E	L	L	■	A	L	L	I	E	■	I	T	A	L
E	S	S	E	■	H	E	L	E	N	■	D	O	D	O

Puzzle 3-8

Page 51

Puzzle 3-9

Page 52

B	B	C	■	S	C	A	R	■	O	G	R	E
A	A	A	■	O	H	I	O	■	D	E	E	D
M	R	B	■	L	A	D	Y	■	I	T	B	E
M	A	S	T	E	R	S	■	S	U	S	A	N
■	■	■	E	M	O	■	B	A	M	M	■	■
C	O	H	A	N	■	D	O	G	■	A	R	A
E	N	O	S	■	R	O	W	■	C	R	O	W
T	O	M	■	P	A	T	■	H	O	T	E	L
■	■	I	C	E	T	■	D	O	W	■	■	■
R	A	C	E	R	■	H	I	L	L	A	R	Y
E	M	I	R	■	F	O	A	L	■	R	A	E
N	O	D	E	■	A	L	L	Y	■	I	N	A
T	R	E	S	■	N	E	S	S	■	A	I	R

Chapter 4

Puzzle 4-1: Great Sports

Page 57

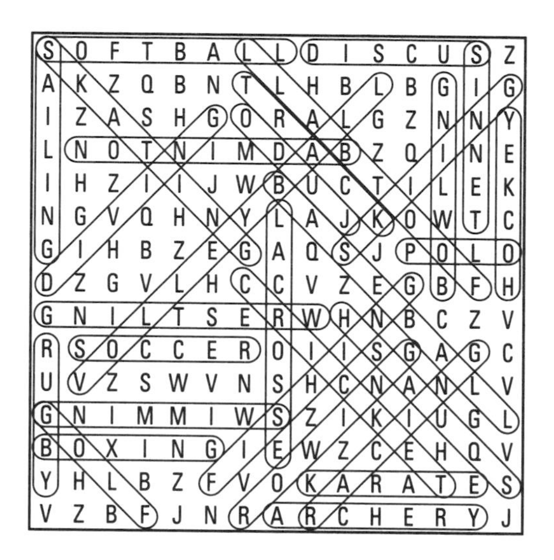

Puzzle 4-2

Page 59

Puzzle 4-3

Page 60

S	O	N	Y	■	G	E	N	A	■	R	A	H
C	L	E	O	■	A	N	E	T	■	E	W	E
H	E	A	D	O	V	E	R	H	E	E	L	S
■	■	■	E	T	E	■	■	A	I	X	■	■
D	E	A	L	T	■	D	O	N	N	A	S	■
E	D	D	S	■	C	O	N	D	E	M	N	■
S	D	I	■	■	E	S	E	■	■	I	I	I
■	A	N	G	E	L	E	S	■	O	N	D	E
■	S	T	U	N	T	S	■	S	N	E	E	R
■	■	E	N	C	■	■	A	M	E	■	■	■
V	E	R	N	A	L	E	Q	U	I	N	O	X
E	L	I	■	M	E	N	U	■	D	A	V	Y
E	L	M	■	P	I	T	A	■	A	T	O	Z

Puzzle 4-4

Page 62

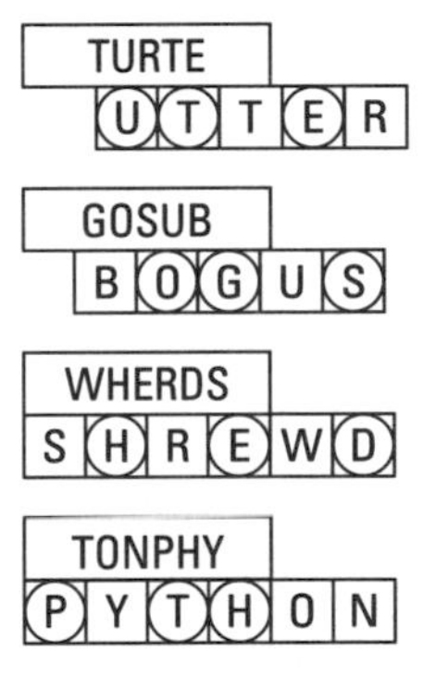

Print your answer here:

"DEEP" THOUGHTS

Puzzle 4-5

Page 64

IF THERE IS A DISPUTE BETWEEN A MUSICIAN AND MYSELF, IT IS SETTLED AMICABLY. I WIN! — DANNY KAYE

Puzzle 4-6

Page 64

WHEN WE REMEMBER WE ARE ALL MAD, THE MYSTERIES DISAPPEAR AND LIFE STANDS EXPLAINED. — MARK TWAIN

Chapter 10

Puzzle 10-1: Pound For Pound

Page 132

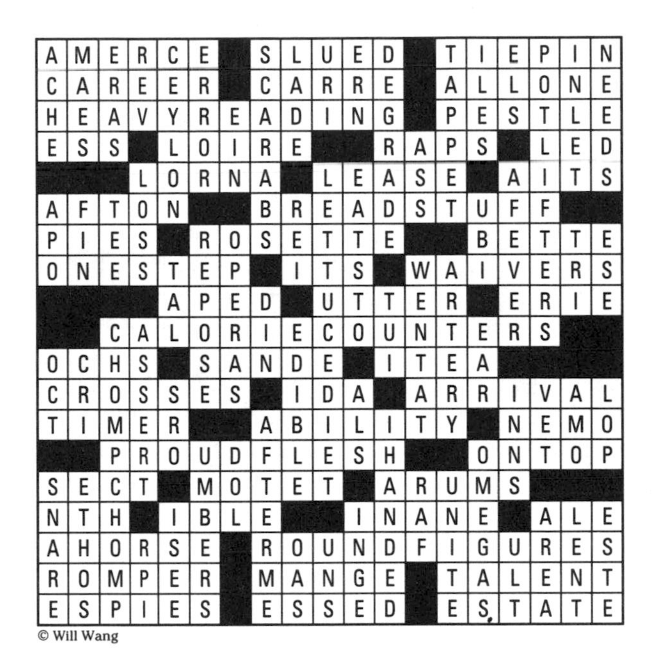

Chapter 11

Puzzle 11-1: 13 x 13 Squares

Page 143

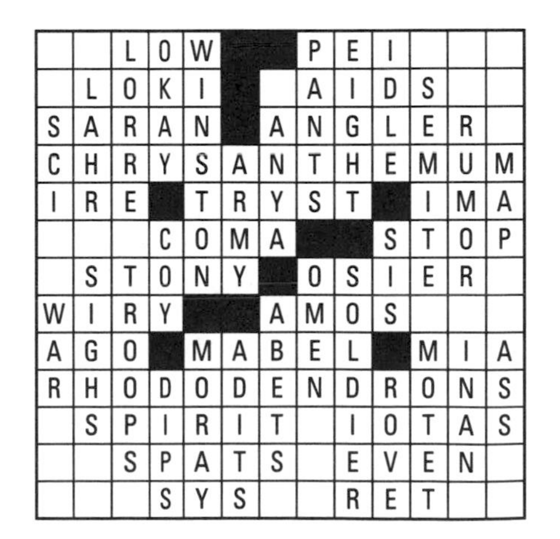

Puzzle 11-2: 17 x 17 Squares

Page 144

			P	T	A									J	O	B
		F	A	I	L	S							B	E	D	E
	R	O	Y	A	L	T	Y					A	R	T	I	E
	A	I	M	■	E	R	E				A	G	A	T	E	
	P	L	E	D	G	E	S			O	M	E	G	A		
		S	N	O	R	E			A	R	I	N	G			
			T	W	O	P	E	R	C	E	N	T				
							Y	A	H	O	O					
						R	E	G	I	S						
					S	A	L	O	N							
				T	A	K	I	N	G	A	C	U	T			
			B	O	N	E	D			S	H	R	E	D		
		B	L	O	T	S			S	T	E	I	N	E	R	
	Q	U	O	T	A				A	R	C	■	F	I	E	
G	U	L	C	H					B	A	K	E	O	F	F	
M	I	L	K							L	O	L	L	Y		
C	D	S									N	O	D			

Chapter 13

Puzzle 13-1

Page 161

I	N	F	E	R	N	O	S	C	A	N	T
M	O	O	R	E	D	V	A	R	D	O	R
P	I	R	I	P	S	O	F	A	C	T	O
E	S	C	R	O	W	I	E	V	I	I	W
L	E	E	R	S	A	D	V	A	N	C	E
C	H	O	L	E	R	A	S	T	A	E	L
H	E	P	S	S	O	L	E	A	T	E	S
O	N	E	T	I	M	E	M	T	R	I	G
I	C	N	O	G	U	C	I	C	A	D	A
C	O	N	G	A	L	I	N	E	N	A	B
E	R	N	I	E	U	G	A	U	C	H	O
R	E	V	E	L	S	U	R	G	E	O	N

Puzzle 11-3

Page 147

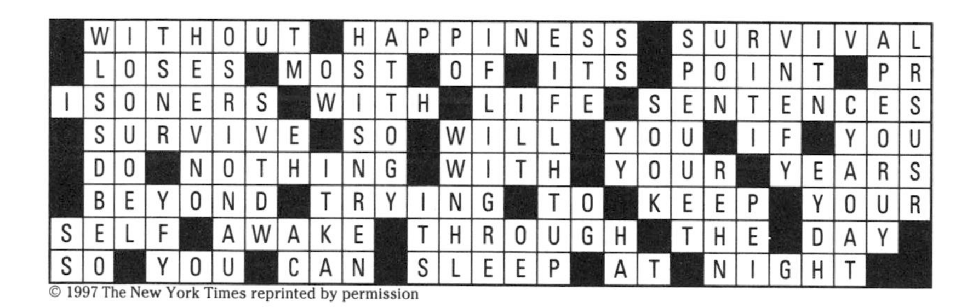

■	W	I	T	H	O	U	T	■	H	A	P	P	I	N	E	S	S	■	S	U	R	V	I	V	A	L
■	L	O	S	E	S	■	M	O	S	T	■	O	F	■	I	T	S	■	P	O	I	N	T	■	P	R
I	S	O	N	E	R	S	■	W	I	T	H	■	L	I	F	E	■	S	E	N	T	E	N	C	E	S
■	S	U	R	V	I	V	E	■	S	O	■	W	I	L	L	■	Y	O	U	■	I	F	■	Y	O	U
■	D	O	■	N	O	T	H	I	N	G	■	W	I	T	H	■	Y	O	U	R	■	Y	E	A	R	S
■	B	E	Y	O	N	D	■	T	R	Y	I	N	G	■	T	O	■	K	E	E	P	■	Y	O	U	R
S	E	L	F	■	A	W	A	K	E	■	T	H	R	O	U	G	H	■	T	H	E	■	D	A	Y	■
S	O	■	Y	O	U	■	C	A	N	■	S	L	E	E	P	■	A	T	■	N	I	G	H	T	■	■

A POLYSTYLE
B ERSTWHILE
C TROUT
D ESCROW
E ROANOAKE
F SUFFUSE
G CUTUPS
H HYSSOP
I WAVY
J ELLIPSIS
K DIVEST
L HAIFA
M ANTHROPOID
N NOTIONS
O GALOSH
P INVIDIOUS
Q NUTRITION
R GIVESAWAY
S INAWINK
T NUMBERS
U THEROOTOF
V HONEYS
W EGYPT
X ROUGHLY
Y EYETEETH

Chapter 15

Puzzle Prep

Page 195

"Hilo volcano" = MAUNA LOA; "Opposite of spring tide" - NEAP; "October gemstone" = OPAL; "Kimono belt" = OBI; "Asian governess" = AMAH; "Lily's cousin?" = ALOE; "Nabokov heroine" = ADA; "Snick's partner" = SNEE; "Leftover, puzzle style" = ORT; "Oolong, e.g." = TEA; "Mosque prayer leader" = IMAM; "Keats' preferred format" = ODE; "Filipino sweetsop" = ATES; "Starchy rootstock" = TARO; "Rhone feeder" = YSER; "Serf" = ESNE; "Heraldic wreath" = ORLE; "Fall bloomer" = ASTER; "Dismounted" = ALIT; "After HST" = DDE

Chapter 19

Puzzle 19-1: Woodsy Cities

Page 230

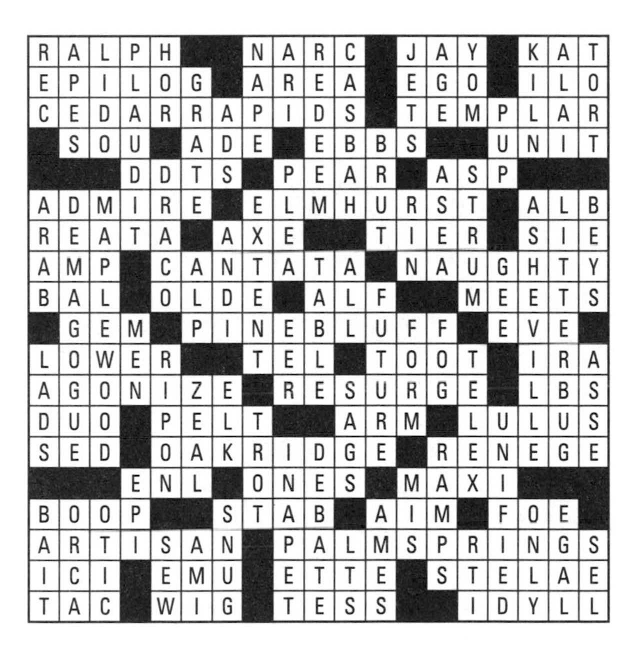

Puzzle 19-2: Open Wide

Page 232

Puzzle 19-3: Paving the Way

Page 234

C	U	E	S		P	O	R	T	S		R	E	S	T
A	B	E	T		A	V	A	I	L		O	L	E	O
L	O	R	I		T	E	R	R	A		C	L	A	M
M	A	I	N	S	T	R	E	E	T		K	A	L	E
S	T	E	E	L	E				S	H	Y			
				O	R	D	E	R		A	R	O	M	A
A	S	A	P		N	A	V	E		T	O	K	E	N
S	I	L	A	S		M	I	T		S	A	R	A	N
I	N	T	R	O		P	A	R	D		D	A	T	E
N	O	O	K	S		S	N	O	O	T				
			P	O	S				O	R	A	T	O	R
O	P	A	L		M	E	M	O	R	Y	L	A	N	E
P	A	R	A		A	L	A	R	M		A	L	I	E
E	R	I	C		L	E	A	S	E		M	O	C	K
C	E	D	E		L	E	M	O	N		O	N	E	S

Puzzle 19-4: Dance Party

Page 235

Puzzle 19-5: Rare Birds

Page 236

Puzzle 19-6: Necessary Items

Page 238

Puzzle 19-7: Heavenly Bodies

Page 240

Puzzle 19-8: In the Cards

Page 241

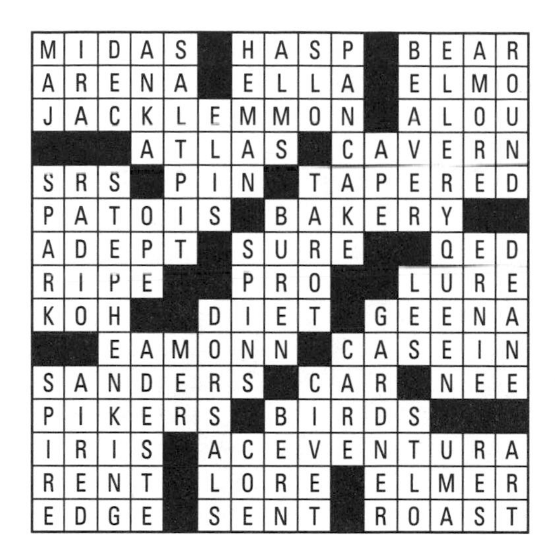

Puzzle 19-10: Chuckles

Page 244

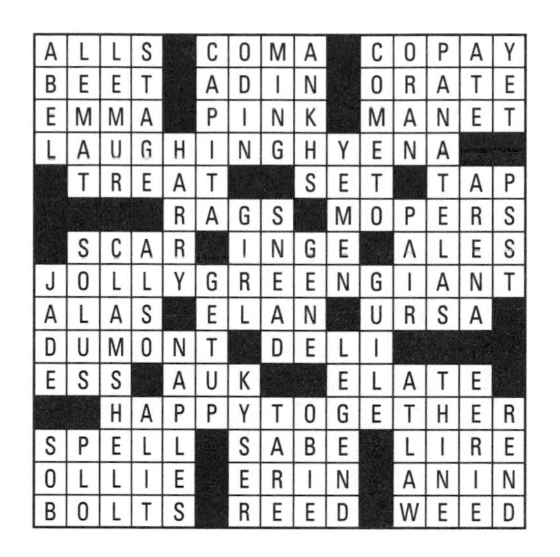

Puzzle 19-9: Crosswordese

Page 242

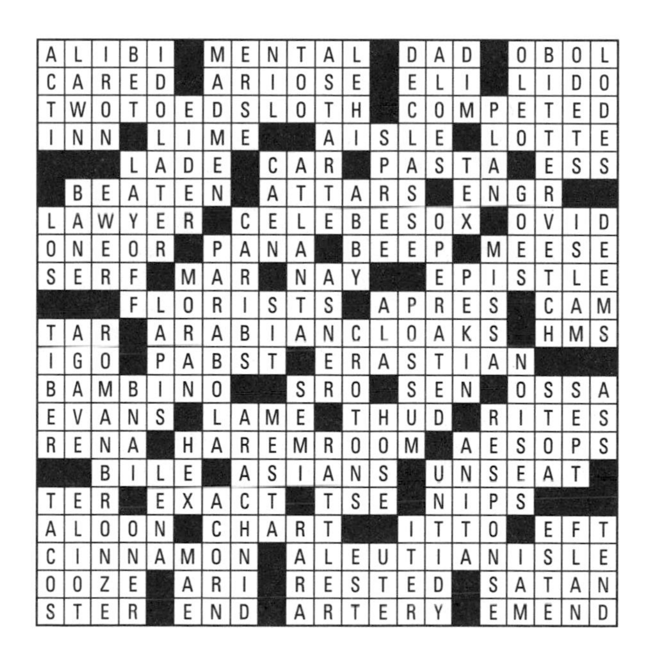

Appendix B
Crossword Repeaters

When you solve often, you start to see the same handy little words frequenting the squares. These crossword cliches *(repeaters)* are familiar to the experienced solver. To the occasional or novice solver, though, they present a hurdle. Allow me to introduce you to them.

In this appendix I give you a handy list of three- and four-letter repeaters that will serve you well through the grids. Next to each entry, I list a typical clue for the repeater. With a star I indicate the most popular of these repeaters, the ones you see most often.

Three-Letter Repeaters

A

AAA = "Narrow foot" or "H'way helper"
AAL = "Mulberry"
ABA = "Lawyer's org."
ACT = "Part of a play"
ADD = "Compute"
ADO* = "Fuss" or "Hubbub"
AFT = "Nautical term" or "Astern"
AGA = "Title for Khan" or "Pasha"
AGE = "Ripen"
AGO* = "Past"
AHA = "Sound of discovery"
AID = "Give alms to" or "— and abet"
AIL = "Feel under the weather"
AIR = "Tune"
AKA = "Pseudonym letters"
A LA* = "—mode"
ALA = "Wings" or "Neighbor of Fla."
ALE* = "Pub order"
ALI = "Baba" or "Actress MacGraw"
ALL = "Complete"
ALP = "Mont Blanc, for one"
ANA = "Collection: suffix"
AMO* = "Latin I verb"
AND = "Common connector"
ANI* = "Blackbird"
ANT* = "Pismire" or "Picnic pest" or "Hill dweller"
ANY = "Have you — wool?"
APE* = "Copy"
APT = "Likely"
ARA* = "Blackbird" or "Coach Parseghian"
ARI* = "Onassis" or "Jackie's ex"
ARC = "Rainbow"
ARM = "Equip with weapons"
ART = "Museum fare"
AS A = "— rule (generally)"
ASA = "Healer"
ASH = "Ember"
ASP = "Poisonous snake"
ASS = "Foolish one"
ATE = "Chowed down" or "Goddess"
AUK* = "Arctic bird"
AVA = "Hawaiian bird" or "Actress Gardner"
AYE = "Verbal vote"

B

BAA = "Bleat" or "Farmyard sound"
BOA* = "Poisonous snake" or "Feather stole"
BRA = "Bikini part"

C

CAB = "Taxi" or "Calloway"
CAD = "Bounder"
CHE = "Guevara"
CHI = "Greek letter" or "Sigma —"
COB = "Swan"
COG = "Gear"
COO* = "Companion to bill"
COT = "Youth's bed"
CRI = "Dernier —"

D

DAB = "Type of fish" or "Flounder"
DAD = "June VIP"
DAM = "Farmyard animal"
DAN = "Anchorman Rather" or "Rather"
DAP = "Fish"
DEA = "Gov't watchdog group"
DEI = "Agnus —"
DES* = "— Moines"
DIN = "Hubbub"
DIS = "Roman god"
DIT = "Morse code"
DNA = "Genetic material" or "Double helix"
DON = "Put on" or "Juan or Giovanni"
DOS = "After uno" or "Author — Passos"
DOT = "Speck"
DUO = "Twosome" or "Dynamic combination"

E

EAR = "Auricle" or "Unit of corn"
EAT = "Bite" or "Corrode"
EBB* = "Type of tide"
ECU = "French coin"
EDO = "Tokyo, once"
EEE = "Foot width"
E'ER = "Poetic contraction"
EFT* = "Salamander"
EGG = "Incite"
EGO = "Self" or "Type of maniac"
EKE* = "Supplement, with "out""
ELA = "Guido's note"
ELI* = "Yalie" or "Actor Wallach" or "Essayist Lamb"
ELK = "Wapiti" or "Member of BPOE"
ELL = "Building addition"
EME = "Dutch uncle"
EMU = "Flightless bird"
EON = "Long time"
ERA = "Age"
ERE = "Poetic word"
ERR* = "Goof" or "Blunder"
ESE = "Vane direction" or "Suffix"
ESS = "Curved shape"
ESP = "Sixth sense"
EST = "Suffix" or "Time zone"
EVA = "A Gabor"

F

FEN = "Bog"
FEY = "Elfin"
FIE = "Oldfashioned exclamation"
FRA = "Brother"

G

GAD = "Roam" or "Prefix with "about""
GAG = "Hoax" or "Muffle"
GAM = "Leg"
GAP = "Rift" or "Word with generation"
GEE = "Word before whiz" or "Command to Nellie"
GET = "Understand"
GNU* = "Wildebeest"

H

HAH = "Sound of discovery"
HAM = "Emoter" or "Noah's son"
HEE = "Haw's partner" or "— Haw"
HEM = "Border"
HIE* = "Hurry"
HOI = "— polloi"
HUE = "Tint"

I

ICI = "Here: Fr." or "Here, in Paris"
IDI = "Ugandan Amin"
ILK = "Type"
ILL = "Unwell" or "Under the weather" or "Neighbor of Ind."
IMP* = "Mischievous one"
IND = "Pol. Party" or "Neighbor of Ill." or "NYC subway"
ION* = "Charged particle"
IRA* = "A Gershwin" or "Retirement fund initials"
IRE* = "Anger" or "Part of the UK"
ITE = "Suffix"

J

JAI* = "— alai"

K

KEN = "Scope"

L

LAG = "Delay" or "Word with jet"
LAM = "Flight" or "On the — (at large)"
LAP = "Circuit"
LEE* = "Robert E. —"
LEI* = "Hawaiian garland"
LET = "Rent"
LIE = "Falsehood"
LOG = "Journal"
LOP = "Cut off"
LOT = "Real estate unit" or "Moab's father"

M

MAA = "Barnyard sound"
MAB = "Queen of the fairies"
MAE* = "Miss West"
MAI = "French month"
MAN = "A British isle"
MEA = "— culpa"
MEG = "Actress Ryan"
MIA* = "Actress Farrow" or "Mamma — !"
MOA = "Flightless bird"

N

NEB = "Beak" or "Neighbor of Mont."
NEE* = "Wedding page word"
NIL* = "Zero" or "Nothing"
NNE* = "Vane direction"
NOD = "Tacit response"

O

ODA = "Harem room"
ODE* = "Poetic form"
OHO = "Sound of discovery"
OLE = "Spanish cheer"
OPT* = "Elect" or "Choose"
ORE = "Lode quarry"
OSE = "Suffix"
OVA = "Eggs"

P

PAR = "Average"
PEI = "Architect I.M."
PER = "— diem"
POE = "Edgar Allan —"
POI = "Hawaiian dish"
PRO* = "For" or "Master"

Q

QED = "Letters in court"
QUM = "Irani city"

R

RAH* = "Arena cheer"
RES = "Matter: Lat."
RIA = "Stream"
RIB = "Tease"
RIO* = "— Grande"
RUE = "Regret" or "Actress McClanahan"

S

SAC = "Pouch"
SAO = "— Paolo"
SIB = "Kin, for short"
SOU = "Worthless coin"
STE* = "Holy woman: abbr."
SUI = "— generis"

T

TAM = "Beret"
TAR = "Sailor"
TEE* = "To a —"
TIC = "Spasm"

U

UNA = "Actress Merkel"
URN = "Ewer"
UTE = "Native American"

V

VIA = "Passage" or "— Air Mail"
VIP = "Top dog"
VUE = "Real estate word"

W

WOE = "Anguish"
WOO = "Court"

Y

YAW = "Veer"
YEN = "Urge" or "Asian currency"

Z

ZAG = "Zig follower"
ZIP = "Type of code"

Four-Letter Repeaters

A

ABBA = "Father" or "Eban"
ABEL = "Cain's brother"
ABET* = "Goad"
ABLE = "Dextrous"
ABRI = "Type of shelter"
ABUT = "Border"
ACTA = "Deeds: Lat."
ACME = "Peak"
AHAB = "Melville's captain"
ADAH = "Wife of Esau"
ADAK = "Aleutian island"
ADAR = "Hebrew month"
AEON = "Eternity: var."
AGAR* = "Seaweed"
AHEM = "Throat clearing sound"
AIDE = "Deputy" or "Helper"
AINE = "Eldest: Fr."
AIRY = "Breezy"
AKIN = "Similar, with "to""
ALAR* = "Winglike" or "Outlawed orchard spray"
ALAS* = "Expression of woe"
ALGA = "Pond cover"
ALLY = "Comrade"
ALMS = "Charity"
ALOE* = "Succulent plant" or "Skin lotion soother"
ALPE = "Slope, in Switzerland"
ALPS = "Swiss range"
ALSO = "Word with ran"
AMAH = "Asian governess"
AMAS = "Latin I verb"
AMEN* = "Last word"
AMID = "Surrounded by"
AMOR = "Roman god of love"
ANEW = "Once more"
ANKH = "Egyptian cross"

ANON = "Before long"
ANTE* = "Bet" or "Feed the kitty"
ANTI = "Opposed"
AONE = "Topnotch"
APER = "Copycat"
APEX = "Apogee" or "Crest"
APIS = "Egyptian animal"
APSE = "Church area"
ARAM = "Syria" or "My Name is — (Saroyan)"
AREA* = "Expanse" or "Word with code"
ARES = "Son of Zeus"
ARGO = "Jason's ship"
ARIA* = "Operatic solo"
ARID* = "Desert-like"
ARLO = "A Guthrie" or "Woody's son"
ARTE = "Commedia dell'—" or "Comedian Johnson"
ASEA* = "Confused"
ASIA = "Altai setting"
ASTA = "Nick and Nora's pooch"
ASTI = "— spumante"
AS TO = "Regarding"
ATKA = "Aleutian island"
ATTU = "Aleutian island"
AURA = "Halo"
AVER* = "State"
AVID* = "Eager"
AVIS* = "Rara —"

B

BAAL = "Deity"
BAIT = "Tempt"
BARA* = "Vamp Theda"
BARD = "Poet"
BEAU = "Suitor"
BEET* = "Borscht basis"
BE IN = "Hippie event"
BETE = "— noire (ogre)"
BOOR = "Churlish one"
BRAC = "Bric-a- —"
BRIC = "— a-brac"
BRIE = "French cheese"

C

CAFE = "Coffee shop"
CAIN = "Brother of Abel"
CANT = "Lingo"
CAN'T = "Coward's lament"
CASA* = "House: Sp." or "Home, to Jose"
CHIT = "Voucher"
CODE = "Zip or area"
COMA* = "Stupor"
CORA = "Mrs. Dithers"
CRAM = "Prepare for an exam"
CZAR = "Ivan, for one: var."

D

DAIS = "Podium"
DALE = "Ravine" or "Roy's partner"
DAME = "Edith Evans, for one"
DDAY = "WWII event"
DEEM = "Surmise" or "Consider"
DEER = "Ruminant" or "Bambi, for one"
DELE* = "Editor's mark"
DIES = "— Irae (hymn)"
DINE = "Have supper" or "Artist Jim"
DIRE = "Grim"
DOER = "Go-getter"
DO IN = "Destroy"
DOLE = "Allot" or "Bob or Elizabeth" or "Name in canned pineapple"

E

EACH = "Apiece"
EARL = "British peer" or "James — Jones"
EARN = "Merit"
EASE = "Relax" or "At — (drill sergeant's command)"
EAST* = "Asia" or "— *of Eden*"
ECHO = "Reverberate" or "Goddess"
ECON = "MBA course"
ECTO* = "Prefix"
EDDY = "Swirl"
EDEN = "Paradise" or "Actress Barbara"
EDIT = "Fix a text"

ELAN* = "Dash"
EMIR* = "Saudi ruler"
EMIT* = "Radiate"
ENDO = "Prefix"
ERGO = "Therefore" or "Cogito — sum"
EROS = "Greek god of love"
ETTE* = "Suffix" or "Major ending"
EWER = "Urn"

F

FAUX = "— pas (goof)"
FETE = "Gala" or "Party, in Paris"
FIAT = "Edict"
FLAK = "Criticism" or "Artillery"

G

GALA* = "Formal party" or "Bash"
GALE = "Squall" or "Actress Storm"
GAPE = "Stare"
GARB* = "Clothing" or "Attire"
GAUL = "France, to Caesar"
GLEE = "Mirth" or "Type of club"
GLEN = "Valley" or "Bandleader Miller"
GLIB = "Facile"
GO AT = "Attack"
GOAT = "Farmyard animal"
GO ON = "Continue talking"
GOON = "Thug"

H

HEIR = "Scion"
HEMP = "Flax" or "Jute"
HERB = "Seasoning" or "Jazzman Alpert"
HERE* = "Roll call response"
HERO = "Type of sandwich" or "Demigod" or "Hercules, for one"
HOMO = "Sapiens"
HONE* = "Sharpen"

I

IBIS = "Wading bird"
IDEA* = "Thought" or "Brainstorm"
IDEE = "Thought: Fr." or "Brainstorm in Paris"
IDLE = "Aimless" or "Monty Python's Eric"
IFFY = "Uncertain"
INGE* = "Playwright William" or "Author of *Bus Stop*"
INTO = "Inside" or "Engaged with"
IOTA* = "Speck" or "Greek letter"
IPSO = "— facto"
IRAN = "Tehran is its capital"
ITEM = "Scoop" or "Gossip columnist's highlight"
IVAN* = "Terrible tsar"

J

JUNO = "Jupiter's wife"

K

KALE = "Cabbage plant"
KEEL = "On an even —"
KEEN = "Eager"
KHAN = "Middle Eastern ruler" or "The Aga —"
KITH = "— and kin"

L

LASS = "Colleen"
LATH = "Slat"
LEAH = "Jacob's wife"
LEAN = "Spare" or "Jack Sprat's diet"
LEAP = "Vault" or "Word with year"
LENS = "Spectacles"
LESE = "— majeste"
LIEN = "Claim"
LIEU = "Substitute, with "in""

M

MAIA = "Mother of Hermes"
MAYA = "Poet Angelou"
MALI = "African country" or "Where the Niger flows"
MENE = "Writing on the wall"
META = "Prefix with physical"
METE* = "Allot"
MOBY = "— *Dick*"

N

NAVE* = "Church area"
NE'ER* = "— -do-well"
NENE = "Hawaiian goose"
NERO = "Husband of Octavia"
NILE = "Longest river"
NOAH = "Ark builder"
NOON = "*High* —"
NOVA = "Type of salmon" or "— Scotia"

O

ODOR = "Scent" or "Reputation"
OGLE* = "Leer"
OGRE = "Fairy tale villain"
OLEO = "Butter substitute"
OLIO* = "Hodgepodge"
OLLA = "Urn"
OMIT = "Delete"
ONER* = "Unique person"
ONTO = "Aware of"
OONA* = "Mrs. Chaplin" or "Charlie's girl"
OPAL = "October birthstone"
OPIE = "Ron Howard role"

P

PAPA = "One of the Three Bears" or "Nickname for Hemingway"
PEON* = "Serf"
PEPO = "Gourd"
POET = "Rhymester" or "Robert Frost, for one"
POOH = "*Winnie the* —"
PUNT = "Boat"

Q

QUID = "— pro quo"

R

RANI* = "Indian princess"
RANT = "Carry on" or "Companion to rave"
RHEA = "Queen of the Titans"
RILE = "Irritate"
RILL = "Stream"
RIOT* = "Uprising"
RITE = "Ceremony"

S

SALT* = "Sailor"
SARI* = "Delhi dress"
SASS* = "Talk back"
SECT = "Clan"
SEMI = "Partial" or "Truck"
SEPT = "Before Oct."
SERE* = "Dry"
SOLO = "Monologue" or "Napoleon —"
SO SO* = "Middling"
STER = "Suffix"
STOA* = "Greek marketplace"

T

TELE* = "Starter with gram"
TETE = "Head: Fr."
TRES = "After dos" or "Very: Fr."
TSAR* = "Despot" or "Ivan, for one"
TYRO = "Novice"

U

UP TO = "Until"
USNA = "Mil. School"

V

VANE = "Barn fixture"
VETO = "Override"
VITA = "Curriculum —" or "Sackville-West"

W

WELD = "Fuse" or "Actress Tuesday"
WHIT = "Shred"

X

XMAS = "Noel, for short"

Y

YOGI = "Mystic" or "Baseball legend Berra"

Z

ZEUS = "King of Mt. Olympus" or "Hera's consort"
ZION = "Heaven"

Index

• A •

• B •

• C •

• H •

• L •

• M •

• O •

• Q •

• R •

• S •

• T •

• U •

• Y •

• Z •

Notes

Notes

Notes

Notes

Notes

Notes

IDG BOOKS WORLDWIDE BOOK REGISTRATION

Register This Book and Win!

We want to hear from you!

Visit **http://my2cents.dummies.com** to register this book and tell us how you liked it!

- Get entered in our monthly prize giveaway.
- Give us feedback about this book — tell us what you like best, what you like least, or maybe what you'd like to ask the author and us to change!
- Let us know any other *...For Dummies*® topics that interest you.

Your feedback helps us determine what books to publish, tells us what coverage to add as we revise our books, and lets us know whether we're meeting your needs as a *...For Dummies* reader. You're our most valuable resource, and what you have to say is important to us!

Not on the Web yet? It's easy to get started with *Dummies 101*®*: The Internet For Windows*® *98* or *The Internet For Dummies*®, 5th Edition, at local retailers everywhere.

Or let us know what you think by sending us a letter at the following address:

...For Dummies Book Registration
Dummies Press
7260 Shadeland Station, Suite 100
Indianapolis, IN 46256-3917
Fax 317-596-5498

BESTSELLING BOOK SERIES